THE MYTH OF THE RATIONAL VOTER

THE MYTH OF
THE RATIONAL VOTER

WHY DEMOCRACIES CHOOSE BAD POLICIES

Bryan Caplan

PRINCETON UNIVERSITY PRESS

PRINCETON AND OXFORD

Library of Congress Cataloging-in-Publication Data

Caplan, Bryan Douglas, 1971–
The myth of the rational voter : why democracies choose
bad policies / Bryan Caplan.
p.   cm.
Includes bibliographical references and index.
ISBN-13: 978-0-691-12942-6 (cloth : alk. paper)
ISBN-10: 0-691-12942-8 (cloth : alk. paper)
1. Economic policy. 2. Democracy. 3. Political sociology. 4. Representative
government and representation. 5. Rationalism. I. Title.
HD87.C36 2006
320.6—dc22   2006030855

British Library Cataloging-in-Publication Data is available

The serious fact is that the bulk of the really important
things economics has to teach are things that people
would see for themselves if they were willing to see.
—*Frank Knight, "The Role of Principles*
in Economics and Politics"

I have often wondered why economists, with these absurd-
ities all around them, so easily adopt the view that men
act rationally. This may be because they study an economic system in which the discipline of the market ensures that, in a business setting, decisions are more or less
rational. The employee of a corporation who buys something for $10 and sells it for $8 is not likely to do so for
long. Someone who, in a family setting, does much the
same thing, may make his wife and children miserable
throughout his life. A politician who wastes his country's
resources on a grand scale may have a successful career.
—*Ronald Coase, "Comment on Thomas W. Hazlett"*

[T]he superstitions to be feared in the present day are
much less religious than political; and of all the forms of
idolatry I know none more irrational and ignoble than this
blind worship of mere numbers.
—*William Lecky,* Democracy and Liberty

CONTENTS

ACKNOWLEDGMENTS

I AM BLESSED with an abundance of argumentative but encouraging colleagues, but there are two to whom I am especially grateful.

The first is Don Boudreaux, who urged me to begin serious research on voter rationality right after the 1998 Public Choice Outreach Seminar. In a discipline where praise is extremely scarce, Don was quick to tell me that he loved my approach, and hasn't stopped telling me since. I really wonder whether I would have written this book—or any of the papers it builds on—without Don's support.

The second is Tyler Cowen, my constant critic. Since I joined the faculty at George Mason, Tyler has never failed to read my work and tell me what I'm doing wrong. No one has reviewed more drafts of this book than Tyler did, or asked harder questions. I can't remember the last time we agreed, but I still feel like he taught me half of everything I know.

I am also eternally grateful to the institution of lunch. Years of debate with lunchtime regulars Tyler, Robin Hanson, and Alex Tabarrok were required to turn my raw ideas into a finished product. And they were only the beginning. Scores of other lunch-goers have heard my views and given me feedback, including Scott Beaulier, David Bernstein, Tim Besley, Pete Boettke, Don Boudreaux, J. C. Bradbury, Geoff Brennan, Corina Caplan, Roger Congleton, Mark Crain, Eric Crampton, Gordon Dahl, Veronique de Rugy, Bill Dickens, Zac Gochenour, Rodolfo Gonzalez, Donald Green, Friedrich Heinemann, Bob Higgs, Randy Holcombe, Dan Houser, Jeff Hummel, Larry Iannaccone, Scott Keeter, Dan Klein, Arnold Kling, Ken Koford, George Krause, Timur Kuran, David Levy, Jacob Levy, Loren Lomasky, John Lott, Daniel Lurker, John Matsusaka, Kevin McCabe, Mitch Mitchell, Nathaniel Paxson, Ben Powell, Ilia Rainer, Carlos Ramirez, Joe Reid, Fab Rojas, Russ Roberts, Charles Rowley, Paul Rubin, Joe Salerno, Jim Schneider, Andrew Sellgren, Thomas Stratmann, Ed Stringham, Tom TerBush, Gordon Tullock, Dick Wagner, Walter Williams, and Donald Wittman.

As much fun as the lunches were, though, I especially want to thank those who read drafts of the manuscript and gave me detailed comments: Scott Beaulier, Pete Boettke, Eric Crampton, Tyler Cowen, Andrew Gelman, David Gordon, Robin Hanson, Michael Huemer, Dan Klein, Arnold Kling, Geoffrey Lea, David Levenstaum, Steve Miller, Nathaniel Paxson, Russ Roberts, Fab Rojas, Russ Sobel, Ilya Somin, Ed Stringham, Koleman Strumpf, Tim Sullivan, Dan Sutter, Alex Tabarrok, Gordon Tullock, Donald Wittman, and the referees at Princeton University Press. I also want to express my appreciation to the Kaiser Family Foundation, for freely sharing the data from the Survey of Americans and Economists on the Economy; Scott Beaulier, Steve Miller, Eric Crampton, Kail Padgitt, and Geoffrey Lea for excellent research assistance; my graduate students in microeconomics and public finance, and readers of my blog, for years of great feedback; and the Mercatus Center for generous support. Finally, I am very lucky that my wife has both a degree in economics and the daily patience to listen to my latest theory.

My apologies to anyone I missed. Can I make it up to you at our next lunch?

THE MYTH OF THE RATIONAL VOTER

Introduction

THE PARADOX OF DEMOCRACY

> A supporter once called out, "Governor Stevenson, all
> thinking people are for you!" And Adlai Stevenson an-
> swered, "That's not enough. I need a majority."
> —*Scott Simon, "Music Cues: Adlai Stevenson"*[1]

IN A DICTATORSHIP, government policy is often appalling, but rarely baffling. The building of the Berlin Wall sparked worldwide outcry, but few wondered, "What are the leaders of East Germany thinking?" *That* was obvious: they wanted to continue ruling over their subjects, who were inconsiderately fleeing en masse. The Berlin Wall had some drawbacks for the ruling clique. It hurt tourism, making it harder to earn hard currency to import Western luxuries. All things considered, though, the Wall protected the interests of elite party members.

No wonder democracy is such a popular political panacea. The history of dictatorships creates a strong impression that bad policies exist because the interests of rulers and ruled diverge.[2] A simple solution is make the rulers and the ruled *identical* by giving "power to the people." If the people decide to delegate decisions to full-time politicians, so what? Those who pay the piper—or vote to pay the piper—call the tune.

This optimistic story is, however, often at odds with the facts. Democracies frequently adopt and maintain policies harmful for most people. Protectionism is a classic example. Economists across the political spectrum have pointed out its folly for centuries, but almost every democracy restricts imports. Even when countries negotiate free trade agreements, the subtext is not, "Trade is mutually beneficial," but, "We'll do you the favor of buying your imports if you do us the favor of buying ours." Admittedly, this is less appalling than the Berlin Wall, yet it is more *baffling*. In theory, democracy is a bulwark against socially harmful policies, but in practice it gives them a safe harbor.[3]

How can this Paradox of Democracy be solved? One answer is that the people's "representatives" have turned the tables on them. Elections might be a weaker deterrent to misconduct than they seem on the surface, making it more important to please special interests than the general public. A second answer, which complements the first, is that voters are deeply ignorant about politics. They do not know who their representatives are, much less what they do. This tempts politicians to pursue personal agendas and sell themselves to donors.[4]

A diametrically opposed solution to the Paradox of Democracy is to deny that it regularly delivers foolish policies. You could insist that the public is right and "the experts" are wrong, openly defending the merits of protection, price controls, and so on. That is straightforward, but risky: It is akin to putting your client on the stand and opening him up to cross-examination. A less direct but safer stance—analogous to keeping your client from testifying—is to pick holes in the alleged *mechanisms* of democratic failure. You don't have to show that your client is innocent if the prosecution lacks a coherent account of how the crime was committed. In the same way, you need not show that a policy is good if there is no coherent account of how it could be bad.

Democracy's cleverest enthusiasts usually take this safer route.[5] Especially in recent years, their strategy has been successful despite the intuitive appeal of stories about electorally safe politicians and ignorant voters. For reasons we will soon explore, these stories buckle or even break when critically analyzed. Without a credible account of *how* democracy falls short of its promise, the insight that it *does* fall short lives on borrowed time.

This book develops an alternative story of how democracy fails. The central idea is that voters are worse than ignorant; they are, in a word, *irrational*—and vote accordingly. Economists and cognitive psychologists usually presume that everyone "processes information" to the best of his ability.[6] Yet common sense tells us that emotion and ideology—not just the facts or their "processing"—powerfully sway human judgment. Protectionist thinking is hard to uproot because it *feels good*. When people vote under the influence of false beliefs that feel good, democracy persistently delivers bad policies. As an old computer programming slogan goes, GIGO—Garbage in, garbage out.

Across-the-board irrationality is not a strike against democracy alone, but all human institutions. A critical premise of this book is that irrationality, like ignorance, is *selective*. We habitually *tune out* unwanted information on subjects we don't care about. In the same vein, I claim that we *turn off* our rational faculties on subjects where we don't care about the truth.[7] Economists have long argued that voter ignorance is a predictable response to the fact that one vote doesn't matter. Why study the issues if you can't change the outcome? I generalize this insight: Why control your knee-jerk emotional and ideological reactions if you can't change the outcome?

This book has three conjoined themes. The first: Doubts about the rationality of voters are empirically justified. The second: Voter irrationality is precisely what economic theory implies once we adopt introspectively plausible assumptions about human motivation. The third: Voter irrationality is the key to a realistic picture of democracy.

In the naive public-interest view, democracy works because it does what voters want. In the view of most democracy skeptics, it fails because it does *not* do what voters want. In my view, democracy fails *because* it does what voters want. In economic jargon, democracy has a built-in *externality.* An irrational voter does not hurt only himself. He also hurts everyone who is, as a result of his irrationality, more likely to live under misguided policies. Since most of the cost of voter irrationality is *external*—paid for by *other people,* why not indulge? If enough voters think this way, socially injurious policies win by popular demand.

When cataloging the failures of democracy, one must keep things in perspective. Hundreds of millions of people under democratic rule enjoy standards of living that are, by historical standards, amazingly good. The shortcomings of the worst democracies pale in comparison with those of totalitarian regimes. At least democracies do not murder millions of their own citizens.[8] Nevertheless, now that democracy is the typical form of government, there is little reason to dwell on the truisms that it is "better than Communism," or "beats life during the Middle Ages." Such comparisons set the bar too low. It is more worthwhile to figure out how and why democracy disappoints.[9]

In the minds of many, one of Winston's Churchill's most famous aphorisms cuts the conversation short: "Democracy is the worst form of government, except all those other forms that have been tried from time to time."[10] But this saying overlooks the fact that the governments vary in *scope* as well as form. In democracies the main alternative to majority rule is not dictatorship, but markets.

Democracy enthusiasts repeatedly acknowledge this.[11] When they lament the "weakening of democracy," their main evidence is that markets face little government oversight, or even usurp the traditional functions of government. They often close with a "wake-up call" for voters to shrug off their apathy and make their voice heard. The heretical thought that rarely surfaces is that weakening democracy in favor of markets could be a good thing. No matter what you believe about how well markets work in absolute terms, if democracy starts to look worse, markets start to look better by comparison.

Economists have an undeserved reputation for "religious faith" in markets. No one has done more than economists to dissect the innumerable ways that markets can fail. After all their investigations,

though, economists typically conclude that the man in the street—
and the intellectual without economic training—underestimates how
well markets work.[12] I maintain that something quite different holds
for democracy: it is widely *over*-rated not only by the public but by
most economists too. Thus, while the general public underestimates
how well markets work, even economists underestimate markets' virtues *relative* to the democratic alternative.

Chapter 1

BEYOND THE MIRACLE OF AGGREGATION

> I am suspicious of all the things that the
> average citizen believes.
> —*H. L. Mencken*, A Second Mencken Chrestomathy[1]

What voters don't know would fill a university library. In the last few decades, economists who study politics have revitalized age-old worries about the people's competence to govern by pointing out that— selfishly speaking—voters are not making a mistake. One vote has so small a probability of affecting electoral outcomes that a realistic egoist pays no attention to politics; he chooses to be, in economic jargon, *rationally ignorant.*[2]

For those who worship at the temple of democracy, this economic argument adds insult to injury. It is bad enough that voters *happen* to know so little. It remains bearable, though, as long as the electorate's ignorance is a passing phase. Pundits often blame citizens' apathy on an elections' exceptionally insipid candidates. Deeper thinkers, who notice that the apathy persists year after year, blame voters' ignorance on lack of democracy itself. Robert Kuttner spells out one version of the story:

> The essence of political democracy—the franchise—has eroded, as voting and face-to-face politics give way to campaign-finance plutocracy . . . [T]here is a direct connection between the domination of politics by special interest money, paid attack ads, strategies driven by polling and focus groups—and the desertion of citizens. . . . People conclude that politics is something that excludes them.[3]

Yet the slogan "The solution for the problems of democracy is more democracy" sounds hollow after you digest the idea of rational ignorance. Voter ignorance is a product of natural human selfishness, not a transient cultural aberration. It is hard to see how initiatives, or campaign finance reform, or any of the popular ways to "fix democracy" strengthen voters' incentive to inform themselves.

As the rational ignorance insight spread, it became an intellectual fault line in the social sciences. Economists, along with economically minded political scientists and law professors, are generally on one side of the fault line.[4] They see voter ignorance as a serious problem, making them skeptical about using government intervention to improve market outcomes. Beneficial government action is possible in theory, but how could hopelessly uninformed voters be expected to elect politicians who follow through? The implication: "Voters don't know what they're doing; just leave it to the market." Thinkers on the other side of the fault line downplay these doubts about government intervention. Once you discount the problem of voter ignorance, it is a short hop from "the policies beneficial in theory" to "the policies democracies adopt in practice."

In time, rational ignorance spawned an expansive research program, known as *public choice* or *political economy* or *rational choice theory*.[5] In the 1960s, finding fault with democracy bordered on heretical, but the approach was hardy enough to take root. Critiques of foolish government policies multiplied during the 1970s, paving the way for deregulation and privatization.[6]

But as these ideas started to change the world, serious challenges to their intellectual foundations surfaced. Earlier criticism often came from thinkers with little understanding of, and less sympathy for, the economic way of thinking. The new doubts were framed in clear economic logic.

The Miracle of Aggregation

> Think about what happens if you ask a hundred people to run a 100-meter race, and then average their times. The average time will not be better than the time of the fastest runners. It will be worse. . . . But ask a hundred people to answer a question or solve a problem, and the average answer will often be at least as good as the answer of the smartest member. With most things, the average is mediocrity. With decision-making, it's often excellence. You could say it's as if we've been programmed to be collectively smart.
> —*James Surowiecki*, The Wisdom of Crowds[7]

If a person has no idea how to get to his destination, he can hardly expect to reach it. He might get lucky, but common sense recognizes a tight connection between knowing what you are doing and successfully doing it. Ubiquitous voter ignorance seems to imply, then, that democracy works poorly. The people ultimately in charge—the voters—are doing brain surgery while unable to pass basic anatomy.

There are many sophisticated attempts to spoil this analogy, but the most profound is that democracy can function well under almost any magnitude of voter ignorance. How? Assume that voters do not make *systematic* errors. Though they err constantly, their errors are random. If voters face a blind choice between X and Y, knowing nothing about them, they are equally likely to choose either.[8]

What happens? With 100% voter ignorance, matters are predictably grim. One candidate could be the Unabomber, plotting to shut down civilization. If voters choose randomly, the Unabomber wins half the time. True, the assumption of zero voter knowledge is overly pessimistic; informed voters are rare, but they do exist. But this seems a small consolation. 100% ignorance leads to disaster. Can 99% ignorance be significantly better?

The surprising answer is yes. The negative effects of voter ignorance are not linear. Democracy with 99% ignorance looks a lot more like democracy with full information than democracy with total ignorance.[9] Why? First, imagine an electorate where 100% of all voters are well informed. Who wins the election? Trivially, *whoever has the support of a majority of the well informed.* Next, switch to the case where only 1% of voters are well informed. The other 99% are so thick that they vote at random. Quiz a person waiting to vote, and you are almost sure to conclude, with alarm, that he has no idea what he is doing. Nevertheless, it is basic statistics that—in a large electorate—each candidate gets about half of the random votes. Both candidates can bank on roughly a 49.5% share. Yet that is not enough to win. For that, they must focus all their energies on the one well-informed person in a hundred. Who takes the prize? *Whoever has the support of a majority of the well informed.* The lesson, as Page and Shapiro emphasize, is that studying the average voter is misleading:

> Even if individuals' responses to opinion surveys are partly random, full of measurement error, and unstable, when aggregated into a collective response—for example, the percentage of people who say they favor a particular policy—the collective response may be quite meaningful and stable.[10]

Suppose a politician takes a large bribe from "big tobacco" to thumb his nose at unanimous demand for more regulation. Pro-tobacco moves do not hurt the candidate's standing among the ignorant— they scarcely know his name, much less how he voted. But his share of the informed vote plummets. Things get more complex when the number of issues rises, but the key to success stays the same: Persuade a majority of the well informed to support you.

This result has been aptly named the "Miracle of Aggregation."[11] It reads like an alchemist's recipe: Mix 99 parts folly with 1 part wisdom to get a compound as good as unadulterated wisdom. An *almost* completely ignorant electorate makes the same decision as a fully informed electorate—lead into gold, indeed!

It is tempting to call this "voodoo politics," or quip, as H. L. Mencken did, that "democracy is a pathetic belief in the collective wisdom of individual ignorance."[12] But there is nothing magical or pathetic about it. James Surowiecki documents many instances where the Miracle of Aggregation—or something akin to it—works as advertised.[13] In a contest to guess the weight of an ox, the average of 787 guesses was off by a single pound. On *Who Wants to Be a Millionaire*, the answer most popular with studio audiences was correct 91% of the time. Financial markets—which aggregate the guesses of large numbers of people—often predict events better than leading experts. Betting odds are excellent predictors of the outcomes of everything from sporting events to elections.[14] In each case, as Page and Shapiro explain, the same logic applies:

> This is just an example of the law of large numbers. Under the right conditions, individual measurement errors will be independently random and will tend to cancel each other out. Errors in one direction will tend to offset errors in the opposite direction.[15]

When defenders of democracy first encounter rational ignorance, they generally grant that severe voter ignorance would hobble government by the people. Their instinctive responses are to (*a*) deny that voters are disturbingly ignorant, or (*b*) interpret voters' ignorance as a fragile, temporary condition. To call these responses "empirically vulnerable" is charitable. Decades of research show they are plain wrong.[16] About half of Americans do not know that each state has two senators, and three-quarters do not know the length of their terms. About 70% can say which party controls the House, and 60% which party controls the Senate.[17] Over half cannot name their congressman, and 40% cannot name either of their senators. Slightly *lower* percentages know their representatives' party affiliations.[18] Furthermore, these low knowledge levels have been stable since the dawn of polling, and international comparisons reveal Americans' overall political knowledge to be no more than moderately below average.[19]

You could insist that none of this information is relevant. Perhaps voters have holistic insight that defies measurement. But this is a desperate route for a defender of democracy to take. The Miracle of Aggregation provides a more secure foundation for democracy. It lets people believe in empirical evidence and democracy at the same time.

The original arguments about rational ignorance took time to spread, but eventually became conventional wisdom. The Miracle of Aggregation is currently in the middle of a similar diffusion process. Some have yet to hear of the Miracle. Backward-looking thinkers hope that if they ignore the objection, it will go away. But the logic is too compelling. Unless someone uncovers a flaw in the Miracle, the fault line in the social sciences will close. Economists and economically minded political scientists and law professors will rethink their doubts about democracy, and go back to the prerational ignorance presumption that if democracies do X, X is a good idea.

The Reality of Systematic Error

> Universal suffrage, which to-day excludes free trade from
> the United States, would certainly have prohibited the
> spinning-jenny and the power-loom.
> —*William Lecky,* Liberty and Democracy[20]

The Miracle of Aggregation proves that democracy can work even with a morbidly ignorant electorate. Democracy gives equal say to the wise and the not-so-wise, but the wise determine policy. Belaboring the electorate's lack of knowledge with study after study is beside the point.

But there is another kind of empirical evidence that *can* discredit the Miracle of Aggregation. The Miracle only works if voters do not make *systematic* errors. This suggests that instead of rehashing the whole topic of voter error, we concentrate our fire on the critical and relatively unexplored question:[21] *Are voter errors systematic?*

There are good reasons to suspect so. Yes, as Surowiecki points out, our average guess about the weight of oxen is dead on. But cognitive psychology catalogs a long list of other questions where our average guess is systematically mistaken.[22] This body of research ought to open our minds to the *possibility* of systematic voter error.

By itself, though, the psychological literature does not get us very far. The link between general cognition and particular political decisions is too loose. People could have poor overall judgment but good task-specific judgment.[23] Voters might be bad statisticians but perceptive judges of wise policy. Thus, we should refine our question: Are voter errors systematic *on questions of direct political relevance?*

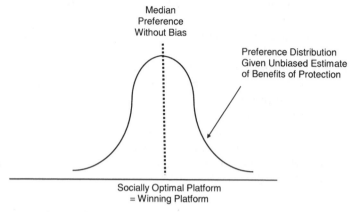

Figure 1.1 The Median Voter Model: Random Error

My answer is an emphatic yes. This book presents robust empirical evidence that—at minimum—beliefs about economics are riddled with severe systematic errors.[24] I strongly suspect that the same holds for beliefs about many other subjects. But as far as economics is concerned, the jury is in. People do not understand the "invisible hand" of the market, its ability to harmonize private greed and the public interest. I call this *antimarket* bias. People underestimate the benefits of interaction with foreigners. I call this *antiforeign* bias. People equate prosperity not with production, but with employment. I call this *make-work* bias. Lastly, people are overly prone to think that economic conditions are bad and getting worse. I call this *pessimistic* bias.

Economic policy is the primary activity of the modern state, making voter beliefs about economics among the most—if not *the* most—politically relevant beliefs. If voters base their policy preferences on deeply mistaken models of the economy, government is likely to perform its bread-and-butter function poorly. To see this, suppose that two candidates compete by taking positions on the degree of protectionism they favor. *Random* voter errors about the effect of protection cause some voters who prefer the effect of free trade to vote for protection. But it is equally common for voters who prefer the effect of protection to vote for free trade.[25] Then the Miracle of Aggregation holds: in spite of voter ignorance, the winning platform is socially optimal.

For anyone who has taught international economics, though, this conclusion is underwhelming. It takes hours of patient instruction to show students the light of comparative advantage. After the final exam, there is a distressing rate of recidivism. Suppose we adopt the

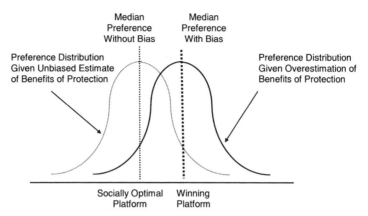

Figure 1.2 The Median Voter Model: Systematic Error

more realistic assumption that voters systematically overestimate the benefits of protection. What happens? Lots of people vote for protection who prefer the effect of free trade, but only a few vote for free trade who prefer the effect of protection. The political scales tilt out of balance; the winning platform is too protectionist. *The median voter would be better off if he received less protection than he asked for.* But competition impels politicians to heed what voters ask for, not what is best for them.

Comparable biases plausibly underlie policy after policy.[26] For example, supply-and-demand says that above-market prices create unsaleable surpluses, but that has not stopped most of Europe from regulating labor markets into decades of depression-level unemployment.[27] The most credible explanation is that the average voter sees no link between artificially high wages and unemployment. Before I studied economics, I failed to see it myself.

Modern Research versus Intellectual Tradition

> Economists have two attitudes toward discourse,
> the official and the unofficial.
> —*Donald McCloskey*, The Rhetoric of Economics[28]

The terminology of "systematic" versus "random" error entered economists' vocabulary about 30 years ago.[29] But the concept of systematic error has a much longer history. Here is how Simon Newcomb began an article in the *Quarterly Journal of Economics* in 1893:

The fact that there is a wide divergence between many of the practical conclusions of economic science, as laid down by its professional exponents, and the thought of the public at large, as reflected in its current discussion and in legislation, is one with which all are familiar.[30]

This was the intellectual climate that Newcomb saw in the contemporary United States and Great Britain. Over a century earlier, in *The Wealth of Nations*, Smith made similar observations about economic beliefs in Britain:

Nothing, however, can be more absurd than this whole doctrine of the balance of trade, upon which, not only these [mercantilist] restraints, but almost all other regulations of commerce are founded. When two places trade with one another, this doctrine supposes that, if the balance be even, neither of them loses or gains; but if it leans in any degree to one side, that one of them loses, and the other gains in proportion to its declension from the exact equilibrium.[31]

The policy consequences, for Smith, are far-reaching:

By such maxims as these, however, all nations have been taught that their interest consisted in beggaring all their neighbors. Each nation has been made to look with an invidious eye upon the prosperity of all the nations with which it trades, and to consider their gain as its own loss. Commerce, which ought naturally to be, among nations, as among individuals, a bond of union and friendship, has become the most fertile source of discord and animosity.[32]

When he affirms that "science is the great antidote to the poison of enthusiasm and superstition,"[33] Smith is not thinking about errors that harmlessly balance out.

In the middle of the 19th century, Frédéric Bastiat, the French popularizer of classical economics, titled one of his most famous books *Economic Sophisms*. "Sophism" is Bastiat's synonym for "systematic error," and he assigns sophisms broad consequences: They "are especially harmful, because they mislead public opinion in a field in which public opinion is authoritative—is, indeed, law."[34] Bastiat attacks dozens of popular protectionist sophisms, for example, but does not bother to criticize any popular free trade sophisms. The reason is not that bad arguments for free trade do not exist, but that—unlike bad arguments for protection—virtually none are popular!

Bastiat's outlook remained respectable well into the 20th century. The eminent economist Frank Knight made no apologies for it:

> The action taken by our own democracy, and the beliefs of the great majority on which the action rests, are often absurd. Nor are they to be explained by economic self-interest, since the measures depend on votes of electors whose interests are directly opposed to them, as well as those benefited.[35]

Yet in recent decades, these ideas have been forced underground. Nearly all modern economic theories of politics begin by assuming that the typical citizen understands economics and votes accordingly—at least on average.[36] As George Stigler, widely known as a stern critic of government regulation, scoffs:

> The assumption that public policy has often been inefficient because it was based on mistaken views has little to commend it. To believe, year after year, decade after decade, that the protective tariffs or usury laws to be found in most lands are due to confusion rather than purposeful action is singularly obfuscatory.[37]

In stark contrast, introductory economics courses still tacitly assume that students arrive with biased beliefs, and try to set them straight, leading to better policy. Paul Samuelson famously remarked, "I don't care who writes a nation's laws—or crafts its advanced treaties—if I can write its economics textbooks."[38] This assumes, as teachers of economics usually do, that students *arrive* with systematic errors.

What a striking situation: As researchers, economists do not mention systematically biased economic beliefs; as teachers, they take their existence for granted. One might blame ossified textbooks for lagging behind research, or teachers for failing to expose their students to cutting-edge work. But the hypothesis that people hold systematically biased beliefs about economics has not been falsified; it has barely been tested.

I maintain that the oral tradition of the teachers of economics offers the researchers of economics a rich mine of scientific hypotheses. At the same time, the oral tradition has been subject to so little analytical scrutiny that it is not hard to refine. Samuelson's is a story of hope; we can sleep soundly as long as he keeps writing textbooks. But pondering two more facts might keep us lying awake at night. Fact 1: The economics the average introductory student absorbs is disappointingly small. If they had severe biases at the beginning, most still have large biases at the end. Fact 2: *below-average students are above-average citizens.* Most voters never take a single course in economics. If it is disturbing to imagine the bottom half of the class voting on economic policy, it is frightening to realize that the general population already does. The typical voter, to whose opinions politicians cater, is probably unable to earn a passing grade in basic economics. No wonder protectionism, price controls, and other foolish policies so often prevail.

Preferences over Beliefs

> The growing obsession in most advanced nations with international competitiveness should be seen, not as a well-founded concern, but as a view held in the face of overwhelming contrary evidence. And yet it is clearly a view that people very much want to hold—a desire to believe that is reflected in a remarkable tendency of those who preach the doctrine of competitiveness to support their cases with careless, flawed arithmetic.
> —*Paul Krugman*, Pop Internationalism[39]

The most common objection to my thesis is theoretical: it contradicts the whole "rational choice approach" of modern social science. My colleague Robin Hanson aptly describes rational choice models as "stories without fools." I put folly—or, in technical terms, "irrationality"—at center stage.

One is tempted to snap: If the facts do not fit rational choice theory, so much the worse for rational choice theory! But this reaction is premature, for there is a satisfying way to reconcile theory and common sense. The preliminary step is to drop specious analogies between markets and politics, between shopping and voting. *Sensible public opinion is a public good.*[40] When a consumer has mistaken beliefs about what to buy, he foots the bill. When a voter has mistaken beliefs about government policy, the whole population picks up the tab.

Dropping false analogies between shopping and voting restores our intellectual flexibility, making the conflict between theory and common sense less daunting. But how can the conflict be resolved? We do not have to turn our backs on economics. It is only necessary to broaden its understanding of human motivation and cognition.

Economists usually presume that beliefs are a means to an end, not an end in themselves. In reality, however, we often have cherished views, valued for their own sake. As Shermer puts it, "Without some belief structure many people find this world meaningless and without comfort."[41] In economic jargon, people have *preferences over beliefs*. Letting emotions or ideology corrupt our thinking is an easy way to satisfy such preferences.[42] Instead of fairly weighing all claims, we can show nepotism toward our favorite beliefs. Ayn Rand calls it "blanking out": "the willful suspension of one's consciousness, the refusal to think—not blindness, but the refusal to see; not ignorance, but the refusal to know."[43]

Outside of economics, the idea that people like some beliefs more than others has a long history. John Locke's *Essay Concerning Human Understanding* inveighs against "enthusiasm, in which reason is taken away." To be an enthusiast is to embrace dubious ideas on emotional grounds:

> For the evidence that any proposition is true (except such as are self-evident) lying only in the proofs a man has of it, whatsoever degrees of assent he affords it beyond the degrees of that evidence, it is plain that *all the surplusage of assurance is owing to some other affection*, and not to the love of truth.[44]

Notice the two components of his analysis. The first is "surplusage of assurance." Locke observes that people assign probabilities to beliefs higher than the evidence warrants. The second is "other affections." The cause of excess confidence, on Locke's account, is conflict of motives. Everyone likes to think that he values truth for its own sake, but there are competing impulses: "conceit," "laziness," "vanity," "the tedious and not always successful labor of strict reasoning," and "fear, that an impartial inquiry would not favour those opinions which best suit their prejudices, lives, and designs."[45]

Thinkers who discuss preferences over beliefs almost invariably bring up religion. Locke is no different:

> In all ages, men in whom melancholy has mixed with devotion, or whose conceit of themselves has raised them into an opinion of a greater familiarity with God, and a nearer admittance to his favour than is afforded to others, have often flattered themselves with a persuasion of an immediate intercourse with the Deity, and frequent communications from the Divine Spirit.[46]

Like most things, enthusiasm comes in degrees. Many who feel no need to convert others take offense if you politely argue that their religion is mistaken. Few dispassionately accept their religious teachings as the "current leading hypothesis." Consider the adjectives that so often appear in the study of religion: fervent, dogmatic, fanatical. Human beings *want* their religion's answers to be true. They often want it so badly that they avoid counterevidence, and refuse to think about whatever evidence falls in their laps. As Nietzsche uncharitably puts it, " 'Faith' means not *wanting* to know what is true."[47]

Once you admit that preferences over beliefs are relevant in religion, it is hard to compartmentalize the insight. As Gustave Le Bon observes in *The Crowd*, there is a close analogy between literal religious belief and fervent ("religious") adherence to any doctrine: "Intolerance and fanaticism are the necessary accompaniments of the religious sentiment. . . . The Jacobins of the Reign of Terror were at bottom as religious as the Catholics of the Inquisition, and their cruel ardor proceeds from the same source."[48] Eric Hoffer famously expands on this point in his short classic *The True Believer*, declaring that "all mass movements are interchangeable": "A religious movement may develop into a social revolution or a nationalist movement; a social revolution, into militant nationalism or a religious movement; a nationalist movement into a social revolution or a religious movement."[49]

It is no accident that both of the substitutes for religion that Hoffer names—nationalism and social revolution—are political. Political/economic ideology is the religion of modernity. Like the adherents of traditional religion, many people find comfort in their political worldview, and greet critical questions with pious hostility.[50] Instead of crusades or inquisitions, the twentieth century had its notorious totalitarian movements.[51] "The religious character of the Bolshevik and Nazi revolutions is generally recognized," writes Hoffer. "The hammer and sickle and the swastika are in a class with the cross. The ceremonial of their parades is as the ceremonial of a religious procession. They have articles of faith, saints, martyrs and holy sepulchers."[52] Louis Fischer confesses that "just as religious conviction is impervious to logical argument and, indeed, does not result from logical processes, just as nationalist devotion or personal affection defies a mountain of evidence, so my pro-Soviet attitude attained complete independence from day-to-day events."[53] George Orwell's *1984* developed the novel vocabulary of Newspeak—words like *doublethink* and *thoughtcrime*—to ridicule the quasireligious nature of totalitarian ideologies.[54] A tour of Nazi or Communist websites can provide the reader with good contemporary examples.

As with religion, extreme ideologies lie at the end of a continuum. One's political worldview might compare favorably with the outlook of the sole member of a Maoist splinter faction, but remain less than rational.[55] To many people, for example, blaming foreigners for domestic woes is a source of comfort or pride. They may not proclaim their protectionism every day, and might acknowledge that foreign trade is beneficial in special circumstances. But they still resist—and resent—those who try change their minds by explaining comparative advantage.

Natural scientists have long known that the majority disbelieves some of their findings because they contradict religion.[56] Social scientists need to learn that the majority disbelieves some of their findings because they contradict quasi religion.

Rational Irrationality

> As we never cease to point out, each man is in practice
> an excellent economist, producing or exchanging
> according as he finds it more advantageous to do
> the one or the other.
> —*Frédéric Bastiat*, Economic Sophisms[57]

Preferences over beliefs is the critical idea that reconciles the theory of rational choice with the facts of voter irrationality. How? Suppose that human beings value *both* their material prosperity and their worldview. In economic jargon, they have two arguments in their utility function: personal wealth and loyalty to their political ideology. What happens if people rationally make trade-offs between their two values?

In any rational choice analysis, prices are the guiding star. If you like both meat and potatoes, you need to know how much meat you must forego in order to get one more potato. It is a mistake, however, to focus exclusively on the price tags at the grocery store. Part of the price of an unhealthy diet is a shorter life span, but the price tag says nothing about it. Economists call the total cost—explicit and implicit—of an activity its "full price." Though less visible than a printed price tag, the full price is the one that matters most.

The more incorrect your beliefs, the more poorly tailored your actions are to actual conditions.[58] What is the full price of ideological loyalty? *It is the material wealth you forego in order to believe.* Suppose that Robinson Crusoe's ideology teaches that native islanders like Friday are unable to farm. It flatters his pride to believe that only Europeans can understand agriculture. If Crusoe's belief is in fact correct, he wisely specializes in agriculture and has Friday do other kinds of work. But if Crusoe's belief is blind prejudice, keeping Friday out of agriculture reduces total production and makes both men poorer. The difference between Crusoe's potential living standard and his actual living standard is the full price of his ideological stance.

On an island with two people, the ideologue's material cost of hewing to his false precepts can be substantial. Under democracy, however, the probability that one vote—however misguided—changes policy rapidly decreases as the number of voters increases. In order to alter the outcome, a vote has to break a tie. The more votes, the fewer ties there are to break. Imagine a thousand Crusoes vote on permissible lines of work for a thousand Fridays. The Crusoes prefer to believe that the Fridays are unfit for agriculture, but the facts are against them. What is the expected loss of material wealth for a

Crusoe who indulges this preference? He forfeits not the per capita reduction in wealth, but the per capita reduction *discounted* by the probability that he flips the outcome of the election. If the per capita cost of keeping Fridays out of agriculture is $1,000, and the probability of being a tiebreaker is 0.1%, then a Crusoe who votes to keep them out pays $1 to adhere to his cherished fallacy.

This example illustrates one of this book's recurring points: In real-world political settings, the price of ideological loyalty is close to zero.[59] So we should *expect* people to "satiate" their demand for political delusion, to believe whatever makes them feel best. After all, it's free. The fanatical protectionist who votes to close the borders risks virtually nothing, because the same policy wins no matter how he votes. Either the borders remain open, and the protectionist has the satisfaction of saying, "I told you so"; or the borders close, and the protectionist has the satisfaction of saying, "Imagine how bad things would have been if we *hadn't* closed the borders!"

There can easily be a large gap between the private and social costs of ideological fealty. Recall that the expected material cost of error for one Crusoe was only $1. If a majority of the individual Crusoes find this price attractive, though, each and every Crusoe loses $1,000. Voting to keep the Fridays out of agriculture sacrifices $1,000,000 in social wealth in order to placate ideological scruples worth as little as $501.

A recurring rejoinder to these alarmist observations is that precisely because confused political ideas are dangerous, voters have a strong incentive to wise up. This makes as much sense as the argument that people have a strong incentive to drive less because auto emissions are unpleasant to breathe. No one faces the choice, "Drive a lot less, or get lung cancer," or "Rethink your economic views, or spiral down to poverty." In both driving and democracy, negative externalities irrelevant to *individual* behavior add up to a large collective misfortune.

The Landscape of Political Irrationality

> Democracy is the theory that the common people know
> what they want, and deserve to get it good and hard.
> —*H. L. Mencken*[60]

Ordinary cynics—and most economists—compare voters to consumers who shrewdly "vote their pocketbooks." In reality, this is atypical. Empirically, there is little connection between voting and material interests. Contrary to popular stereotypes of the rich Republican and the poor Democrat, income and party identity are only loosely re-

lated. The elderly are if anything slightly less supportive of Social Security and Medicare than the rest of the population. Men are *more*
pro-choice than women.[61]

If self-interest does not explain political opinion, what does? Voters
typically favor the policies they perceive to be in the general interest
of their nation. This is, however, no cause for democratic optimism.
The key word is *perceive*. Voters almost never take the next step by
critically asking themselves: "Are my favorite policies *effective means*
to promote the general interest?" In politics as in religion, faith is a
shortcut to belief.

What are the implications for democracy? Standard rational choice
theory rightly emphasizes that politicians woo voters by catering to
their preferences. But this means one thing if voters are shrewd policy
consumers, and almost the opposite if, as I maintain, voters are like
religious devotees. In the latter case, politicians have a strong incentive to do what is popular, but little to competently deliver results.
Alan Blinder cuttingly refers to "a compliant Congress, disdainful of
logic, but deeply respectful of public opinion polls."[62] If one politician
fails to carry out the people's wishes, a competing politician will. Le
Bon makes the same point in sweeping terms:

> The masses have never thirsted after truth. They turn aside from
> evidence that is not to their taste, preferring to deify error, if error
> seduce them. Whoever can supply them with illusions is easily their
> master; whoever attempts to destroy their illusions is always their
> victim.[63]

Thus, it is in *mind-set*, not practical influence, that voters resemble
religious believers. Given the separation of church and state, modern
religion has a muted effect on nonbelievers. Scientific progress continues with or without religious approval. Political/economic misconceptions, in contrast, have dramatic effects on everyone who lives under
the policies they inspire—even those who see these misconceptions
for what they are. If most voters think protectionism is a good idea,
protectionist policies thrive; if most believe that unregulated labor
markets work badly, labor markets will be heavily regulated.

The conventional complaint about politicians is "shirking"—their
failure to do what voters want.[64] I maintain that "shirking" should be
dethroned in favor of "demagoguery." *Merriam-Webster's Collegiate
Dictionary* defines a *demagogue* as "a leader who makes use of popular prejudices and false claims and promises in order to gain power."[65]
Put bluntly, rule by demagogues is not an aberration. It is the natural
condition of democracy. Demagoguery is the winning strategy as long
as the electorate is prejudiced and credulous. Indeed, while *dema-*

gogue normally connotes insincerity, this is hardly necessary. "Religious" voters encourage politicians to change their behavior by *feigning* devotion to popular prejudices, but also prompt entry by the *honestly prejudiced* into the political arena.[66]

Shirking should be dethroned, not but disowned. Elections are imperfect disciplinary devices.[67] Some deviation from voter wishes is bound to occur. But how much? How strictly do elections constrain politicians? My view is that it depends on voters themselves. If they care deeply about an issue—like public use of racial slurs—politicians have almost no slack. One wrong word costs them the election. In contrast, if voters find a subject boring—like banking regulation—if emotion and ideology provide little guidance, their so-called representatives have "wiggle room" to maneuver.

Politicians' wiggle room creates opportunities for special interest groups—private and public, lobbyists and bureaucrats—to get their way. On my account, though, interest groups are unlikely to directly "subvert" the democratic process. Politicians rarely stick their necks out for unpopular policies because an interest group begs them—or pays them—to do so. Their careers are on the line; it is not worth the risk. Instead, *interest groups push along the margins of public indifference.*[68] If the public has no strong feelings about how to reduce dependence on foreign oil, ethanol producers might finagle a tax credit for themselves. No matter how hard they lobbied, though, they would fail to ban gasoline.

Lastly, for all the power ascribed to them, the media are also consumer-driven. Competition induces them to cover news that viewers want to watch. In the standard rational choice account, this reduces political information costs and so helps democracy work. Yet I am skeptical that much useful information flows from media to viewers. Instead, like politicians, the media show viewers what they want to see and tell them what they want to hear.[69]

Admittedly, the media, like politicians, have wiggle room. Yet once again, it is slack along the margins of indifference. If a shocking disaster story, bundled with mild liberal reporting bias, remains highly entertaining to a mainstream audience, then predominantly Democratic newscasters can mix in a little left-wing commentary. But if the media stray too far from typical viewer opinion—or just get too pedantic—the audience flies away. So while the conventional view gives the media too much credit—the private good of entertainment vitiates the public good of information—it is even more wrongheaded to treat the media as the source of popular fallacies. As we shall see, the fallacies preceded modern media; they continue to flourish because the audience is *predisposed* to be receptive.

To recap, my story is voter-driven. Voters have beliefs—defensible or not—about how the world works. They tend to support politicians who favor policies that, in the voters' own minds, will be socially beneficial. Politicians, in turn, need voter support to gain and retain office. While few are above faking support for popular views, this is rarely necessary: Successful candidates usually sincerely share voters' worldview. When special interests woo politicians, they tailor their demands accordingly. They ask for concessions along policy margins where the voice of public opinion is silent anyway. The media, finally, do their best to entertain the public. Since scandalous behavior by politicians and interest groups is entertaining, the media are watchdogs. Like all watchdogs, though, the media have a subordinate role. If their coverage, however sound, conflicts with viewers' core beliefs, they change the channel.

Conclusion

To undermine the Miracle of Aggregation, this book focuses on the empirical evidence that voters' beliefs about *economics* are systematically mistaken. This does not imply that their beliefs about other topics are any sounder. In fact, I hope that experts in other fields will use my framework to explain how biased beliefs about *their* area of specialty distort policy.

The reason why I emphasize economics is that it is at the heart of most modern policy disputes. Regulation, taxes, subsidies—they all hinge on beliefs about how policy affects economic outcomes. The modal respondent in the National Election Studies ranks economic issues as "the most important problem" in most election years. In fact, if you classify "social welfare" issues like welfare, the environment, and health care as economic, then economic issues were "the most important problem" in *every* election year from 1972 to 2000.[70] Biased beliefs about economics make democracy worse at what it does most. Understanding these biases is therefore important not just for economists, but for everyone who studies politics. If that is not motivation enough, economists' love/hate relationship with the Miracle of Aggregation—official embrace, punctuated by exasperated under-the-table complaints about economic illiteracy—makes for a juicy story.

The empirics of economic beliefs serve as the springboard for a new perspective on democracy. How can economic theory accommodate the empirical evidence on systematic bias? Conceptually, the necessary change is not radical: Just add one new ingredient—preferences over beliefs—to the rational choice stew. Yet substantively, my account almost reverses the rational choice consensus. I see neither well-functioning democracies nor democracies highjacked by special interests. Instead, I see democracies that fall short because voters get the foolish policies they ask for. Adding one new ingredient to the rational choice stew gives it a starkly different flavor.

Chapter 2

SYSTEMATICALLY BIASED BELIEFS

ABOUT ECONOMICS

> Logical minds, accustomed to being convinced by a chain
> of somewhat close reasoning, cannot avoid having re-
> course to this mode of persuasion when addressing
> crowds, and the inability of their arguments always sur-
> prises them.
> —*Gustave Le Bon*, The Crowd[1]

In their modern theoretical work, economists look almost uniformly hostile to the view that people suffer from systematic bias. Nearly every formal model takes for granted that whatever individuals' limitations, on average they get things right. The approach that Gary Becker championed is now the norm:

> I find it difficult to believe that most voters are systematically fooled about the effects of policies like quotas and tariffs that have persisted for a long time. I prefer instead to assume that voters have unbiased expectations, at least of policies that have persisted. They may overestimate the dead weight loss from some policies, and underestimate it from others, but on the average they have a correct perception.[2]

Journals regularly reject theoretical papers that explicitly take the opposite position on methodological grounds: "You can't assume that." Papers that *covertly* introduce systematic bias risk being "outed."[3] In a well-known piece in the *Journal of Political Economy,* Stephen Coate and Stephen Morris worry that other economists are smuggling in the "unreasonable assumptions" that voters "have biased beliefs about the effects of policies" and "could be persistently fooled."[4] Dani Rodrik similarly laments, "The bad news is that the habit of attributing myopia or irrationality to political actors—whether explicitly or, more often, implicitly—persists."[5] Translation: These eminent social scientists are demanding that their colleagues honor the ban on irrationality in deed as well as word.

Evidence of Bias from Psychology and Public Opinion Research

Economists' theoretical aversion to systematic bias has fortunately not prevented empirical work from moving forward. Beyond the confines of their discipline, economists' strictures have been largely ignored. Psychologists like Daniel Kahneman and Amos Tversky have unearthed a diverse list of biases to which humans are prone.[6] For example, individuals overestimate the probability of vivid, memorable events such as airplane crashes. Other studies confirm that markedly more than 50% of people put themselves in the upper half of the distribution of many favorable attributes.[7] Numerous economists have built on psychologists' work, giving rise to the field of Psychology and Economics.[8]

This body of research proves that systematic mistakes exist. It is a powerful argument for keeping an open mind about the frailty of human understanding. Nevertheless, moving from laboratory to real life is somewhat perilous.[9] It is one thing to show that people fall short of a theoretical ideal of rationality in contrived experimental conditions. It is another to infer that irrational beliefs undermine their real-world choices—the decisions that human beings make in the environment where they were "born and raised."[10] After all, people might be *good at what they do* even though their general cognitive skills make logicians and statisticians cringe. Psychologists call this "ecological rationality"—the ability to choose sensibly in your natural habitat.[11] A mechanic who fails to notice correlations in a laboratory experiment may ably diagnose your car trouble. Voters might have sensible views about the issues of the day even though the clunkiest computer on the market beats them in chess.

It is hard to remain cavalier, however, if your mechanic affirms that cars run on sand instead of gasoline. How could anyone who holds this belief be trusted with a car? The error is directly relevant to practical decisions, and points its adherent in a dangerous direction. Roughly the same is true if voters think that the biggest item in the federal budget is foreign aid. With such a distorted picture of where their tax dollars go, they are likely to spurn responsible politicians with realistic proposals in favor of demagogues who promise to painlessly balance the budget.

The question that naturally presents itself, then, is: Do voters have biased beliefs about questions directly relevant to policy? While economists have shied away from this topic, public opinion researchers have not. They find voter bias to be common and quantitatively significant.[12] To escape their conclusion, one must reject the whole idea of "grading" the quality of public opinion—effectively letting the public act as the judge in its own case.

The simplest way to test for voter bias is to ask questions with objective quantitative answers, like the share of the federal budget dedicated to national defense or Social Security. Since researchers know the true numbers, they can statistically compare respondents' expressed beliefs to the facts. One high-quality example is the National Survey of Public Knowledge of Welfare Reform and the Federal Budget.[13] It presents strong evidence that the public systematically overestimates the share of government spending on welfare and foreign aid, and underestimates the share devoted to national defense and especially Social Security.

The main drawback of these studies is that many interesting questions are only answerable with a degree of ambiguity. Suppose you wonder if the public systematically underestimates the benefits of free trade. You cannot simply compare public opinion to Known Fact from the *Statistical Abstract of the United States*.[14] But several political scientists propose and apply a creative alternative. They estimate voters' "enlightened preferences"—the preferences they would have if they were "fully informed," or, to be more precise, far better informed.[15] This is a three-step process:

1. Administer a survey of policy preferences *combined with* a test of objective political knowledge.
2. Statistically estimate individuals' policy preferences as a function of their objective political knowledge and their demographics—such as income, race, and gender.
3. Simulate what policy preferences *would* look like if all members of all demographic groups had the *maximum* level of objective political knowledge.

Thus, you begin by collecting data on respondents' preferred policies—whether they want more or less government spending, whether they want to reduce the deficit by raising taxes, whether they are pro-choice or pro-life. Next, you test respondents' objective political knowledge. Think of it as a test of their "Political I.Q." See if they know how many senators each state has, who the chief justice of the Supreme Court is, whether Russia is a member of NATO, and so on.

Once you know respondents' Political I.Q., you can use it—along with information on respondents' income, race, gender, and so on—to statistically predict their policy preferences. You can see whether, for example, the average person with high Political I.Q. favors more or less government spending than the average person with low Political I.Q.

Table 2.1
Average Policy Preferences

Income	Knowledge	% of Population	Average Response
High	High	25	3
High	Low	25	5
Low	High	25	4
Low	Low	25	6
Average Preference			4.5
Enlightened Preference			3.5

Armed with this information, you can guesstimate what an individual *would* think if his demographics stayed the same but his Political I.Q. rose to godly heights. If a poor man with a low Political I.Q. learned a lot more about politics but stayed poor, would he change his mind about welfare policy? If so, how?

Finally, once you know how *one individual* would revise his opinions, you can calculate how the *whole distribution* of opinions would change if *everyone* had the maximum Political I.Q. All you have to do is figure out what each and every individual would want given maximum political knowledge, then compare the new distribution to the old.

To work through a simple example, imagine there are two demographic groups—rich and poor—and two knowledge levels—low and high, for a total of four categories. Each category has the same fraction of people—25% each. Respondents rate their preferred welfare policy on the scale from 0 to 10, where 0 means drastic cuts and 10 means drastic increases. The average response for the whole population is 4.5.

To calculate the enlightened preferences of the whole population, replace the actual answers of the low-knowledge respondents with the average answer of high-knowledge respondents *with the same income*. Assign the average preference of the high-knowledge rich respondents—3—to *all* rich respondents. Assign the average preference of the high-knowledge poor respondents—4—to *all* poor respondents. The new average—3.5—is the population's enlightened preference.

One key feature of the enlightened preference approach is that *in the absence of systematic effects of knowledge on policy preferences*, there would be nothing to report. The distribution of enlightened preferences would equal the distribution of actual, "unenlightened" preferences.

In practice, though, the enlightened preference approach has a big payoff: Systematic effects of knowledge on policy preferences are large and ubiquitous. As Althaus explains: "Contrary to the predictions of collective rationality models, the aggregate opinions of ill-informed respondents are usually more one-sided than those of the well informed."[16] He goes on to provide an excellent summary of the three most noteworthy patterns in the data:

1. "First, fully informed opinion on foreign policy issues is relatively more interventionist than surveyed opinion but slightly more dovish when it comes to the use and maintenance of military power."[17] If the public's knowledge of politics magically increased, isolationism would be less popular. More knowledgeable individuals favor an active international role for the United States. At the same time, they are less hawkish: They want to be involved in world affairs, but see a greater downside of outright war.

2. "The second pattern among policy questions is for fully informed opinion to hold more progressive attitudes on a wide variety of social policy topics, particularly on those framed as legal issues."[18] Most notably, a more knowledgeable public would be more pro-choice, more supportive of gay rights, and more opposed to prayer in school.

3. "The third pattern in policy questions is for simulated opinions to be more ideologically conservative on the scope and applications of government power. In particular, fully informed opinion tends to be fiscally conservative when it comes to expanding domestic programs, to prefer free market solutions over government intervention to solve policy problems, to be less supportive of additional government intervention to protect the environment, and to prefer a smaller and less powerful federal government." For example, the 1996 American National Election Study asks which of the following two positions is closer to the respondent's views: "One, we need a strong government to handle today's complex economic problems; or two, the free market can handle these problems without government becoming involved."[19] Fully informed opinion was more promarket. Beliefs about welfare and affirmative action fit the same pattern: While political knowledge increases support for equal opportunity, it decreases support for equal results.

It is hard to swallow the idea that if people knew more, they would agree with you less. Particularly for Althaus's third pattern, it is tempting to dismiss the results. After all, riches and knowledge go together. Why not conclude that more informed people favor free-market poli-

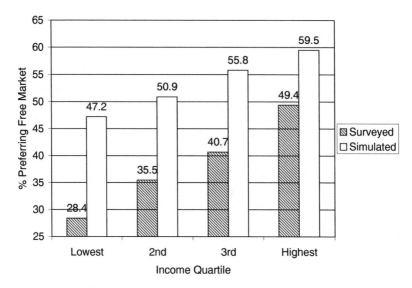

Figure 2.1 "Enlightened Preferences" for Free Market vs. Government
Source: Althaus (2003: 111)

cies because the rich correctly identify their own interests? This objection misses the whole point. The distribution of enlightened preferences is more promarket than the actual distribution of preferences primarily because people of *all income levels* become more promarket as their political knowledge increases. In fact, Althaus shows that as knowledge rises, promarket views increase disproportionately in the *bottom* half of the income distribution.

The effects that Althaus reports are often large. Of those surveyed, 62% expressed a preference for strong government over the free market; 38% took the contrary position. But estimated "enlightened preferences" were 15 percentage points more promarket; the split went from 62/38 to 47/53. The same holds for many other basic policy questions, on everything from deficit reduction (69/31 opposed becomes 52/48 in favor) to abortion on demand (54/46 opposed becomes 56/44 in favor).[20]

Getting Economics Back on Track

Political scientists' findings are frankly embarrassing for economists who study politics. While economists learn more and more about how government would work in theory if voters were immune to system-

atic error, public opinion researchers convincingly show that in practice, systematic voter error is quite real. Indeed, bias is the rule, not the exception.

Economists' blind spot is particularly hard to excuse because they stand at the end of a long tradition with a lot to say about bias. Many of the most famous economists of the past, like Adam Smith and Frédéric Bastiat, obsessed over the public's wrongheaded beliefs about economics, its stubborn resistance to basic principles like opportunity cost and comparative advantage. Today's economists have not merely failed to follow relevant empirical work in a related discipline. They have also turned their backs on what economists used to know.

At least this is what economists have done as researchers. *As teachers*, curiously, most economists honor the wisdom of their forebears. When the latest batch of freshmen shows up for Econ 1, textbook authors and instructors still try to separate students from their prejudices—in the words of Paul Krugman, "to vaccinate the minds of our undergraduates against the misconceptions that are so predominant in educated discussion."[21]

This peculiar disconnect between research and teaching has an important upside. The problem is not that economists have nothing to say about bias. On the contrary, the problem is that economists have a lot to say, but are reluctant to go public, to put their scientific credibility on the line. If this reluctance could be overcome, however, economics would have much to offer. Great economists have been studying systematic bias for centuries, but modern economists have failed to notify psychologists, public opinion specialists, or anyone else. Furthermore, teaching experience has given many living economists shrewd insight into the public's biases. Human knowledge would take several steps forward if economists merely revealed what they already know.

So the glass is half full. Economics is not living up to its potential, but it has a lot of potential. Few economists are currently interested in the vital questions that public opinion researchers are asking. But economists of the past have thought profoundly about these matters, and economists of the present have more to add, even if they keep their cards close to their chest.

Psychologists and public opinion researchers have made an impressive effort to educate economists about the realities of systematic bias. The communication has been largely one-way. It may be jarring, then, to hear that economists can repay the favor. After all their stern admonitions against the assumption of systematic bias, are we to believe that economists have original insights on the topic? It is out of character for economists to hold back.

There is a logical explanation. Few modern economists care about the history of thought, so many of the most penetrating discussions have been ignored or forgotten.[22] Furthermore, in their dual roles as researchers and teachers, economists face starkly different incentives. It is professionally risky to emphasize systematically biased beliefs in the journals, but perfectly respectable to do so in the classroom. This is an ideal climate for ideas to quietly endure.

Very well: What do economists—past and present—have to say about systematic error? Out of all the complaints that economists lodge against laymen, four families of beliefs stand out.[23] This book will refer to these families as *antimarket bias, antiforeign bias, make-work bias,* and *pessimistic bias.* Economists have long seen them as widely accepted but sadly mistaken. The rest of this chapter describes the systematic errors that economists accuse the public of making, and briefly explains why economists think they are right and the public is wrong. Formal statistical evidence waits in the next chapter.

Antimarket Bias

> Commerce is, by its very essence, satanic.
> —*Charles Baudelaire*[24]

I first learned about farm price supports in the produce section of the grocery store. I was in kindergarten. My mother explained that price supports *seemed* to make fruits and vegetables more expensive, but assured me that this conclusion was simplistic. If the supports went away, so many farms would go out of business that prices would soon be higher than ever. If I had been more precocious, I would have asked a few questions. Were there price support programs for the other groceries? Why not? As it happened, though, I accepted what she told me, and felt a lingering sense that price competition is bad for buyer and seller alike.

This was one of my first memorable encounters with **antimarket bias**, *a tendency to underestimate the economic benefits of the market mechanism.*[25] The public has severe doubts about how much it can count on profit-seeking business to produce socially beneficial outcomes. They focus on the *motives* of business, and neglect the discipline imposed by competition. While economists admit that profit-maximization plus market imperfections can yield bad results, non-economists tend to view successful greed as socially harmful per se.

Near the end of his life, Joseph Schumpeter eloquently captured the essence of antimarket bias:

> Capitalism stands its trial before judges who have the sentence of death in their pockets. They are going to pass it, whatever the defense they may hear; the only success victorious defense can possibly produce is a change in the indictment.[26]

Arguably the greatest historian of economic thought, Schumpeter elsewhere matter-of-factly speaks of "the ineradicable prejudice that every action intended to serve the profit interest must be anti-social by this fact alone."[27] Considering his encyclopedic knowledge, this remark speaks volumes. Antimarket bias is not a temporary, culturally specific aberration. It is a deeply rooted pattern of human thinking that has frustrated economists for generations.[28]

Economists across the political spectrum criticize antimarket bias. Liberal Democratic economists echo and amplify Schumpeter's theme. Charles Schultze, head of Jimmy Carter's Council of Economic Advisors, proclaims, "Harnessing the 'base' motive of material self-interest to promote the common good is perhaps *the* most important social invention mankind has yet achieved." But politicians and voters fail to appreciate this invention. "The virtually universal characteristic of [environmental] policy . . . is to *start* from the conclusion that regulation is the obvious answer; the pricing alternative is never considered."[29]

Projecting your own preferences onto the majority is a cliché of democratic politics. Pundits rarely proclaim, "The American people want X, but they're wrong." In the face of antimarket bias, however, many economists loudly defy public opinion. It would be hard to find an economist more in favor of free markets than Ludwig von Mises. Yet does he argue that unresponsive elites *force* big government on an unwilling majority? No, he freely grants that the policies he opposes reflect the will of the people: "There is no use in deceiving ourselves. American public opinion rejects the market economy."[30] The problem with democracy is not politicians' shirking, but the public's antimarket bias:

> For more than a century public opinion in Western countries has been deluded by the idea that there is such a thing as "the social question" or "the labor problem." The meaning implied was that the very existence of capitalism hurts the vital interests of the masses, especially those of the wage earners and the small farmers. The preservation of this manifestly unfair system cannot be tolerated; radical reforms are indispensable.
>
> The truth is that capitalism has not only multiplied population figures but at the same time improved the people's standard of living in an unprecedented way.[31]

There are too many variations on antimarket bias to list them all. Probably the most common is to *equate market payments with transfers*, ignoring their incentive properties.[32] (A "transfer," in economic jargon, is a no-strings-attached movement of wealth from one person to another.) All that matters, then, is how much you empathize with the transfer's recipient compared to the transfer's provider. To take the classic case: People tend to see profits as a gift to rich. So unless you perversely pity the rich more than the poor, limiting profits seems like common sense.

Economists across the ideological spectrum find it hard to respond to this outlook with anything but derision. Profits are not a handout, but a quid pro quo: "*If* you want to get rich, *then* you have to do something people will pay for." Profits give incentives to reduce production costs, move resources from less-valued to more-valued industries, and dream up new products. This is the central lesson of *The Wealth of Nations*: the "invisible hand" quietly persuades selfish businessmen to serve the public good:

> Every individual is continually exerting himself to find out the most advantageous employment for whatever capital he can command. It is his own advantage, indeed, and not that of the society, which he has in view. But the study of his own advantage naturally, or rather necessarily leads him to prefer that employment which is most advantageous to the society.[33]

For modern economists, these are truisms, but they usually miss the deeper lesson. If Adam Smith's observations are only truisms, why did he bother to write them? Why do teachers of economics keep quoting and requoting this passage? *Because Smith's thesis was counterintuitive to his contemporaries, and remains counterintuitive today.* A truism for the few is heresy for the many. Smith, being well aware of this fact, tries to shock readers out of their dogmatic slumber: "By pursuing his own interest he frequently promotes that of the society more effectually than when he really intends to promote it. I have never known much good done by those who affected to trade for the publick good."[34] Business profit appears to be a transfer but benefits society; business philanthropy appears to benefit society but is at best a transfer.

The same applies to other unpopular "windfalls." Attacks on "obscene profits" dominate antimarket thought in recent centuries, but in earlier times the leading culprit was interest or "usury."[35] In popular imagination, interest has but one effect: enriching moneylenders and impoverishing those who depend upon them. In his classic *Capital and Interest*, Eugen von Böhm-Bawerk observes that prejudice against debt markets goes back millennia:

The creditor is usually rich, the debtor poor, and the former appears in the hateful light of a man who squeezes from the little that the poor man has, something, in the shape of interest, that he can add to his own superfluous riches. It is not to be wondered at, then, that both the ancient world and especially the Christian Middle Ages were exceedingly unfavorable to interest.[36]

Timur Kuran's dissection of Islamic economics reports that opposition to interest has recently enjoyed a powerful revival:

To be recognized as an Islamic economist it is not sufficient to be a learned Muslim who contributes to economic debates. One must be opposed in principle to all interest.[37]

Interest is economic enemy number one throughout the Muslim world, and many governments actively favor interest-free "Islamic banking":

The objective is not simply to make Islamic banking more accessible. It is to make all banking Islamic. Certain campaigns against conventional banking have succeeded in making "interest-laden" banking illegal. In Pakistan all banks were ordered in 1979 to purge interest from their operations within five years, and in 1992 the Sharia court removed various critical exemptions. Interest prohibitions have gone into effect also in Iran and the Sudan.[38]

What is everyone from ancient Athens to modern Islamabad missing? Like profit, interest is not a gift, but a quid pro quo: The lender earns interest in exchange for *delaying* his consumption. A government that successfully stamped out interest payments would be no friend to those in need of credit, for the same stamp would crush lending as well.

Skipping ahead to the present, Alan Blinder blames opposition to tradable pollution permits on antimarket bias.[39] Why let people "pay to pollute," when we can force them to cease and desist? The textbook answer is that tradable permits get you more pollution abatement for the same cost. The firms able to cheaply cut their emissions do so, selling their excess pollution quota to less flexible polluters. End result: More abatement bang for your buck. A price for pollution is therefore not a pure transfer; it creates incentives to improve environmental quality as cheaply as possible. But noneconomists disagree—including relatively sophisticated policy insiders. Blinder discusses a fascinating survey of 63 environmentalists, congressional staffers, and industry lobbyists. *Not one* could explain economists' standard rationale for tradable permits.[40]

The second most prominent avatar of antimarket bias is *monopoly theories of price.* Economists obviously acknowledge that monopolies exist. But the public habitually makes "monopoly" a scapegoat for scarcity.[41] The idea that supply and demand *usually* controls prices is hard to accept. Even in industries with many firms, noneconomists treat prices as a function of their CEO's intentions and conspiracies. Economists understand, however, that collusion is a Prisoners' Dilemma.[42] If an industry has more than a handful of firms, industry-wide conspiracies are unlikely to succeed.

Historically, it has been especially common for the public to pick out middlemen as uniquely vicious "monopolists." *Look* at these parasites: They buy products, "mark them up," and then resell us the "exact same thing." Bastiat attacks contemporary socialists for "hate speech" against the middleman:

> They would willingly eliminate the capitalist, the banker, the speculator, the entrepreneur, the businessman, and the merchant, accusing them of interposing themselves between producer and consumer in order to fleece them both, without giving them anything of value. . . . Then, with the aid of those high-sounding words: *Exploitation of man by man, speculation in hunger, monopoly,* they set themselves to blackening the name of business and throwing a veil over its benefits.[43]

What could these so-called benefits possibly be? Economists have a standard response. Transportation, storage, and distribution are valuable services—a fact that becomes obvious whenever you need a cold drink in the middle of nowhere. And like most valuable services, they are not costless. The most that is reasonable to ask, then, is not that middlemen work for free, but that they face the daily test of competition. Given the large number of firms one typically sees in these markets, economists find accusations of "monopoly" fairly bizarre.[44]

While we are on the subject, we should not forget a conspiracy theory that is as popular as it is preposterous: Capitalists join forces to keep wages at the subsistence level. Many still see Third World economies through this lens, and tell a watered-down version of the same story for the First. But there are literally millions of employers in the First World. Just imagining the logistics of such a plot is laughable. Its more literate defenders point out that Adam Smith himself worried about employer conspiracies,[45] conveniently overlooking the fact that in Smith's time, high transportation and communication costs left workers with far fewer alternative employers.

What about the Third World? The number of employment options is often substantially lower. But if there really were a vast employer conspiracy to hold down wages, the Third World would be an especially profitable place to invest. Query: Does investing your life savings in poor countries seem like a painless way to get rich quick? If not, you at least tacitly accept economists' sad-but-true theory of Third World poverty: Its workers earn low wages because their productivity is low.[46]

Collusion aside, the public's implicit model of price determination is that businesses are monopolists of variable altruism. If a CEO feels greedy when he wakes up, he raises his price—or puts low-quality merchandise on the shelves. Nice guys charge fair prices for good products; greedy scoundrels gouge with impunity for junk. It is only a short step for market skeptics to add, "And nice guys finish last." As John Mueller emphasizes, the public links greed with almost everything bad: Capitalism is "commonly maligned for the deceit, unfairness, dishonesty, and discourtesy that are widely taken to be the inevitable consequences of its apparent celebration of greed."[47] Or as villainous innkeeper Thenardier sings in *Les Misérables*:

> Charge 'em for the lice,
> Extra for the mice,
> Two percent for looking in the mirror twice!
> Here a little slice,
> There a little cut,
> Three percent for sleeping with the window shut!
> When it comes to fixing prices,
> There are a lot of tricks he knows.
> How it all increases,
> All those bits and pieces,
> Jesus! It's amazing how it grows![48]

Never mind that Thenardier is bankrupt before the end of the first act. Presumably he was run out of business by an even greedier competitor.

Where does the public go wrong? For one thing, *asking* for more can *get* you less. Giving your boss the ultimatum, "Double my pay or I quit" usually ends badly. The same holds in business: raising price and cutting quality often leads to lower profits, not higher. Mueller makes the deeper point that many strategies that work as a one-shot scam backfire as routine policies.[49] It is hard to make a profit if no one sets foot in your store twice. Intelligent greed militates against "deceit, unfairness, dishonesty, and discourtesy" because they damage the seller's reputation.

An outsider who eavesdrops on Krugman's or Stiglitz's debates with other economists might get the impression that the benefits of markets remain controversial.[50] To understand the conversation, you have to notice what economists are *not* debating. They are not debating whether prices give incentives, or if a vast business conspiracy runs the world. Almost all economists recognize the core benefits of the market mechanism; they disagree only at the margin.

Antiforeign Bias

> The impressive fact about ordinary Americans is that, despite years of education and propaganda, they still cling stubbornly to their skepticism about the global economy. With their usual condescension, elite commentators dismiss the popular expressions of concern as uninformed and nativist, the misplaced fears of people ill equipped to grasp the larger dimensions of economics.
> —*William Greider,* Who Will Tell the People?[51]

A shrewd businessman I know has long thought that everything wrong in the American economy could be solved with two expedients:

1. A naval blockade of Japan.
2. A Berlin Wall at the Mexican border.

This is only a mild caricature of his position, which is all the more puzzling because he usually gets the mutual benefits of trade. He does well on eBay. But like most noneconomists, he suffers from **antiforeign bias**, *a tendency to underestimate the economic benefits of interaction with foreigners.*[52] When outsiders emerge on the economic scene, they do a mental double take: "Foreigners? Could it really be mutually beneficial for us to trade with *them*?"

Popular metaphors equate foreign trade with racing and warfare, so you might say that antiforeign views are embedded in our language. Perhaps foreigners are sneakier, craftier, or greedier. Whatever the reason, they supposedly have a special power to exploit us. As Newcomb explains:

> It has been assumed as an axiom which needs no proof, because none would be so hardy as to deny it, that foreign nations cannot honestly be in favor of any trade with us that is not to our disadvantage; that the very fact that they want to trade with us is a good reason for receiving their overtures with suspicion and obstructing their wishes by restrictive legislation.[53]

Alan Blinder echoes Newcomb's lament a century later. People around the world scapegoat foreigners:

> When jobs are scarce, the instinct for self-preservation is strong, and the temptation to blame foreign competitors is all but irresistible. It was not only in the United States that the bunker mentality took hold. That most economists branded the effort to save jobs by protectionism shortsighted and self-defeating was beside the point. Legislators are out to win votes, not intellectual kudos.[54]

There is probably no other popular opinion that economists have found so enduringly objectionable. In *The Wealth of Nations*, Smith admonishes his countrymen:

> What is prudence in the conduct of every private family, can scarce be folly in a great kingdom. If a foreign country can supply us with a commodity cheaper than we ourselves can make it, better buy it of them with some part of the produce of our own industry, employed in a way in which we have some advantage.[55]

As far as his peers were concerned, Smith's arguments won the day. Over a century later, Newcomb could securely observe in the *Quarterly Journal of Economics* that "one of the most marked points of antagonism between the ideas of the economists since Adam Smith and those which governed the commercial policy of nations before his time is found in the case of foreign trade."[56] There was a little backsliding during the Great Depression,[57] but economists' pro-foreign views abide to this day. Even theorists like Paul Krugman who specialize in exceptions to the optimality of free trade frequently downplay their findings as curiosities:

> This innovative stuff is not a priority for today's undergraduates. In the last decade of the 20th century, the essential things to teach students are still the insights of Hume and Ricardo. That is, we need to teach them that trade deficits are self-correcting and that the benefits of trade do not depend on a country having an absolute advantage over its rivals.[58]

Economists are especially critical of the antiforeign outlook because it does not just *happen* to be wrong; it frequently conflicts with elementary economics. Textbooks teach that total output increases if producers specialize and trade. On an individual level, who could deny it? Imagine how much time it would take to grow your own food, when a few hours' wages spent at the grocery store feed you for weeks. Analogies between individual and social behavior are at times misleading, but this is not one of those times. International trade is, as Steven Landsburg explains, a technology:

> There are two technologies for producing automobiles in America. One is to manufacture them in Detroit, and the other is to grow them in Iowa. Everybody knows about the first technology; let me tell you about the second. First you plant seeds, which are the raw materials from which automobiles are constructed. You wait a few months until wheat appears. Then you harvest the wheat, load it onto ships, and sail the ships westward into the Pacific Ocean. After a few months, the ships reappear with Toyotas on them.[59]

And this is one amazing technology. The Law of Comparative Advantage, one of most fascinating theorems in economics, shows that mutually beneficial international trade is possible even if one nation is *less productive in every way*.[60] Suppose an American can make 10 cars or five bushels of wheat, and a Mexican can make one car or two bushels of wheat. Though the Americans are better at both tasks, specialization and trade increase production. If one American switches from wheat to cars, and three Mexicans switch from cars to wheat, world output goes up by two cars *plus* one bushel of wheat.

How can anyone overlook trade's remarkable benefits? Adam Smith, along with many 18th- and 19th-century economists, identifies the root error as misidentification of money and wealth: "A rich country, in the same manner as a rich man, is supposed to be a country abounding in money; and to heap up gold and silver in any country is supposed to be the best way to enrich it."[61] It follows that trade is zero-sum, since the only way for a country to make its balance more favorable is to make another country's balance less favorable.

Even in Smith's day, however, his story was probably too clever by half. The root error behind 18th-century mercantilism was unreasonable distrust of foreigners. Otherwise, why would people focus on money draining out of "the nation," but not "the region," "the city," "the village," or "the family"? Anyone who consistently equated money with wealth would fear *all* outflows of precious metals. In practice, human beings then and now commit the balance-of-trade fallacy only when *other countries* enter the picture. No one loses sleep about the trade balance between California and Nevada, or me and Tower Records. The fallacy is not treating *all* purchases as a cost, but treating *foreign* purchases as a cost.[62]

Modern conditions do make antiforeign bias easier to spot. To take one prominent example, immigration is far more of an issue now than it was in Smith's time. Economists are predictably quick to see the benefits of immigration. Trade in labor is roughly the same as trade in goods. Specialization and exchange raise output—for instance, by letting skilled American moms return to work by hiring Mexican nannies.

In terms of the balance of payments, immigration is a nonissue. If an immigrant moves from Mexico City to New York, and spends all his earnings in his new homeland, the balance of trade does not change. Yet the public still looks on immigration as a bald misfortune: jobs lost, wages reduced, public services consumed. Many see a *larger* trade deficit as a fair price to pay for *reduced* immigration. One peculiar *pro*-NAFTA argument is that if we admit more Mexican goods, we will have fewer Mexicans.[63] It should be evident, then, that the general public sees immigration as a distinct danger—independent of, and more frightening, than an unfavorable balance of trade. People feel all the more vulnerable when they reflect that these foreigners are not just selling us their products. *They live among us.*

It is misleading, however, to think about "foreignness" as either/or. From the viewpoint of the typical American, Canadians are less foreign than the British, who are in turn less foreign than the Japanese. During 1983–87, 28% of Americans in the General Social Survey admitted they disliked Japan, but only 8% disliked England, and a scant 3% disliked Canada.[64] It is not surprising, then, that the degree of anti-foreign bias varies by country. Objective measures like the volume of trade or the trade deficit are often secondary to physical, linguistic, and cultural similarity. Trade with Canada or Great Britain generates only mild alarm compared to trade with Mexico or Japan. U.S. imports from, and trade deficits with, Canada exceeded those with Mexico *every* year from 1985 to 2004.[65] During the anti-Japan hysteria of the eighties, British foreign direct investment in the United States always exceeded that of the Japanese by at least 50%.[66] Foreigners who look like us and speak English are hardly foreign at all.

Calm reflection on the international economy reveals much to be thankful for, and little to fear. On this point, economists past and present agree. But an important proviso lurks beneath the surface. Yes, there is little to fear about the international economy itself. But modern researchers—unlike economists of the past and teachers of the present—rarely mention that *attitudes* about the international economy are another story. Paul Krugman hits the nail on the head: "The conflict among nations that so many policy intellectuals imagine prevails is an illusion; but it is an illusion that can destroy the reality of mutual gains from trade."[67]

Make-Work Bias

> What we should wish for, clearly, is that each hectare
> of land produce little wheat, and that each kernel of
> wheat contain little sustenance—in other words, that our
> land should be unfruitful. . . . [O]ne could even say that
> job opportunities would be in direct proportion to this
> unfruitfulness. . . . What we should desire still more is
> that human intelligence should be enfeebled or
> extinguished; for, so long as it survives, it ceaselessly
> endeavors to increase the *ratio of the end to the means*
> *and of the product to the effort.*
> —*Frédéric Bastiat*, Economic Sophisms[68]

I was an undergraduate when the Cold War ended, and I can still remember talking about military spending cuts with a conservative student. The whole idea made her nervous. Why? Because she had no idea how a market economy would absorb the discharged soldiers. She did not even distinguish between short-term and long-term consequences of the cuts; in her mind, to layoff 100,000 government employees was virtually equivalent to disemploying 100,000 people for life. Her position is particularly striking if you realize that her objection applies equally well to spending on government programs that— as a conservative—she opposed.

If a well-educated individual ideologically opposed to wasteful government spending thinks like this, it is hardly surprising that she is not alone. The public often literally believes that labor is better to use than conserve. Saving labor, producing more goods with fewer manhours, is widely perceived not as progress, but as a danger. I call this **make-work bias**, *a tendency to underestimate the economic benefits of conserving labor.*[69] Where noneconomists see the destruction of jobs, economists see the essence of economic growth—the production of more with less. Alan Blinder explains:

> If you put the question directly, "Is higher productivity better than lower productivity?," few people will answer in the negative. Yet policy changes are often sold as ways to "create jobs." . . . Jobs can be created in two ways. The socially beneficial way is to enlarge GNP, so that there will be more useful work to be done. But we can also create jobs by seeing to it that each worker is less productive. Then more labor will be required to produce the same bill of goods. The latter form of job creation does raise employment; but it is the path to rags, not riches.[70]

For an individual to prosper, he only needs to *have* a job. But society can only prosper if individuals *do* a job, if they create goods and services that someone wants.

Economists have been at war with make-work bias for centuries. Bastiat ridicules the equation of prosperity with jobs as "Sisyphism," after the mythological fully-employed Greek who was eternally condemned to roll a boulder up a hill. In the eyes of the public:

> Effort itself constitutes and measures wealth. To progress is to increase the *ratio of effort to result.* Its ideal may be represented by the toil of Sisyphus, at once barren and eternal.[71]

In contrast, for the economist:

> Wealth . . . increases proportionately to the increase in the *ratio of result to effort.* Absolute perfection, whose archetype is God, consists in the widest possible distance between these two terms, that is, a situation in which no effort at all yields infinite results.[72]

In the 1893 *Quarterly Journal of Economics,* Simon Newcomb explains:

> The divergence between the economist and the public is by no means confined to foreign trade. We find a direct antagonism between them on nearly every question involving the employment of labor. . . . The idea that the utility and importance of an industry are to be measured by the employment which it gives to labor is so deeply rooted in human nature that economists can scarcely claim to have taken the first step towards its eradication.[73]

His last remark is particularly striking. Nineteenth-century economists believed they had diagnosed enduring economic confusions, not intellectual fads, and they were right. Almost a hundred years after Newcomb, Alan Blinder makes the same lament. But Blinder's critique of make-work bias, unlike Newcomb's, did not appear in a leading academic journal like the *QJE.* He had to venture beyond the ivory tower with a popular book to find his audience. Referees would almost certainly have taken issue with Blinder—not because modern economists agree with make-work bias, but because it is disreputable to claim that *anyone* embraces such folly.

But embrace it they do. The crudest form of make-work bias is Luddite fear of the machine. Common sense proclaims that machines make life easier for human beings. The public qualifies this "naive" position by noting that machines also make people's lives harder by throwing them out of work. And who knows? Maybe the second effect dominates the first. During the Great Depression, intellectual fads like Howard Scott's "technocracy" movement blamed the nation's woes on technological progress.

As Scott saw the future, the inexorable increase in productivity, far outstripping opportunities for employment or investment, must mean permanent and growing unemployment and permanent and growing debt, until capitalism collapsed under the double load.[74]

Economists' love of qualification is notorious, but most doubt that the protechnology position needs to be qualified. Technology often *creates* new jobs; without the computer, there would be no jobs in computer programming or software development. But the fundamental defense of labor-saving technology is that employing more workers than you need wastes valuable labor. If you pay a worker to twiddle his thumbs, you could have paid him to do something socially useful instead.

Economists add that market forces readily convert this *potential* social benefit into an actual one. After technology throws people out of work, they have an incentive to find a new use for their talents. Cox and Alm aptly describe this process as "churn": "Through relentless turmoil, the economy re-creates itself, shifting labor resources to where they're needed, replacing old jobs with new ones."[75] They illustrate this process with history's most striking example: The drastic decline in agricultural employment:

> In 1800, it took nearly 95 of every 100 Americans to feed the country. In 1900, it took 40. Today, it takes just 3. . . . The workers no longer needed on farms have been put to use providing new homes, furniture, clothing, computers, pharmaceuticals, appliances, medical assistance, movies, financial advice, video games, gourmet meals, and an almost dizzying array of other goods and services. . . . What we have in place of long hours in the fields is the wealth of goods and services that come from allowing the churn to work, wherever and whenever it might occur.[76]

These arguments sound harsh. That is part of the reason why they are so unpopular: people would rather feel compassionately than think logically. Many economists advocate government assistance to cushion displaced workers' transition, and retain public support for a dynamic economy. Alan Blinder recommends extended unemployment insurance, retraining, and relocation subsidies.[77] Other economists disagree. But almost all economists grant that stopping transitions has a grave cost.

Exasperating as the Luddite mentality is, countries rarely move beyond rhetoric and turn back the clock of technology. But you cannot say the same about another controversy infused with make-work bias: hostility to downsizing. What could possibly be *good* about downsizing? Every time we figure out how to accomplish a goal using fewer workers, it enriches society, because labor is a valuable resource.

> We have a tremendous stake in allowing the churn to grind forward, putting our labor resources to work raising living standards, to give us more for less. We can't get around it: The churn's promise of higher living standards can't be reaped without job losses. . . . Downsizing companies will be vilified for making what appear to be hardhearted decisions. When passions cool, however, there ought to be time to recognize that, in most cases, the dirty work had to be done.[78]

Inside of a household, everyone understands what Cox and Alm call "the upside of downsizing."[79] You do not worry about how to spend the hours you save when you buy a washing machine. There are always other ways to spend your time. Bastiat insightfully observes that a loner would never fall prey to make-work bias:

> No solitary man would ever conclude that, in order to make sure that his own labor had something to occupy it, he should break the tools that save him labor, neutralize the fertility of the soil, or return to the sea the goods it may have brought him. . . . He would understand, in short, that a *saving in labor* is nothing else than *progress*.[80]

The existence of an exchange economy is a necessary condition for make-work confusion to arise.

> But *exchange* hampers our view of so simple a truth. In society, with the division of labor that it entails, the production and the consumption of an object are not performed by the same individual. Each person comes to regard his own labor no longer as a means, but as an end.[81]

If you receive a washing machine as a gift, the benefit is yours; you have more free time and the same income. If you get downsized, the benefit goes to other people; you have more free time, but your income temporarily falls. In both cases, though, society conserves valuable labor.

Pessimistic Bias

> Two [more] generations should saturate the world with
> population, and should exhaust the mines. When that
> moment comes, economical decay, or the decay of
> economical civilization, should set in.
> —*Henry Adams, 1898*[82]

I first encountered antidrug propaganda in second grade. It was called "drug education," but it was mostly scary stories. I was told that kids around me were using drugs, and that a pusher would soon offer me some, too. Teachers warned that more and more kids would become addicts, and by the time I was in junior high I would be surrounded by them. Authority figures would occasionally speculate about our adulthood, and wonder how a country could function with such a degenerate workforce. Yet another reason, they mused, that this country is going downhill.

The junior high dystopia never materialized. I am still waiting to be offered drugs. By the time I reached adulthood, it was apparent that most people were not going to their jobs high on PCP. Generation X used its share of illegal narcotics, but its entry into the workforce accompanied the marvels of the Internet age, not a stupor-induced decline in productivity and innovation.

My teachers' predictions about America's economic future turned out to be laughable. But they fit nicely into a larger pattern. As a general rule, the public believes economic conditions are not as good as they really are. It sees a world going from bad to worse; the economy faces a long list of grim challenges, leaving little room for hope. I refer to the public's leanings as **pessimistic bias**, *a tendency to overestimate the severity of economic problems and underestimate the (recent) past, present, and future performance of the economy.*[83]

Adam Smith famously ridiculed such attitudes with a one-liner: "There is a great deal of ruin in a nation."[84] His point, which economists often echo, is that the public lacks perspective. A large economy can and usually does progress despite interminable setbacks. While economists debate about *how much* growth to expect, public discourse thinks in terms of stagnation versus decline.

Suppose a congenitally pessimistic doctor examines a patient. There are two kinds of errors to watch out for. For one thing, he would exaggerate the severity of the patient's *symptoms*. After finding a body temperature of 100 degrees, the doctor might exclaim that the patient has a "dangerous fever." But the doctor might also err in his *overall* judgment, giving the patient two weeks to live.

Pessimism about the economy exhibits the same structure. You may be pessimistic about *symptoms*, overblowing the severity of everything from the deficit to affirmative action. But you can also be pessimistic *overall*, seeing negative trends in living standards, wages, and inequality. Public opinion is marked by pessimism in both its forms. Economists constantly advise the public not to lose sleep over the latest economic threat in the news.[85] But they also make a habit of explaining how far mankind has come in the last hundred years, pointing out massive gains we take for granted.[86]

A staple of pessimistic rhetoric is to idealize conditions in the more distant past in order to put recent conditions in a negative light. Arthur Herman's *The Idea of Decline in Western History* asserts that "Virtually every culture past or present has believed that men and women are not up to the standards of their parents and forebears," and asks, "Why is this sense of decline common to all cultures?"[87] In *Primitivism and Related Ideas in Antiquity*, Arthur Lovejoy and George Boas second the view that this pessimistic illusion is nearly universal:

> It is a not improbable conjecture that the feeling that humanity was becoming over-civilized, that life was getting too complicated and over-refined, dates from the time when the cave-men first became such. It can hardly be supposed—if the cave-men were at all like their descendants—that none among them discoursed with contempt on the cowardly effeminacy of living under shelter or upon the exasperating inconvenience of constantly returning for food and sleep to the same place instead of being free to roam at large in wide-open spaces.[88]

Pessimistic bias has a smaller role in the oral tradition of economics than antimarket, antiforeign, or make-work bias. Famous economists of the past frequently overlook it; teachers of economics spend relatively little time rooting it out. But while the voice of oral tradition is softer than usual, it is not silent. Though he did not live to see the Industrial Revolution, Adam Smith declares progress the normal course of events:

> The uniform, constant, and uninterrupted effort of every man to better his condition . . . is frequently powerful enough to maintain *the natural progress of things toward improvement*, in spite both of the extravagance of government, and of the greatest errors of administration. Like the unknown principle of animal life, it frequently restores health and vigour to the constitution, in spite, not only of the disease, but of the absurd prescriptions of the doctor.[89]

However, progress is so gradual that a few pockets of decay hide it from the public view:

> To form a right judgment of it, indeed, we must compare the state of the country at periods somewhat distant from one another. The progress is frequently so gradual that, at near periods, the improvement is not only not sensible, but from the declension either of certain branches of industry, or of certain districts of the country,

things which sometimes happen though the country in general be in great prosperity, *there frequently arises a suspicion that the riches and industry of the whole are decaying.*[90]

David Hume—economist, philosopher, and Adam Smith's best friend—blames popular pessimism on our psychology, not the slow and uneven nature of progress: "The humour of blaming the present, and admiring the past, is strongly rooted in human nature, and has an influence even on persons endued with the profoundest judgment and most extensive learning."[91] Hume elsewhere appeals to pessimistic bias to account for superstition: "Where real terrors are wanting, the soul, active to its own prejudice, and fostering its predominant inclination, finds imaginary ones, to whose power and malevolence it sets no limits."[92]

Despite these promising beginnings, 19th-century economists did little to develop the theme of pessimistic bias. Bastiat and Newcomb say little about it. Nineteenth-century socialists who predicted "immiseration" of the working class met intellectual resistance from economists. But the root of the socialists' forecast was hostility to markets, not pessimism as such. Economists often ridiculed socialists for their wild *optimism* about the impending socialist utopia.[93]

Nineteenth-century opponents of doom and gloom are easier to find in sociology. Alexis de Tocqueville attacks pessimism as "the great sickness of our age."[94] Herbert Spencer finds it exasperating that "the more things improve the louder become the exclamations about their badness."[95] When problems—from mistreatment of women to illiteracy to poverty—are serious, people take them for granted. As conditions improve, the public believes ever more strongly that things have never been worse.

> Yet while elevation, mental and physical, of the masses is going on far more rapidly than ever before—while the lowering of the death-rate proves that the average life is less trying, there swells louder and louder the cry that the evils are so great that nothing short of a social revolution can cure them. In presence of obvious improvements . . . it is proclaimed, with increasing vehemence, that things are so bad that society must be pulled to pieces and re-organised on another plan.[96]

Even leading optimists grant that pessimistic bias has grown worse in the modern era. Herman maintains that it peaked soon after the end of World War I, when "Talking about the end of Western civilization had become as natural as breathing. The only subject left to debate was not whether the modern West was doomed but why." But pessimism remains at strangely high levels: "While intellectuals have been predicting the imminent collapse of Western civilization for more than one hundred and fifty years, its influence has grown faster during that period than at any time in history."[97]

How can high levels of pessimism coexist with constantly rising standards of living?[98] Though pessimism has abated since World War I, the *gap* between objective conditions and subjective perceptions is arguably greater than ever.[99] Gregg Easterbrook ridicules the failure of the citizens of the developed world to appreciate their good fortune:

> Our forebears, who worked and sacrificed tirelessly in their hopes their descendants would someday be free, comfortable, healthy, and educated, might be dismayed to observe how acidly we deny we now are these things.[100]

Like David Hume, economists Cox and Alm appeal to fundamental human psychology to explain our pessimism: "The present almost always pales when measured against 'the good old days.' " Mild forms of this bias sustain lingering economic malcontent: "Nostalgists often ignore improvements in goods and services, yet remember fondly the prices they paid long ago for the cheapest versions of products."[101] Strong forms make us "open-minded" to paranoid fantasies:

> Some part of human nature connects with the apocalyptic. Time and again, pessimists among us have envisioned the world going straight to hell. Never mind that it hasn't: A lot of us braced for the worst. Whether the source is the Bible or Nostradamus, Thomas Malthus, or the Club of Rome, predictions of calamity aren't easily ignored, no matter how many times we wake up in the morning after the world was supposed to end.[102]

There is an ongoing debate about growth *slowdown*. This is what *relatively* pessimistic economists like Paul Krugman mean when they say that "the U.S. economy is doing badly."[103] Other economists counter that standard numbers inadequately adjust for the rising quality and variety of the consumption basket, and the changing composition of the workforce. The rapid growth of the 1990s raised more doubts.[104] Either way, the worst-case scenario GDP statistics permit—a lower speed of progress—is no disaster. In the face of popular economic pessimism, Krugman, too, exclaims: "I have seen the present, and it works!"[105]

The intelligent pessimist's favorite refuge is to argue that standard statistics like GDP miss important components of our standard of living. The leading candidate is environmental quality, where negative thinking is firmly ensconced—to put it mildly.[106] Pessimists often add that our failure to deal with environmental destruction will soon morph into economic disaster as well. In the 1960s, über-pessimist Paul Ehrlich notoriously predicted that environmental neglect would shortly lead to mass starvation.[107] If resources are rapidly vanishing as our numbers multiply, human beings are going to be poor and hungry, not just out of touch with Mother Earth.

A number of economists have met these challenges. The most wide-ranging is Julian Simon, who argues that popular "doom and gloom" views of resource depletion, overpopulation, and environmental quality are exaggerated, and often the opposite of the truth.[108] Past progress does not *guarantee* future progress, but it creates a strong presumption:

> Throughout the long sweep of history, forecasts of resource scarcity have always been heard, and—just as now—the doomsayers have always claimed that the past was no guide to the future because they stood at a turning point in history. . . . In every period those who would have bet on improvement rather than deterioration in fundamental aspects of material life—such as the availability of natural resources—would usually have been right.[109]

Simon has been a lightning rod for controversy, but his main theses— that natural resources are getting cheaper, population density is not bad for growth, and air quality is improving—are now almost mainstream in environmental economics.[110] Since Michael Kremer's seminal paper "Population Growth and Technological Change: One Million B.C. to 1990," even Simon's "extreme" view that population growth *raises* living standards has gained wide acceptance.[111] The upshot: Refining measures of economic welfare does not revive the case for pessimism. In fact, more inclusive measures cement the case for optimism, because life has also been getting better on the neglected dimensions.[112] The question "Aren't you worried that declining environmental quality is going to destroy our material prosperity?" is therefore reminiscent of "Do you still beat your mother?"

Conclusion

Economists have a love/hate relationship with systematic bias. As theorists, they deny its existence. As empiricists, they increasingly import it from other fields. But when they teach, address the public, or wonder what is wrong with the world, they dip into their own "private stash." On some level, economists not only recognize that systematically biased beliefs exist. They think they have discovered virulent strains in their own backyard— systematically biased beliefs *about economics.*[113]

Antimarket bias, antiforeign bias, make-work bias, and pessimistic bias are the most prominent specimens. Indeed, they are so prominent that one can hardly teach economics without bumping into them. Students of economics are not a blank slate for their teachers to write on. They arrive with strong prejudices. They underestimate the benefits of markets. They underestimate the benefits of dealing with foreigners. They underestimate the benefits of conserving labor. They underestimate the performance of the economy, and overestimate its problems.

But economists' love/hate relationship with systematic bias raises some doubts. If the leading figures in the history of economics took the existence of these biases for granted, if teachers of economics grapple with them over and over in the classroom, what happens when we put these biases under the microscope of modern research? Do they hold up to empirical scrutiny? Or are they just stories that economists have been telling themselves all these years?

Chapter 3

EVIDENCE FROM THE SURVEY OF AMERICANS AND ECONOMISTS ON THE ECONOMY

> It seems, then, that I am asserting that the conventional wisdom about international trade is dominated by entirely ignorant men, who have managed to convince themselves and everyone else who matters that they have deep insights, but are in fact unaware of the most basic principles of and facts about the world economy; and that the disdained academic economists are at least by comparison fonts of wisdom and common sense. And that is indeed my claim.
> —*Paul Krugman,* Pop Internationalism[1]

ECONOMISTS from Smith, Bastiat, and Newcomb to Mises, Blinder, and Krugman maintain that the public suffers from systematically biased beliefs about economics. Are they right? We can judge an argument about, say, comparative advantage, on its own merits. But that is not enough to establish the existence of a systematic bias. Once you know that economic view X is correct, you still have to verify that, by and large, (a) economists believe X, and (b) noneconomists believe not-X. Is it really the case, for example, that economists are more upbeat about the effects of international competition than noneconomists?

These are quintessentially empirical questions. Teaching experience carries some weight: Can economists have been misreading their students for centuries? But personal impressions are not good enough. When psychologists and political scientists talk about bias, they back up their claims with hard data. Economists who want to join the discussion have to do the same.

There are numerous surveys of the economic beliefs of both economists and the general public.[2] They broadly confirm the "wide divergence" with which Newcomb maintained "all are familiar." Take the case of free trade versus protection. A long-running survey initiated by J. R. Kearl and coauthors has repeatedly asked economists whether they agree that "tariffs and import quotas usually reduce the general welfare of society."[3] In 2000, 72.5% mainly agreed, and an additional 20.1% agreed with provisos; only 6% generally disagreed. The breakdowns for 1990 and the late 1970s are even more lopsided in favor of free trade.

What about the public's views on this matter? The carefully constructed Worldviews survey[4] has repeatedly asked a random sample of Americans the following:

> It has been argued that if all countries would eliminate their tariffs and restrictions on imported goods, the costs of goods would go down for everyone. Others have said that such tariffs and restrictions are necessary to protect certain manufacturing jobs in certain industries from the competition of less expensive imports. Generally, would you say you sympathize more with those who want to eliminate tariffs or those who think such tariffs are necessary?[5]

The public always leans decidedly in favor of protection. Support for free trade bottomed out in 1977, when only 18% sympathized with eliminating tariffs, and 66% thought they were necessary. But public opinion remains protectionist in absolute terms. In 2002, sympathy for ending tariffs reached a historic high of 38%—versus 50% who took the opposite view. Furthermore, 85% of the respondents that year held that "protecting the jobs of American workers" should be a "very important" goal of foreign policy—an all-time high![6]

If antiforeign bias really exists, these are the patterns you would expect. Comparable evidence can be marshaled for the other biases explored in the last chapter. Take antimarket bias. In the late 1970s, Kearl et al. asked economists whether "wage-price controls should be used to control inflation."[7] Almost three-quarters of economists generally disagreed. In contrast, the General Social Survey (henceforth, GSS) reports that solid majorities of noneconomists think it should be government's responsibility to "keep prices under control."[8] Those who agree outnumber those who disagree by at least 2:1 and often 3:1. Casual empiricism and formal empiricism are in sync. Economists trust competition; noneconomists want government to leash rapacious businesses.

Nevertheless, the evidence is not rock solid, because the survey results are not strictly comparable. The Kearl questions on free trade and price controls are similar to their counterparts in the Worldviews survey and the GSS, not identical. Moreover, the surveys were rarely performed at exactly the same time. The Kearl data on price controls come from the late seventies; the GSS data, from the eighties and nineties.

Getting data on the economic beliefs of economists and the public is therefore deceptively easy. Surveys of both groups abound. The catch is that almost none samples *both* laymen and experts on the *same* questions at the *same* time. A skeptic could attribute differences to wording: If you ask economists a question loaded one way, and the public a question loaded in the other, you can "find" any pattern you like.

Analyzing the SAEE: The Public, the Economists, and the "Enlightened Public"

Fortunately, one large and well-crafted study is largely immune to this critique. In 1996, the *Washington Post*, Kaiser Family Foundation, and Harvard University Survey Project collaborated to create the Survey of Americans and Economists on the Economy (henceforth, SAEE).[9] Based on interviews with 1,510 randomly selected members of the American public and 250 economics Ph.D.'s, the SAEE is ideally structured to test for systematic lay-expert belief differences.[10] It also features remarkably diverse questions, which lets us explore belief differences in depth. A further advantage of the SAEE is its rich set of respondent characteristics. One can use this information to test theories about the origin of lay-expert belief gaps.

The rest of this book draws heavily on the SAEE, so it is worth exploring at length. Its 37 questions break down into four categories.[11] Questions in the first two categories ask whether various factors are a "major reason," "minor reason," or "not a reason at all" why "the economy is not doing better than it is." There are 18 questions of this form. Questions in the third category ask whether something is good, indifferent, or bad for the economy. There are seven questions with this structure. The last category is a grab bag of a dozen miscellaneous questions.

The next three sections walk the reader through the entire survey. But before proceeding, it is vital to address the most serious objection to this approach: *Experts can be biased, too.* There are large belief gaps between economists and the public. They cannot both be right. But is it legitimate to infer the existence of systematic *biases* in the public's thinking from the mere existence of systematic *differences* between economists and noneconomists?

Elitist though it sounds, this is the standard practice in the broader literature on biases. As the great cognitive psychologists Kahneman and Tversky describe their method: "The presence of an error of judgment is demonstrated by comparing people's responses either with an established fact . . . or with an accepted rule of arithmetic, logic, or statistics."[12] "Established" or "accepted" by whom? By experts, of course.

In principle, experts could be mistaken instead of the public. But if mathematicians, logicians, or statisticians say the public is wrong, who would dream of "blaming the experts"? Economists get a lot less respect. Many maintain, like William Greider, that even that is more than they deserve:

> Democracy is now held captive by the mystique of "rational" policymaking, narrow assumptions about what constitutes legitimate political evidence. It is a barrier of privilege because it effectively discounts authentic political expressions from citizens and elevates the biases and opinions of the elites.[13]

From this standpoint, using economists' views to impugn the public's backfires. There are no "experts in economics," only " 'experts' in economics."

The most common doubt about economists stems from their apparent inability to agree, best captured by George Bernard Shaw's line "If all economists were laid end to end, they would not reach a conclusion."[14] But economists' hard-core detractors recognize the superficiality of this complaint. They know that economists regularly see eye-to-eye with one another. A quip from Steven Kelman directly contradicts Shaw:

> The near-unanimity of the answers economists give to public policy questions, highly controversial among the run of intelligent observers, but which share the characteristic of being able to be analyzed in terms of microeconomic theory, reminds one of the unanimity characterizing bodies such as the politburo of the Soviet Communist Party.[15]

It is not lack of consensus that incenses knowledgeable critics, but the way economists unite behind *unpalatable* conclusions—such as doubts about the benefits of regulation. Kelman bemoans the fact that even economists in the Carter administration were economists first and liberals second:

> At the government agency where I have worked and where agency lawyers and agency microeconomists interact with each other . . . the lawyers are often exasperated, not only by the frequency with which agency economists attack their proposals but also by the unanimity among the agency economists in their opposition. The lawyers tend to (incorrectly) attribute this opposition to failure to hire "a broad enough spectrum" of economists, and to beg the economists, if they can't support the lawyers' proposals, at least to give them "the best economic arguments" in favor of them. . . . The economists' answer is typically something like, "There are no good economic arguments for your proposal."[16]

As usual, it is a rare person who seriously considers, "Maybe others disagree with me because they *know more* than me." For detractors, the most plausible explanation for economists' distinctive outlook is that these so-called experts are biased.

But how? Baldly asserting, "They're wrong because they're biased" explains nothing. Even critics feel compelled to specify the source of the bias. Challenges to economists' scientific objectivity take on two main forms.

The first is *self-serving bias.* A large literature claims that human beings gravitate toward selfishly convenient beliefs.[17] Since economists have high incomes and secure jobs, perhaps they are biased to believe that whatever benefits them, benefits all. Marx famously ridiculed economists as apologists for the capitalist system that suckled them, denouncing Jeremy Bentham, for instance, as "that insipid, pedantic, leather-tongued oracle of the ordinary bourgeois intelligence of the 19th century."[18] Ludwig von Mises colorfully recalls that in interwar Germany "all that the students of the social sciences learned from their teachers was that economics is a spurious science and that the so-called economists are, as Marx said, sycophantic apologists of the unfair class interests of bourgeois exploiters, ready to sell the people to big business and finance capital."[19] Brossard and Pearlstein, writing half a century later for the *Washington Post,* remark, "The disconnect between economists and typical Americans reflects, at least in part, the fact that economists tend to be members of a social, intellectual, and economic elite that has fared relatively well over the past 20 years. . . . And many of the economists hold down tenured teaching positions that afford them a lifetime of job security."[20] One could even equate economists' cushy jobs with a tacit bribe. Why rock the boat when you enjoy a lavish stateroom?

The second doubt about economists' objectivity is less sordid but equally damaging: *ideological bias.*[21] Robert Kuttner disapprovingly observes that "Much of the economics profession, after an era of embracing the mixed economy, has reverted to a new fundamentalism cherishing the virtues of markets."[22] A consensus of fundamentalists hardly inspires confidence. It sound like an intellectual chain letter: Maybe each batch of graduate students was brainwashed by the previous generation of ideologues.

By appealing to these two specific biases, the critics take a risk. Both the self-serving and the ideological bias hypotheses are, *in principle,* empirically testable. Economists' views are the product of their affluence? Then rich economists and rich noneconomists should agree. Economists are blinded by conservative ideology? Then conservative economists and conservative noneconomists should agree. The SAEE is a remarkable resource because it has enough information to test both hypotheses. It measures all the leading social cleavages: family income, job security, race, gender, age, even income growth. It also has two measures of ideology.

One can use this information to estimate what the average belief would be after statistically *adjusting* for both self-serving and ideological biases. I term this the belief of the *Enlightened Public*. The Enlightened Public's belief is the answer to the question, "What would the average person believe if he had a Ph.D. in economics?" Or equivalently: "What would Ph.D. economists believe if their finances and political ideology matched those of the average person?"[23]

Imagine, then, that laymen and experts had identical income, job security, income growth, race, gender, age, ideology, and party identification. Would they still disagree? If either self-serving bias or ideological bias is a *full explanation* for the belief gap, the estimated beliefs of the Enlightened Public will match the observed beliefs of the typical noneconomist.[24] You could make laymen and experts see eye-to-eye by adding the right control variables. Contrarily, if the hypotheses of self-serving and ideological bias are *totally without merit*, the beliefs of the Enlightened Public would match the observed views of economists. Whatever control variables you used, the lay-expert gap would persist unscathed.

Note the parallel with political scientists' analysis of "enlightened preferences," as discussed in chapter 2. In the enlightened preference approach, one estimates what a person would think if you increased his level of political knowledge to the maximum level, keeping his other characteristics fixed. Using the SAEE, similarly, I estimate what a person would think if you turned him into a Ph.D. economist, keeping his other characteristics fixed. The key difference is that political scientists usually measure knowledge directly, while my approach proxies it using educational credentials.

The next four sections travel through the entire Survey of Americans and Economists on the Economy, analyzing responses question by question. Each of these questions has three summary statistics:

- First, the "raw" average belief for the general public.
- Second, the "raw" average belief for Ph.D. economists.
- Last, the estimated belief of the Enlightened Public.

To repeat, if self-serving and/or ideological bias *fully* accounts for the lay-expert belief gap, the Enlightened Public's average answer equals the public's. If self-serving and/or ideological bias explains *none* of the lay-expert belief gap, the Enlightened Public's average answer equals the economists'. If the truth lies somewhere in the middle, the Enlightened Public's average answer lies between the public's and the economists'.

If the self-serving and ideological bias hypotheses fail, it remains conceivable that economists suffer from a totally different bias. The same is true for any empirical result. No matter how airtight an explanation now appears, the truth conceivably belongs to another theory, so startlingly original that no one has been smart enough to propose it. Conceivable, but unlikely. If the two main efforts to undermine economists' objectivity fail, this shifts the burden of proof back onto their critics. After adding all these controls, belief *differences* that remain are best interpreted as *biases* of the public.

To preview, it turns out that the beliefs of the Enlightened Public are usually far closer to economists' than to the public's. Self-serving and ideological bias *combined* cannot account for more than 20% of the lay-expert belief gap. The remaining 80% should be attributed to the experts' greater knowledge. The naive "Experts are right, laymen are wrong" theory fits the data; the "Experts are deluded, laymen get it right" theory does not.

This does not mean that the average belief of the economics profession is an infallible oracle. I have never seen it that way. There are cases where I think that the public is closer to the truth. There are topics that I think *both* groups badly misunderstand. My claim, rather, is that—after correcting for measurable biases—economists should not change their minds just because noneconomists think differently.

Veteran teachers of Econ 1—along with economically literate laymen—will deem much of the question-by-question walkthrough to be obvious, but there are periodic surprises. Sheltered economists who teach only upper-division or graduate classes will probably have a sense of déjà vu as they progress through the SAEE. Even if they have never discussed economics with a noneconomist since they were college freshman, neglected memories of their pre-econ outlook will bubble up. Readers with little or no background in economics may react with astonishment, puzzlement, or outrage. There is not much I can do about the outrage. But I try to point readers in the right direction by sketching the main reasons why economists think as we do.

The SAEE Examined, Part I

The SAEE's first 11 questions all use the following prompt:

> Regardless of how well you think the economy is doing, there are always some problems that keep it from being as good as it might be. I am going to read you a list of reasons some people have given

for why the economy is not doing better than it is. For each one, please tell me if you think it is a major reason the economy is not doing better than it is, a minor reason, or not a reason at all.

Question 1. You are reading figure 3.1 correctly: economists are *less* concerned about the economic damage of excessive taxation than the general public. If you think that economists are far-right ideologues, this is the first sign that you should think again. The Enlightened Public takes the same view, with slightly more moderation. The reason is that the rich and securely employed worry *less* about taxation than the rest of the population—presumably the opposite of what self-serving bias predicts.

The most plausible explanation for the gap is pessimistic bias. The public is convinced it is getting a bad deal; taxes could be significantly reduced without cutting back on popular government functions. But economists recognize that locating clear-cut "waste" is difficult, and unpopular programs like foreign aid are only a tiny fraction of the budget. They also know that slashing taxes while holding spending steady spells trouble.[25]

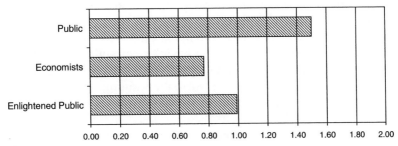

Figure 3.1 Question 1: "Taxes are too high"
0 = "not a reason at all"   1 = "minor reason"   2 = "major reason"

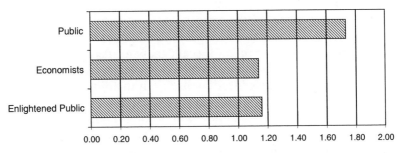

Figure 3.2 Question 2: "The federal deficit is too big"
0 = "not a reason at all"   1 = "minor reason"   2 = "major reason"

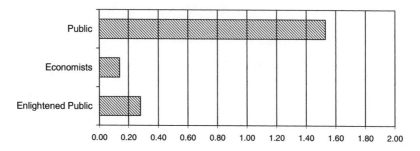

Figure 3.3 Question 3: "Foreign aid spending is too high"
0 = "not a reason at all"   1 = "minor reason"   2 = "major reason"

Question 2. The public is frequently chided for simultaneously opposing tax increases, spending cuts, and budget deficits. Responses to the question on budget deficits strongly confirm the third part of this triad (fig. 3.2). No other problem in the SAEE inspires more pessimism. Economists take the deficit seriously too, but view this woe as minor and manageable. Note that the Enlightened Public sides completely with the economists; economists' personal circumstances and ideology do nothing to explain their dissent.

Question 3. The belief gap on foreign aid (fig. 3.3) is larger than on any other, and remains almost as large after correcting for bias. The public sees foreign aid spending as a serious problem. Economists virtually to a man believe it is not worth mentioning, and the Enlightened Public is nearly as extreme. Given many economists' strong criticisms of foreign aid, this is surprising at first.[26] But economists normally criticize the effects of foreign aid on the countries that *receive* it. It is one thing to assert that foreign aid subsidizes foolish policies in the Third World and props up corrupt regimes. It is another to insist that foreign aid is bankrupting the United States. It is the latter claim that the public whole-heartedly endorses.

It is hard not to link these misconceptions with antiforeign bias. The elderly are the most quantitatively important drain on the federal budget,[27] but people *like* them. If scapegoats for fiscal distress must be found, why not focus on people who rub you the wrong way? Ungrateful foreigners smugly bleeding us dry fit the bill.

Question 4. To a person who suffers from antiforeign bias, immigration is scary. Unskilled foreigners "flood" into the country, "steal" jobs from Americans, depress wages, and gobble up public services. Economists take almost the opposite position—and the Enlightened Public is willing to cosign (fig. 3.4). International trade in goods increases

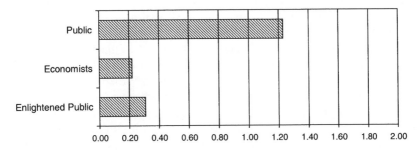

Figure 3.4 Question 4: "There are too many immigrants"
0 = "not a reason at all"   1 = "minor reason"   2 = "major reason"

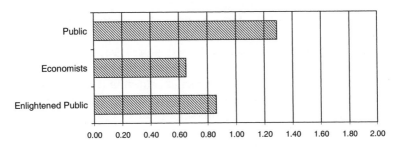

Figure 3.5 Question 5: "Too many tax breaks for business"
0 = "not a reason at all"   1 = "minor reason"   2 = "major reason"

the size of the pie, even if one trading partner has an absolute advantage in everything, and even if the good is *labor*. The case is not airtight; immigrants might prefer mugging or collecting welfare to working. But economists recognize, as the public does not, that one more self-supporting worker is a net benefit, no matter where he was born.

What about the public's fears? Some are overstated; others are flat wrong. Above all, there is no fixed number of jobs. Labor markets have often absorbed far larger infusions into the workforce than the United States is doing today. Although immigration is currently a high fraction of our population *growth*, the main reason is the low U.S. birth rate. Measured as a fraction of the population, the rate of immigration is not all that high. Empirical economists also know that there is weak evidence that immigrants depress wages, and considerable evidence that immigrants consume less in public services than they pay in taxes.[28]

Question 5. The question in figure 3.5 primarily taps into antimarket bias. Taxes are too high, thinks the public—except taxes on greedy businesses. They must be shirking their fair share, indirectly wreaking havoc on the rest of the economy. Economists see matters differently, and the Enlightened Public leans in its direction.

If you look at the facts rather than judging business guilty by reason of greedy intent, the popular view has several weaknesses. Probably the main one is that tax breaks for business are small relative to the budget.[29] Another underlying factor is that economists know that corporate income is already double taxed. Tax breaks or "loopholes" partially mitigate the inefficiencies of double taxation. The public, moreover, typically ignores the complexities of tax incidence. Consumers or workers might ultimately bear the burden that the tax code assigns to business.

Question 6. The public sees inadequate education as a serious problem, and economists agree (fig. 3.6). Indeed, economists see this as the single most serious economic problem for the United States. The leading rationale is that education has positive externalities, making the market's level of output smaller than optimal. The public presumably lacks such a sophisticated argument, but happens to reach the same conclusion.[30]

Question 7. In figure 3.7, economists again defy their conservative reputation. Yes, they habitually point out the hidden disincentive effects of government programs. But the public is already comfortable with the idea that if you help the poor, they are less likely to help themselves. The dispute is one of magnitude. Swayed by their pessimistic bias, noneconomists imagine that welfare disincentives are an implausibly large burden.

Where does the public go wrong? Its greatest error is numerical. Poverty programs, even broadly interpreted, add up to only 10% of federal spending.[31] This is many times larger than foreign aid, but still too small to be a "major reason" for subpar economic performance.

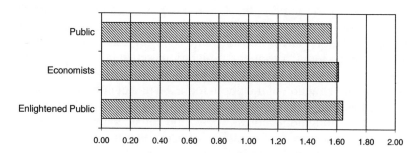

Figure 3.6 Question 6: "Education and job training are inadequate"
0 = "not a reason at all"   1 = "minor reason"   2 = "major reason"

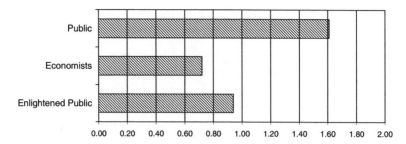

Figure 3.7 Question 7: "Too many people are on welfare"
0 = "not a reason at all"   1 = "minor reason"   2 = "major reason"

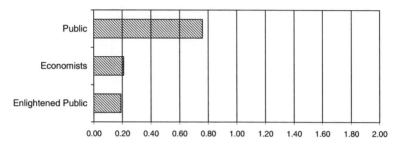

Figure 3.8 Question 8: "Women and minorities get too many advantages under affirmative action"
0 = "not a reason at all"   1 = "minor reason"   2 = "major reason"

Furthermore, welfare recipients come from the least skilled segment of the population. This tightly caps the economic damage of their absence from the workforce.

Question 8. Economists know about the negative efficiency consequences of affirmative action. Giving special categories of employees the right to sue their employers makes them less likely to be hired in the first place. But economists nevertheless assign the problem less overall significance than the public (figure 3.8). The reason is probably quantitative: Despite the public's pessimism, there are too few discrimination lawsuits to be more than a minor problem.[32]

Question 9. The question on the work ethic (fig. 3.9) taps straight into noneconomists' pessimistic bias. It fits their image of a society falling apart due to steadily declining virtue. For economists, in contrast, relaxed attitudes toward work are a symptom of progress, not decay. As people get richer, economists expect them to consume more luxury goods—including more free time. In a well-functioning econ-

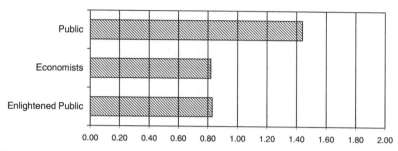

Figure 3.9 Question 9: "People place too little value on hard work"
0 = "not a reason at all"   1 = "minor reason"   2 = "major reason"

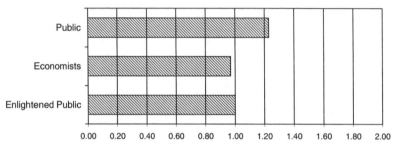

Figure 3.10 Question 10: "The government regulates business too much"
0 = "not a reason at all"   1 = "minor reason"   2 = "major reason"

omy, if individuals want more leisure and less stuff, the labor market gives them what they want.

Yet this cannot be the whole story. Economists' *relative* rating for this problem is high, and so is the Enlightened Public's. The simplest explanation is that economists are thinking in terms of measured gross domestic product, which has the widely acknowledged defect that it puts no value on leisure. By this metric, more work is always economically beneficial.[33]

Question 10. Economists' reputation as dogmatic deregulators appears to be overstated (fig. 3.10). They rate the problem of overregulation less seriously than the ever-pessimistic public.[34] But note that *relatively* speaking, stereotypes work. It is economists' fifth largest problem, versus third smallest for the public. Economists frequently hold that many perceived problems are all in the public's head, but overregulation is not one of them.

Does this not cut against the thesis of antimarket bias? To a degree, but evidence outside the SAEE helps triangulate the public's position. The public frets about regulation in the abstract, but favors it the particular, from minimum wages to farm subsidies to drug testing.[35] Even

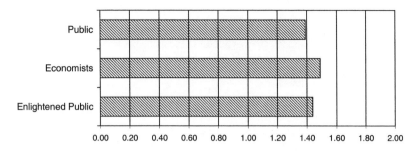

Figure 3.11 Question 11: "People are not saving enough"
0 = "not a reason at all"   1 = "minor reason"   2 = "major reason"

drastic measures like overall price controls are not unpopular.[36] For the public, the primary cost of regulation seems to be burdensome paperwork and red tape. Economists' often have the more fundamental worry that *regulation is counterproductive*. Price controls create shortages and black markets; drug efficacy tests mandated by the Food and Drug Administration delay the introduction of life-saving drugs. Economists also harbor doubts about regulators' goals: they know, as few noneconomists do, that the goal of much regulation is to shield existing firms from competition.[37]

Question 11. Laymen and experts are almost equally distressed by the low savings rate (fig. 3.11). Fear is the public's default position; this is a rare case where economists concur. There are two main reasons for the experts' high level of concern. First, savings is double taxed. You pay one tax when you earn income, and a further tax if you earn any interest on your after-tax income. This suggests an unusually large gap between the efficient, untaxed level of savings and the actual level. Second, many economists think that savings has positive externalities, so without taxes the level of savings would still be too low.

The SAEE Examined, Part II

The prompt for the SAEE's next seven questions changes slightly:

Now I am going to read you another list of reasons, having to do with businesses, that some people have given for why the economy is not doing better than it is. For each one, please tell me if you think it is a major reason the economy is not doing better than it is, a minor reason, or not a reason at all.

Question 12. Are the critics right about self-serving bias? Economists scoff at the idea that excessive profits are hurting the economy (fig.

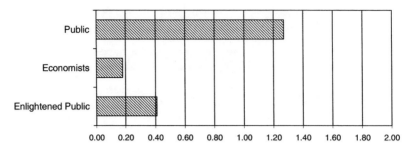

Figure 3.12 Question 12: "Business profits are too high"
0 = "not a reason at all"   1 = "minor reason"   2 = "major reason"

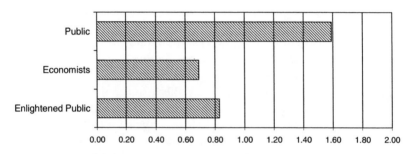

Figure 3.13 Question 13: "Top executives are paid too much"
0 = "not a reason at all"   1 = "minor reason"   2 = "major reason"

3.12). Who would be so insensitive, other than malefactors of great wealth? The results for the Enlightened Public support a curt rejoinder. *Anyone with a Ph.D. in economics,* rich or poor, would tell you the same. Economists' contrarian position is not a rentier's rationalization.

The real problem is not that greed blinds economists but that anti-market bias blinds the public. Part of the public's error is quantitative. It wildly overestimates the rate of profit enjoyed by the typical business, with an average guess near 50%.[38] But the disagreement is deeper. Through the prism of antimarket bias, the public perceives profit as a lump-sum transfer to business. Economists, in contrast, recognize it as the motor of progress as well as flexibility.

Question 13. Beliefs about excessive executive pay (fig. 3.13) parallel those about excessive profits. The numbers for the Enlightened Public fit the "experts right, laymen wrong" story. Once again, we should stop worrying about economists' self-serving bias, and start worrying about noneconomists' antimarket bias. For the public, executive pay is a transfer to high-level managers: When they earn more, underlings

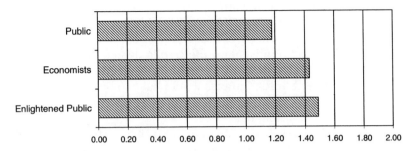

Figure 3.14 Question 14: "Business productivity is growing too slowly"
0 = "not a reason at all"   1 = "minor reason"   2 = "major reason"

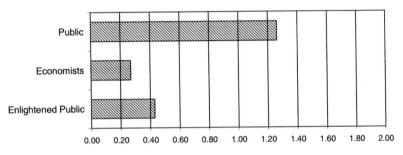

Figure 3.15 Question 15: "Technology is displacing workers"
0 = "not a reason at all"   1 = "minor reason"   2 = "major reason"

get less. Economists reject this fixed-pie mentality.[39] The salaries of the captains of industry provide incentives to cut costs, create and improve products, and accurately predict consumer demand.

Question 14. Business productivity (fig. 3.14) is the only problem that clearly worries economists more than the general public, but one can plausibly argue that this dispute is semantic. "Business productivity" sounds vaguely desirable to laymen. But it has a precise meaning for economists: It is the part of production unaccounted for by labor or capital. Intuitively, business productivity growth means the *same* inputs give you *more* output. If noneconomists understood economists' jargon, maybe their judgments would match.

Question 15. It is hard not to notice that machines make us richer. Technology is one of the most blatant differences between the present and the past, and the First World and the Third. The data show, however, that many embrace make-work bias in its crudest form: fear of the machine (fig. 3.15). Indeed, they probably resent those who are *not* afraid, especially egghead economists who fail to "feel the pain" of the untenured man in the street. But this accusation falls flat; the Enlightened Public embraces economists' "extreme" position with only a hint of moderation.

Question 16. If economists and the public agreed about the economic dangers of "sending jobs overseas" (fig. 3.16), claims that the public suffers from antiforeign bias would have to be abandoned. In fact, this is the second-largest gap in the SAEE, overshadowed only by the belief gap on foreign aid.

Economists' dismissal of the foreign aid problem stems from their knowledge of the budget. If the United States spent 50 times as much on foreign aid, they would admit it to be a major drain on Americans' standard of living. The lack of concern with jobs going overseas is more theory-driven. According to the Law of Comparative Advantage, jobs "go overseas" because there are more remunerative ways to use domestic labor.[40]

Question 17. When a profitable company cuts its workforce, the typical person treats it as clearly bad for the economy (fig. 3.17). It is

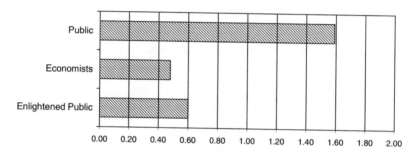

Figure 3.16 Question 16: "Companies are sending jobs overseas"
0 = "not a reason at all"   1 = "minor reason"   2 = "major reason"

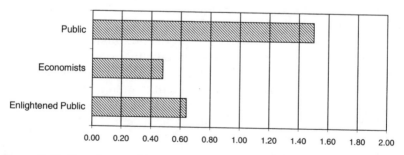

Figure 3.17 Question 17: "Companies are downsizing"
0 = "not a reason at all"   1 = "minor reason"   2 = "major reason"

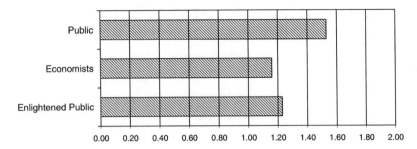

Figure 3.18 Question 18: "Companies are not investing enough money in education and job training"
0 = "not a reason at all"   1 = "minor reason"   2 = "major reason"

excusable if a firm lets workers go in order to avoid bankruptcy; then you are sacrificing some jobs to save the rest. But everyone reviles a profitable firm that downsizes in order to be *more* profitable.

Everyone, that is, who suffers from make-work bias. The popular stance rests on the illusion that employment, not production, is the measure of prosperity. In contrast, for economists and the Enlightened Public, downsizing proves the rule that private greed and the public interest point in the same direction.[41] Downsizing superfluous workers leads them to search for more socially productive ways to apply their abilities. Imagine what would have happened if the farms of the 19th century never "downsized." Greed drove these changes, but they remained changes for the better.

Question 18. There is a broad consensus (see fig. 3.6) that inadequate education is a major economic problem. The item in figure 3.18 advances a hypothesis about *why* we are insufficiently educated: lack of spending by business. This story would appeal to people with anti-market bias, and the shoe fits: Economists and the Enlightened Public do not dismiss this explanation, but the public is noticeably more sympathetic.

The SAEE Examined, Part III

All of the previous questions focused on perceived economic *problems*. The next batch of questions is more open-ended.

Generally speaking, do you think each of the following is good or bad for the nation's economy, or don't you think it makes much difference?

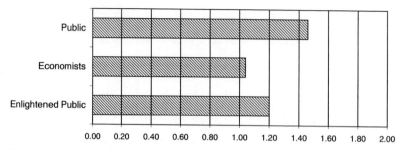

Figure 3.19 Question 19: "Tax cuts"
0 = "bad"   1 = "doesn't make much difference"   2 = "good"

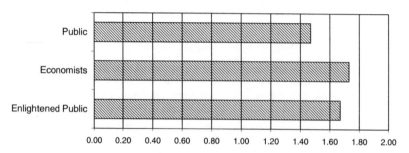

Figure 3.20 Question 20: "More women entering the workforce"
0 = "bad"   1 = "doesn't make much difference"   2 = "good"

Question 19. The public thinks that taxes are too high, and infers that tax cuts are a good thing (fig. 3.19). My interpretation is that noneconomists, avid pessimists, are convinced that government squanders their money. They therefore naively hope to pay for tax cuts by cutting unpopular programs and "waste." Economists, contrary to their laissez-faire image, are skeptical. Unpopular programs are only a small fraction of the budget,[42] and "waste" cannot be identified in an uncontroversial way.

Question 20. Economists and noneconomists both see increased female labor force participation as a good thing (fig. 3.20), but—ever the pessimists—the latter are less unanimous. It is striking that the public is so upbeat about increased female labor supply but so downbeat about increased immigrant labor supply. Presumably their economic effects are similar. One explanation for the inconsistency is that political correctness makes people too nervous to lament that women are "stealing jobs" from men.

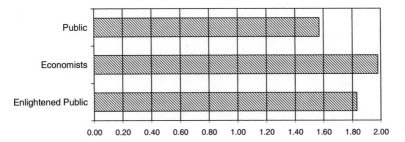

Figure 3.21 Question 21: "Increased use of technology in the workplace"
0 = "bad" 1 = "doesn't make much difference" 2 = "good"

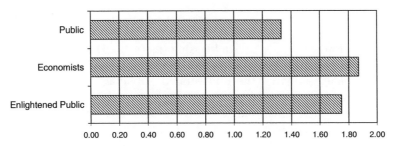

Figure 3.22 Question 22: "Trade agreements between the United States and other countries"
0 = "bad"   1 = "doesn't make much difference"   2 = "good"

Question 21. Despite make-work bias, the public is not completely crazy. A comfortable majority acknowledges the economic benefits of technological progress (fig. 3.21). A sizable belief gap arises because economists embrace new technology with one voice, while the public has reservations. According to popular stereotypes, economists fail to give a straight answer, but now the shoe is on the other foot. A noneconomist is many times *more* likely to say, "Yes, technology can be good, but on the other hand. . . . "

Question 22. Looking only at the public's average response in figure 3.22, one might be puzzled by how positive the public is about trade agreements. Where has its antiforeign bias gone? Compared to economists and the Enlightened Public, though, the public's support is half-hearted. Noneconomists tend to think, "Exports good, imports bad." So they wonder whether trade agreements "give too much" to the other side. Economists lack the public's ambivalence because they think imports are good; *unilateral* free trade is better than mutual protection.[43]

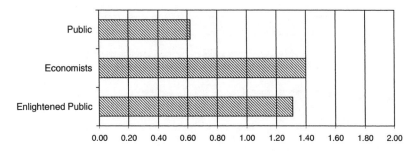

Figure 3.23 Question 23: "The recent downsizing of large corporations"
0 = "bad"   1 = "doesn't make much difference"   2 = "good"

Question 23. Economists do not just say that the danger of downsizing is overblown; they see it as a blessing (fig. 3.23). Doing more with less is the definition of progress. Is this a modern version of "Let them eat cake"? The results for the Enlightened Public say otherwise. If a person of average means got an econ Ph.D., he would change his mind.

Question 24. The most plausible way to defend the public's grasp of economics is to blame lay-expert disagreement on varying time horizons. Economists emphasize the "long run"; the public cares about here and now. Perhaps experts and laymen covertly agree about facts, but have different levels of patience. Many economists who acknowledge the reality of lay-expert belief gaps opt for this interpretation. One is Schumpeter:

> Rational recognition of the economic performance of capitalism and of the hopes it holds out for the future would require an almost impossible moral feat by the have-not. That performance stands out only if we take a long-run view; any pro-capitalism argument must rest on long-run considerations. . . . For the masses, it is the short-run view that counts. Like Louis XV, they feel *après nous le déluge.*[44]

By asking about effects 20 years in the future (fig. 3.24), we can test Schumpeter's hypothesis. If different levels of impatience are the full explanation, laymen and experts would think exactly alike. In fact, this belief gap is unusually big. Both groups are less negative about the long run, but economists are more positive both now and later. They expect a mixed blessing to become a pure gain; the public expects a pure bad to fade out.

Question 25. When the SAEE asks about the effect of trade agreements on U.S. employment (fig. 3.25), antiforeign bias and make-work bias join forces, opening up a very wide gap between

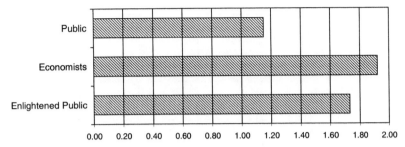

Figure 3.24 Question 24: "Some people say that these are economically unsettled times because of new technology, competition from foreign countries, and downsizing. Looking ahead 20 years, do you think these changes will eventually be good or bad for the country or don't you think these changes will make much difference?"
0 = "bad"   1 = "doesn't make much difference"   2 = "good"

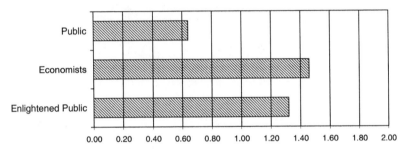

Figure 3.25 Question 25: "Do you think that trade agreements between the United States and other countries have helped create more jobs in the U.S., or have they cost the U.S. jobs, or haven't they made much of a difference?"
0 = "cost jobs" 1 = "haven't made much difference" 2 = "helped create jobs"

economists and the public. Whatever noneconomists think about trade agreements overall, they are convinced that the effect on domestic employment is negative. Economists and the Enlightened Public deny this, as expected.[45]

The Saee Examined, Part IV

The remaining questions vary in form and content, but continue to exhibit large and robust systematic belief differences.

Question 26. A key form of antimarket bias is to deny or downplay the role of competition. It is telling, then, that economists overwhelmingly attribute the 1996 rise in the price of gas to supply and demand

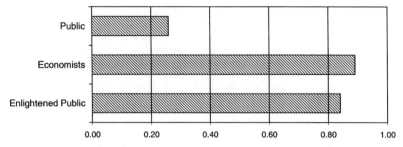

Figure 3.26 Question 26: "Which do you think is more responsible for the recent increase in gasoline prices?"
0 = "oil companies trying to increase their profits"   1 = "the normal law of supply and demand"

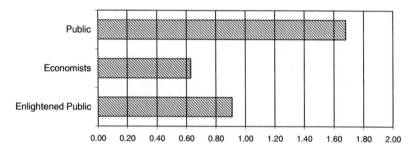

Figure 3.27 Question 27: "Do you think the current price of gasoline is too high, too low, or about right?"
0 = "too low"   1 = "about right"   2 = "too high"

(fig. 3.26), but barely a quarter of the public agrees.[46] Where economists see prices governed by market forces, the public sees monopoly or collusion. The numbers for the Enlightened Public confirm that economists do not dissent just because they are too rich to worry about how much it costs to fill their gas tank.

The real problem is not that economists are out of touch, but that the public's story makes no sense. If gas prices rise because "oil companies are trying to increase their profits," why do gas prices ever fall? Do oil companies feel generous and decide to cut their profits? Basic economics, in contrast, has an elegant explanation: If the cost of inputs falls, so does the profit-maximizing price.

Question 27. The wording of question 27 (fig. 3.27) leaves something to be desired; as a consumer, you might trivially maintain that any price is "too high." But responses to the previous question suggest

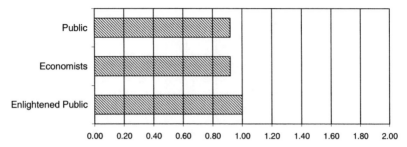

Figure 3.28 Question 28: "Do you think improving the economy is something an effective president can do a lot about, do a little about, or is that mostly beyond any president's control?"
0 = "beyond president's control"   1 = "do a little about"
2 = "can do a lot about"

that few respondents read the question so literally. When people answer "too high," they probably mean that some kind of monopoly holds prices above the competitive level. "Too low," in contrast, probably means that higher fuel taxes are necessary to correct for pollution, congestion, and other negative externalities of car use.

The "too high" position is a classic form of antimarket bias. But opposition to the "too low" thesis arguably stems from the same root. Suppose you want to reduce pollution and congestion. You could do it by command-and-control: emissions regulations, annual inspections, carpool lanes. But economists realize that the market mechanism is a more efficient method. A tax on gas gives people an incentive to reduce pollution and congestion without specifically dictating anyone's behavior.[47]

Question 28. A rare issue where economists and the public agree is on the president's capacity to improve the economy (fig. 3.28). It is most curious because economists criticize the public for mechanically linking economic conditions to incumbent presidents. What about the Federal Reserve, Congress, other governments, secular trends, and random shocks?

When economists only criticize errors in one direction, there is normally a good reason: errors in that direction predominate. This is the exception that proves the rule. Perhaps those who minimize the president's influence are less outspoken, creating the illusion of a systematic difference.

Question 29. The public's default is to expect things to get worse. The good old days are gone; since the 1970s, stagnation and decline have been our lot. "McJobs" fit neatly into this worldview. As usual, economists think that the numbers contradict the public's extreme

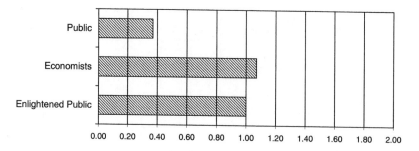

Figure 3.29 Question 29: "Do you think most of the new jobs being created in the country today pay well, or are they mostly low-paying jobs?" 0 = "low-paying jobs"   1 = "neither"   2 = "pay well"

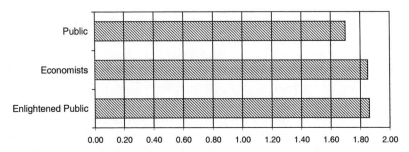

Figure 3.30 Question 30: "Do you think the gap between the rich and the poor is smaller or larger than it was 20 years ago, or is it about the same?" 0 = "smaller"   1 = "about the same"   2 = "larger"

pessimism (fig. 3.29).[48] But the belief gap runs deeper than the latest data set. The progress of recent centuries implies that it is *abnormal* for new jobs to be low-paying. A temporary setback is possible, but it merits an intellectual double-take.

Question 30. The public sees two decades of rising inequality (fig. 3.30). Given its antimarket and pessimistic reflexes, how could it not? But playing against type, economists are more convinced than the public. The data on inequality are solid enough, and economists have no strong presumptions about inequality.[49] They know that living standards rise over time, but have little reason to expect a trend in the distribution of income and wealth.

Question 31. It is tempting to interpret "pessimistic bias" as semantic. Maybe the public says "The economy is doing badly *compared to my hopes*" and economists counter "The economy is doing well *considering its constraints.*" But if they are just talking past each other,

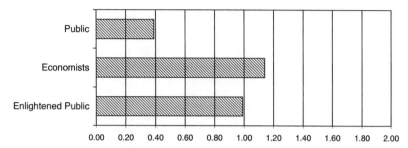

Figure 3.31 Question 31: "During the past 20 years, do you think that, in general, family incomes for average Americans have been going up faster than the cost of living, staying about even with the cost of living, or falling behind the cost of living?"
0 = "falling behind"   1 = "staying about even"   2 = "going up"

apparent pessimism would fall for less ambiguous topics. It does not. The question about family incomes (fig. 3.31) is one of the least ambiguous in the SAEE—and has one of the larger belief gaps.

Shouldn't the belief gap be larger? Economists' average response is slightly above 1; does a substantial minority of the profession deny that mean income went up? No. Rising inequality is a confounding factor. The question asks about median income ("family incomes for average Americans"), not mean income ("average American family incomes"). If inequality is rising, the first can go down as the second goes up.

But while almost every economist grasps the distinction between mean and median income, it is doubtful that many noneconomists do. Members of the general public who said "falling behind" probably think that *mean* income fell from 1976 to 1996. However, even economists who said "falling behind" know that mean income rose. The upshot: residual ambiguity in this question *masks* the full size of the lay-expert gap.

Question 32. The belief gap for real wages (fig. 3.32) is much narrower than for real income, a change almost entirely attributable to the economists. The public gives the same answer twice in a row, probably because it equates income and wages. Economists know that the two are different, and that some of the data on average real wages contradict the presumption of progress. If average real wages are stagnant and inequality is rising, it follows that the wages of the average American worker are falling. Still, a substantial minority of economists stands behind the presumption of progress on wages, pointing to serious flaws that bias official numbers downwards.[50]

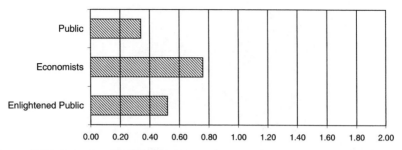

Figure 3.32 Question 32: "Thinking just about wages of the average American worker, do you think that during the past 20 years they have been going up faster than the cost of living, staying about even with the cost of living, or falling behind the cost of living?"
0 = "falling behind"   1 = "staying about even"   2 = "going up"

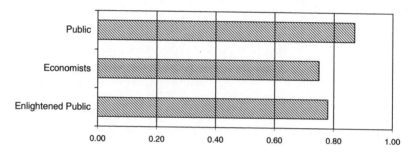

Figure 3.33 Question 33: "Some people say that in order to make a comfortable living, the average family must have two full-time wage earners. Do you agree with this, or do you think the average family can make a comfortable living with only one full-time wage earner?"
0 = "can make living with one wage earner"   1 = "need two wage earners"

Question 33. Ample majorities of both economists and the public agree that the average American family needs two incomes to live comfortably (fig. 3.33), but economists are less sure. This does not reflect economists' above-average income, because the Enlightened Public says the same. Economists are probably less pessimistic because they practice marginal thinking. Being a stay-at-home mom or having a full-time job are not the only choices. Lower income means some sacrifices, but a family with one full-time and one part-time earner has ways to "comfortably" adjust: buy a moderately less expensive home, or delay purchase of a new car for a year or two.

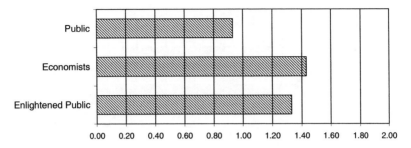

Figure 3.34 Question 34: Over the next five years, do you think the average American's standard of living will rise, or fall, or stay about the same?" 0 = "fall" 1 = "stay about the same" 2 = "rise"

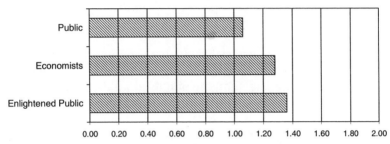

Figure 3.35 Question 35: "Do you expect your children's generation to enjoy a higher or lower standard of living than your generation, or do you think it will be about the same?" 0 = "lower" 1 = "about the same" 2 = "higher"

Question 34. With enough data, you can convince an economist that improvements in living standards failed to materialize some time in the past, or that an impending recession will pull them down. But it is hard to stop an economist from expecting rising living standards in the medium- or long-term future (fig. 3.34). Critics hail this as proof of their dogmatism. Yet the presumption of progress does not come out of thin air. Two centuries of awesome economic growth back it up.[51] Is it not more dogmatic for noneconomists to remain pessimistic in spite of this track record?

Question 35. Here is an ideal prompt to tap respondents' beliefs about long-run growth (fig. 3.35). Economists' beliefs about the economic future are of course more upbeat than noneconomists', though the gap is smaller than you would expect. Surprisingly, the Enlightened Public is more optimistic than either. The reason: high-income

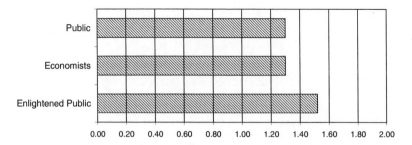

Figure 3.36 Question 36: [If you have any children under the age of 30] "When they reach your age, do you expect them to enjoy a higher or lower standard of living than you do now, or do you expect it to be about the same?" 0 = "lower"   1 = "about the same"   2 = "higher"

males are uncharacteristically pessimistic on this topic. Since economists tend to be high-income males, their demographics dilute their optimism.

Question 36. It seems especially odd that economists and the public agree about their own children's economic future (fig. 3.36). If economists are more optimistic than the public about the prospects of the next generation, why are the two groups equally optimistic about their own children? On closer examination, though, economists are more optimistic—*after controlling for income.* If a person of ordinary means had an economist's education, he would see a brighter future for his children.

There is a logical explanation for this pattern. The question asks respondents to compare *their own* current situation to their children's. The better you are doing, the more successful your children have to be to equal you. Many SAEE respondents appear to grasp this subtle point: As income goes up, optimism steeply declines. The upshot is that economists' income camouflages their optimism.

Question 37. When asked about the current state of the economy (fig. 3.37), economists give more upbeat answers than the rest of the public. The root of the disagreement is not, however, economic training. Economists see eye to eye with noneconomists who happen to have high job security and growing incomes. After controlling for these characteristics, the belief gap is no longer statistically significant.[52]

Three Doubts

Everything that follows in this book takes the reality of systematically biased beliefs about economics for granted. So before moving on, it

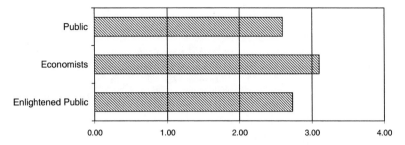

Figure 3.37 Question 37: "When you think about America's economy today, do you think it is. . ."
0 = "in a depression"   1 = "in a recession"   2 = "stagnating"   3 = "growing slowly"   4 = "growing rapidly"

is worth plugging some holes by considering leading challenges. My findings may not be watertight, but they are more than seaworthy. The objections are not strong enough to reverse the conclusion that the public's economic beliefs are riddled with large systematic errors.

Vagueness. One problem with the "experts right, laymen wrong" view of the SAEE is the vagueness or "fuzziness" of the responses. Who knows what it means to be a "major" versus a "minor" reason for subpar economic performance? Perhaps the public is partial to superlative adjectives, and Ph.D.s signal their levelheadedness with measured language.

The most telling counterevidence comes from other public opinion studies that ask for exact numbers. If you compare numerical responses to actual figures, systematic bias still leaps out at you. Take the budget. The National Survey of Public Knowledge of Welfare Reform and the Federal Budget finds that the public's numerical perceptions are almost the reverse of the truth.[53] This survey presented a list of six federal program categories: foreign aid, welfare,[54] interest on the debt, defense, Social Security, and health. It then asked respondents to name the two largest items.

Table 3.1 shows responses, providing the actual numbers from 1993 for the sake of comparison. Foreign aid—by far the *smallest*—was absurdly the most frequently named! Only 14% realized that the most expensive federal program—Social Security—is in the top two. The public's picture of the budget is upside down.[55] Furthermore, it is upside down in the expected way. In the SAEE, respondents qualitatively overestimate the damage of foreign aid and welfare; in the National Survey respondents quantitatively overestimate the fraction of the budget spent on foreign aid and welfare.

Table 3.1
Americans' Views of the Two Largest Areas of Federal Government Spending

Item	% Selecting Area as One of the Two Largest Areas of Federal Spending	Actual Federal Budget Share (1993)
Foreign aid	41%	1.2%
Welfare	40%	10.2%
Interest on the federal debt	40%	14.1%
Defense	37%	20.7%
Social Security	14%	21.6%
Health	8%	10.9%

Sources: Kaiser Family Foundation and Harvard University School of Public Health (1995), tables 15 and 16; Office of Management and Budget (2005: 51)

Insincerity. The SAEE measures what people *say* they believe. It is possible that when they affirm strange beliefs, they are lying. As Gordon Tullock explains:

> A man may inform a social scientist that he is trying to achieve some goal by a given course of action although the course of action does not seem well chosen in view of the stated goal. An incautious social scientist may then conclude that the man is irrational. The real explanation may simply be that the goals aimed at are different from the stated goals.[56]

This is an internally consistent but highly implausible way to interpret my results. Respondents in the SAEE have no material incentive to lie. They are not politicians whose candor could cost them an election. And there is not much emotional impetus to lie either. Respondents might hide their true feelings about race out of embarrassment, but few economic beliefs bear such a stigma. After years of teaching economics, I cannot recall a single case where I suspected that a student was only *pretending* to disagree with me. (Pretending to agree is another matter!)

Question Selection Bias. Systematic belief differences are so common in the SAEE that you might get suspicious. Did the authors select questions where they *expected* disagreement? There is no evidence that they did. They picked questions on the basis of public and media attention. Here, for example, is how the authors wrote the first part of the survey: "Based on a review of almost two decades of public opinion polling on the economy, we chose 18 of the reasons most frequently mentioned as possible reasons for the economy not doing better. . . "[57] They were looking for *common* explanations, not explanations with large lay-expert gaps. The same holds for the rest of the SAEE.[58]

Rethinking Systematic Error

Once they realize that a theory implicitly depends on systematic error, most economists are incredulous: "You are assuming irrationality!" Being explicit wins you a little credit for candor, but the main effect is to hasten your dismissal. The goal of this chapter has been to bypass a priori objections with direct empirical evidence.

In the process, we have amassed an embarrassment of riches. There are too many details to digest in one sitting. What does an aerial view of the SAEE tell us?

First and foremost, *the SAEE strongly confirms the reality of large and systematic belief differences between economists and the public.* In fact, there are almost no areas where large, systematic belief differences do *not* exist. The Miracle of Aggregation is not merely false every now and then. At least in economics, it barely works more often than most "miracles" do.

The findings are especially compelling because, with few exceptions, *differences go in the predicted directions.* This is the second of the SAEE's lessons. Economists and the public disagree in the *way* that economists—in conversation, lectures, and textbooks—have long maintained. The public really holds, for starters, that prices are not governed by supply and demand, protectionism helps the economy, saving labor is a bad idea, and living standards are falling. Educators are not beating a dead horse when they argue against antimarket bias, antiforeign bias, make-work bias, or pessimistic bias.

If A and B disagree, there are three logical possibilities. The first is that A is right and B is wrong. The second is that A is wrong and B is right. The third is that both A and B are wrong. But we can rule out the possibility that both A and B are right. Systematic differences between laymen and experts do not logically entail systematic errors on the part of the public. Continuing with my aerial summary, though, the third lesson from the SAEE is that *the naive "economists right, public wrong" interpretation is usually the best.*

We all share a presumption that when an expert disagrees with a nonexpert, the expert is right. This holds in math, science, history, and car repair. Yes, the experts have been wrong before. An amusing book by Cerf and Navasky, *The Experts Speak: The Definitive Compendium of Authoritative Misinformation*,[59] provides hundreds of embarrassing examples. Notice, however, that they did not write a companion volume entitled *The Public Speaks: The Definitive Compendium of Amateur Misinformation*. It would be too easy. How startling would it be to read hundreds of inane comments by the unqualified? *The Experts Speak* is funny precisely because experts are *ordinarily* right.

If you want to criticize the experts, the burden is on you to overcome the standard presumption. The detractors of the economics profession try, pointing to economists' self-serving and ideological biases. But they do not meet their burden of proof. The SAEE reveals that *both of the leading accounts of the experts' biases are wrong*.

Economists are richer than noneconomists, but millionaires without economics degrees think like other people, and economists who drive taxis think like other economists. In fact, the paltry evidence of self-serving bias should be taken at *less* than face value. Income has a small influence on beliefs, but is the direction really selfish? The rich worry less about foreign aid and welfare, not just excessive profits and executive pay.

Ideological bias is an even weaker reed. Controlling for individuals' party identification and ideology makes the lay-expert belief gap a little *larger*. Ideologically moderate, politically independent economists are totally at odds with ideologically moderate, politically independent noneconomists. How can this be? *Economics only looks conservative compared to other social sciences*, like sociology, where leftism reigns supreme. Compared to the general public, the typical economist is left of center.[60] Furthermore, contrary to critics of the economics profession, economists do not reliably hold right-wing positions. They accept a *mix* of "far right" and "far left" views. Economists are more optimistic than very conservative Republicans about downsizing or excessive profits—and more optimistic about immigration and welfare than very liberal Democrats.[61]

Shooting down the leading opponents of the "economists right, public wrong" position does not *prove* that it is true. But it significantly increases the probability. Think of it this way: Common sense advises us to trust the experts. Critics challenge the experts' objectivity, and their complaints turn out to be in error. The sensible response is to reaffirm the commonsense position. Indeed, after the strongest challengers fail, we should become more confident that economists are right and the public is wrong.

There is no reason, then, to deny economists a normal level of deference in their field of expertise. But the profession also deserves an affirmative defense. Frankly, the strongest reason to accept its reliability is to flip through a basic economics text, then read the SAEE questions for yourself. You may not be fully convinced of economists' wisdom. I, too, doubt it on occasion. But it is hard to avert your gaze from the public's folly. Time and again, it gravitates toward answers that are positively silly.

If that is too subjective for you, an impressive empirical regularity points in the same direction: *Education makes people think like economists.* Out of the SAEE's 37 questions, there are 19 where economic training and education move together, and only two where they move apart. It is not merely members of one inbred discipline who diverge from mainstream opinion. So do educated Americans in general, with the degree of divergence rising with the level of education. And the magnitude is substantial. Moving from the bottom of the educational ladder to the top has more than half of the (enormous) effect of an econ Ph.D.[62]

This pattern is all the more compelling because it has parallels in other fields. Take political knowledge. Delli Carpini and Keeter report that education substantially improves performance on objective tests about government structure, leaders, and current events.[63] Kraus, Malmfors, and Slovic similarly find that education makes members of the general public "think more like toxicologists."[64] Perhaps education just increases exposure to brainwashing. But it is more likely that educated people think clearer and know more.

Conclusion

Appearances can be revealing. Noneconomists and economists appear to systematically disagree on an array of topics. The SAEE shows that they do. Economists appear to base their beliefs on logic and evidence. The SAEE rules out the competing theories that economists primarily rationalize their self-interest or political ideology. Economists appear to know more about economics than the public. The SAEE weighs heavily in favor of this conclusion.

The SAEE is hardly the only empirical evidence for these propositions. As mentioned at the beginning of this chapter, there are numerous studies of economic beliefs. The advantage of the SAEE is its craftsmanship. It has been constructed to deflect the main objections that skeptics could levy against earlier empirics. Now that the SAEE has cleared these hurdles, it is fair to look back and recognize that the earlier literature—including both statistical work and economists' centuries of observation and reflection—is basically sound.

The rest of this book takes the public's systematically biased beliefs as an established fact. There is much more work to be done on the details, but the overall story is unlikely to change. The task at hand is to figure out how these biases fit into the big picture. How can social science account for the ubiquity of these systematic errors? And what effects do these systematic errors have in the world?

TECHNICAL APPENDIX

The Enlightened Public

To estimate the beliefs of the Enlightened Public, the data for the general public and economists were pooled. *Each* of the 37 beliefs in the SAEE, reproduced in table 3.2, was regressed on *all* of the variables in table 3.3.

Strictly speaking, of course, simple regression is not the best method for discrete dependent variables, but the coefficients are easier to interpret, and redoing everything with ordered logits yields virtually identical predictions.[65] The regression equations were then used to predict the beliefs of the Enlightened Public, who by definition are *average* members of the general public in every way *except* in education and economic training. Those values are, by assumption, respectively equal to 7 and 1. Equivalently, since the public's average Education = 4.54 and its average Econ = 0, the Enlightened Public holds the beliefs an average person would hold if his Education score were (7 – 4.54) = 2.46 higher and his Econ score were 1.00 higher.

To reproduce the complete results for all 37 equations would be overkill. Table 3.4 instead displays the results of greatest interest: the coefficients and *t*-stats for Education and Econ, controlling for the other variables in table 3.3. Table 3.4's results can be used to calculate how beliefs respond to *changes* in education and economic training.

Example. What is the predicted effect of sending a noneconomist with the average level of education (4.54) to graduate school in economics? Upon completion, his Education will be 2.46 higher and his Econ will be 1 instead of 0. His predicted belief on any given question is therefore his initial belief *plus* 2.46 times the coefficient on Education *plus* the coefficient on Econ.[66] On TAXHIGH, for instance, the coefficient on Education is –.09, and the coefficient on Econ is –.32. The estimated belief change is therefore –2.46 * .09 –.32 = –.54.

Table 3.2
Questions and Mean Answers

Regardless of how well you think the economy is doing, there are always some problems that keep it from being as good as it might be. I am going to read you a list of reasons some people have given for why the economy is not doing better than it is. For each one, please tell me if you think it is a major reason the economy is not doing better than it is, a minor reason, or not a reason at all.

0 = "Not a reason at all"; 1 = "Minor reason"; 2 = "Major reason"

#	Variable	Question	Mean (Public)	Mean (Economists)	Enlightened Public
1	TAXHIGH	Taxes are too high	1.50	0.77	0.99
2	DEFICIT	The federal deficit is too big	1.73	1.14	1.16
3	FORAID	Foreign aid spending is too high	1.53	0.14	0.28
4	IMMIG	There are too many immigrants	1.23	0.22	0.31
5	TAXBREAK	Too many tax breaks for business	1.29	0.65	0.86
6	INADEDUC	Education and job training are inadequate	1.56	1.61	1.64
7	WELFARE	Too many people are on welfare	1.61	0.72	0.94
8	AA	Women and minorities get too many advantages under affirmative action	0.76	0.21	0.19
9	HARDWORK	People place too little value on hard work	1.44	0.82	0.83
10	REG	The government regulates business too much	1.23	0.97	1.00
11	SAVINGS	People are not saving enough	1.39	1.49	1.44

Now I am going to read you another list of reasons, having to do with businesses, that some people have given for why the economy is not doing better than it is. For each one, please tell me if you think it is a major reason the economy is not doing better than it is, a minor reason, or not a reason at all.

0 = "Not a reason at all"; 1 = "Minor reason"; 2 = "Major reason"

#	Variable	Question	Mean (Public)	Mean (Economists)	Enlightened Public
12	PROFHIGH	Business profits are too high	1.27	0.18	0.41
13	EXECPAY	Top executives are paid too much	1.59	0.69	0.83
14	BUSPROD	Business productivity is growing too slowly	1.18	1.43	1.49

Table 3.2 (*cont'd*)

#	Variable	Question	Mean (Public)	Mean (Economists)	Enlightened Public
15	TECH	Technology is displacing workers	1.26	0.27	0.43
16	OVERSEAS	Companies are sending jobs overseas	1.59	0.48	0.60
17	DOWNSIZE	Companies are downsizing	1.50	0.48	0.64
18	COMPEDUC	Companies are not investing enough money in education and job training	1.53	1.16	1.23

Generally speaking, do you think each of the following is good or bad for the nation's economy, or don't you think it makes much difference?
  0 = "Bad"; 1 = "Doesn't make much difference"; 2 = "Good"

#	Variable	Question	Mean (Public)	Mean (Economists)	Enlightened Public
19	TAXCUT	Tax cuts	1.46	1.04	1.20
20	WOMENWORK	More women entering the workforce	1.47	1.73	1.67
21	TECHGOOD	Increased use of technology in the workplace	1.57	1.98	1.83
22	TRADEAG	Trade agreements between the United States and other countries	1.33	1.87	1.75
23	DOWNGOOD	The recent downsizing of large corporations	0.62	1.40	1.31

Some people say that these are economically unsettled times because of new technology, competition from foreign countries, and downsizing. Looking ahead 20 years, do you think these changes will eventually be good or bad for the country or don't you think these changes will make much difference?

#	Variable	Coding	Mean (Public)	Mean (Economists)	Enlightened Public
24	CHANGE20	0 = "Bad"; 1 = "Won't make much difference"; 2 = "Good"	1.15	1.92	1.73

Table 3.2 (*cont'd*)

Do you think that trade agreements between the United States and other countries have helped create more jobs in the U.S., or have they cost the U.S. jobs, or haven't they made much of a difference?

#	Variable	Coding	Mean (Public)	Mean (Economists)	Enlightened Public
25	TRADEJOB	0 = "Cost the U.S. jobs"; 1 = "Haven't made much difference"; 2 = "Helped create jobs in the U.S."	0.64	1.46	1.32

Which do you think is more responsible for the recent increase in gasoline prices?

#	Variable	Coding	Mean (Public)	Mean (Economists)	Enlightened Public
26	WHYGASSD	0 = "Oil companies trying to increase their profits"; 1 = "The normal law of supply and demand" ["both" coded as 1; "neither" as 0]	0.26	0.89	0.84

Do you think the current price of gasoline is too high, too low, or about right?

#	Variable	Coding	Mean (Public)	Mean (Economists)	Enlightened Public
27	GASPRICE	0 = "Too low"; 1 = "About right"; 2 = "Too high"	1.68	0.63	0.91

Do you think improving the economy is something an effective president can do a lot about, do a little about, or is that mostly beyond any president's control?

#	Variable	Coding	Mean (Public)	Mean (Economists)	Enlightened Public
28	PRES	0 = "Beyond any president's control"; 1 = "Do a little about"; 2 = "Something president can do a lot about"	0.92	0.92	1.00

Table 3.2 (*cont'd*)

Do you think most of the new jobs being created in the country today pay well, or are they mostly low-paying jobs?

#	Variable	Coding	Mean (Public)	Mean (Economists)	Enlightened Public
29	NEWJOB	0 = "Low-paying jobs"; 1 = "Neither"; 2 = "Pay well"	0.37	1.07	1.00

Do you think the gap between the rich and the poor is smaller or larger than it was 20 years ago, or is it about the same?

#	Variable	Coding	Mean (Public)	Mean (Economists)	Enlightened Public
30	GAP20	0 = "Smaller"; 1 = "About the same"; 2 = "Larger"	1.70	1.85	1.86

During the past 20 years, do you think that, in general, family incomes for average Americans have been going up faster than the cost of living, staying about even with the cost of living, or falling behind the cost of living?

#	Variable	Coding	Mean (Public)	Mean (Economists)	Enlightened Public
31	INCOME20	0 = "Falling behind"; 1 = "Staying about even"; 2 = "Going up"	0.39	1.14	0.99

Thinking just about wages of the average American worker, do you think that during the past 20 years they have been going up faster than the cost of living, staying about even with the cost of living, or falling behind the cost of living?

#	Variable	Coding	Mean (Public)	Mean (Economists)	Enlightened Public
32	WAGE20	0 = "Falling behind"; 1 = "Staying about even"; 2 = "Going up"	0.34	0.76	0.52

Some people say that in order to make a comfortable living, the average family must have two full-time wage earners. Do you agree with this, or do you think the average family can make a comfortable living with only one full-time wage earner?

#	Variable	Coding	Mean (Public)	Mean (Economists)	Enlightened Public
33	NEED2EARN	0 = "Can make living with one wage earner"; 1 = "Agree that need two wage earners"	0.87	0.75	0.78

Table 3.2 (*cont'd*)

Over the next five years, do you think the average American's standard of living will rise, or fall, or stay about the same?

#	Variable	Coding	Mean (Public)	Mean (Economists)	Enlightened Public
34	STAN5	0 = "Fall"; 1 = "Stay about the same"; 2 = "Rise"	0.93	1.43	1.33

Do you expect your children's generation to enjoy a higher or lower standard of living than your generation, or do you think it will be about the same?

#	Variable	Coding	Mean (Public)	Mean (Economists)	Enlightened Public
35	CHILDGEN	0 = "Lower"; 1 = "About the same"; 2 = "Higher"	1.06	1.28	1.36

[If you have any children under the age of 30] When they reach your age, do you expect them to enjoy a higher or lower standard of living than you do now, or do you expect it to be about the same?

#	Variable	Coding	Mean (Public)	Mean (Economists)	Enlightened Public
36	CHILDSTAN	0 = "Lower"; 1 = "About the same"; 2 = "Higher"	1.30	1.30	1.52

When you think about America's economy today, do you think it is. . .

#	Variable	Coding	Mean (Public)	Mean (Economists)	Enlightened Public
37	CURECON	0 = "In a depression"; 1 = "In a recession"; 2 = "Stagnating"; 3 = "Growing slowly"; 4 = "Growing rapidly"	2.59	3.10	2.73

Table 3.3
Control Variables

What is your race? Are you white, black or African-American, Asian-American or some other race?

Variable	Coding	Mean (Public)	Mean (Economists)	Enlightened Public
Black	= 1 if black, 0 otherwise	.08	.004	.08
Asian	= 1 if Asian, 0 otherwise	.06	.05	.06
Othrace	= 1 if other race, 0 otherwise	.05	.03	.05
Age	= 1996 – birthyear	44.40	48.74	44.40
Male	= 1 if male, 0 otherwise	.46	.94	.46

How concerned are you that you or someone else in your household will lose their job in the next year?

Variable	Coding	Mean (Public)	Mean (Economists)	Enlightened Public
Jobsecurity	0 = "very concerned" 1 = "somewhat concerned" 2 = "not too concerned" 3 = "not at all concerned"	1.88	2.32	1.88

During the past five years, do you think that your family's income has been going up faster than the cost of living, staying about even with the cost of living, or falling behind the cost of living?

Variable	Coding	Mean (Public)	Mean (Economists)	Enlightened Public
Yourlast5	0 = "Falling behind" 1 = "Staying about even" 2 = "Going up"	.74	1.59	.74

Over the next five years, do you expect your family's income to grow faster or slower than the cost of living, or do you think it will grow at about the same pace?

Variable	Coding	Mean (Public)	Mean (Economists)	Enlightened Public
Yournext5	0 = "Slower" 1 = "About the same" 2 = "Faster"	.94	1.33	.94

Table 3.3 (*cont'd*)

If you added together the yearly incomes, before taxes, of all the members of your household for the last year, 1995, would the total be

Variable	Coding	Mean (Public)	Mean (Economists)	Enlightened Public
Income	1 = $10,000 or less	5.09	8.44	5.09
	2 = $10,000-$19,999			
	3 = $20,000-$24,999			
	4 = $25,000-$29,999			
	5 = $30,000-$39,999			
	6 = $40,000-$49,999			
	7 = $50,000-$74,999			
	8 = $75,000-$99,999			
	9 = $100,000 or more			

In politics today, do you consider yourself a Republican, a Democrat, or an Independent?

Variable	Coding	Mean (Public)	Mean (Economists)	Enlightened Public
Dem	Dem = 1 if Democrat, 0 otherwise	.33	.38	.33
Rep	Rep = 1 if Republican, 0 otherwise	.29	.19	.29
Othparty	Othparty = 1 if member of another party, 0 otherwise	.04	.02	.04

Would you say that your views in most political matters are very liberal, liberal, moderate, conservative, or very conservative?

Variable	Coding	Mean (Public)	Mean (Economists)	Enlightened Public
Othideol	1 = "don't think in those terms", 0 otherwise	.02	.03	.02
Ideology* (1-Othideol)	−2 = "very liberal" −1 = "liberal" 0 = "moderate" 1 = "conservative" 2 = "very conservative"	.13	-.04	.13

Table 3.3 (*cont'd*)

What is the last grade or class that you COMPLETED in school?

Variable	Coding	Mean (Public)	Mean (Economists)	Enlightened Public
Education	1 = "None, or grade 1–8" 2 = "High school incomplete (grades 9–11) 3 = "High school graduate (grade 12 or GED certificate)" 4 = "Business, technical, or vocational school AFTER high school" 5 = "Some college, no 4-year degree" 6 = "College graduate (B.S., B.A., or other 4-year degree)" 7 = "Post-graduate training or professional schooling after college (e.g. toward a master's degree or Ph.D.; law or medical school)"	4.54	7.00	7.00
Econ	= 1 if economist, 0 otherwise	0.00	1.00	1.00

Table 3.4
Coefficients on Education and Econ

#	Variable	Education Coefficient	Education t-stat	Econ Coefficient	Econ t-stat
1	TAXHIGH	−0.09	−7.47	−0.32	−5.61
2	DEFICIT	−0.01	−.63	−0.58	−10.91
3	FORAID	−0.09	−7.64	−1.02	−17.21
4	IMMIG	−0.12	−9.13	−0.59	−8.96
5	TAXBREAK	−0.07	−5.66	−0.25	−3.95
6	INADEDUC	−0.01	−.88	0.10	1.62
7	WELFARE	−0.07	−5.79	−0.48	−8.62
8	AA	−0.08	−6.69	−0.35	−5.72
9	HARDWORK	−0.04	−2.74	−0.50	−7.39

Table 3.4 (*cont'd*)

#	Variable	Education Coefficient	Education t-stat	Econ Coefficient	Econ t-stat
10	REG	−0.07	−5.50	−0.06	−1.00
11	SAVINGS	0.01	1.09	0.08	1.24
12	PROFHIGH	−0.07	−5.25	−0.72	−11.50
13	EXECPAY	−0.04	−3.41	−0.69	−12.01
14	BUSPROD	−0.01	−.96	0.33	5.18
15	TECH	−0.10	−8.40	−0.51	−8.41
16	OVERSEAS	−0.05	−4.46	−0.87	−15.57
17	DOWNSIZE	−0.03	−2.44	−0.81	−13.76
18	COMPEDUC	−0.02	−1.53	−0.27	−4.63
19	TAXCUT	0.00	.17	−0.30	−4.21
20	WOMENWORK	0.03	2.32	0.15	2.68
21	TECHGOOD	0.04	3.06	0.16	2.47
22	TRADEAG	0.09	6.03	0.24	3.22
23	DOWNGOOD	0.01	.54	0.68	8.72
24	CHANGE20	0.04	2.74	0.45	5.94
25	TRADEJOB	0.07	4.74	0.59	8.63
26	WHYGASSD	0.03	3.85	0.52	13.26
27	GASPRICE	−0.04	−4.36	−0.66	−13.04
28	PRES	0.02	1.44	0.11	1.54
29	NEWJOB	0.02	1.47	0.63	8.68
30	GAP20	0.03	3.15	0.07	1.46
31	INCOME20	−0.01	−.78	0.66	10.96
32	WAGE20	−0.02	−1.83	0.30	5.54
33	NEED2EARN	−0.01	−1.38	−0.08	−2.54
34	STAN5	−0.03	−2.37	0.55	8.53
35	CHILDGEN	−0.07	−5.24	0.57	8.03
36	CHILDSTAN	−0.02	−.80	0.28	3.41
37	CURECON	0.01	.40	0.12	1.25

Chapter 4

CLASSICAL PUBLIC CHOICE AND THE FAILURE OF RATIONAL IGNORANCE

> Apparently irrational cultural beliefs are quite remarkable:
> They do not appear irrational by slightly departing from
> common sense, or timidly going beyond what the
> evidence allows. They appear, rather, like down-right
> provocations against common sense rationality.
> —*Richard Shweder*[1]

ANTHONY DOWNS's *An Economic Theory of Democracy* (1957) turned *rational ignorance* into a basic element of the economics of politics. Gordon Tullock did not coin the phrase until 10 years later,[2] but Downs's one-sentence explanation remains definitive: "it is irrational to be politically well-informed because the low returns from data simply do not justify their cost in time and other resources."[3]

The logic is simple. Time is money, and acquiring information requires time. Individuals balance the benefit of learning against its cost.[4] In markets, if individuals know too little, they pay the price in missed opportunities; if they know too much, they pay the price in wasted time. The prudent path is to find out enough to make a tolerably good decision.

Matters are different in politics. One vote is extraordinarily unlikely to change an election's outcome.[5] So suppose an ignorant citizen votes randomly. Except in the freak case where he casts the decisive vote, flipping an otherwise deadlocked election, the *marginal* effect is zero. If time is money, acquiring political information takes time, and the expected personal benefit of voting is roughly zero, a rational, selfish individual chooses to be ignorant.

The civics textbook motto, "If everybody thought that way, democracy would produce horrible results," could well be true. But as an appeal to citizen self-interest, the motto is a bald fallacy of composition. If everyone knows nothing about politics, we are worse off; but it does not follow that if *I* know nothing about politics, *I* am worse off. If one person stands up at a concert, that person sees better, but if everyone stands up, no one sees better.

In the fifties and sixties, economists got used to calling imperfect information a "market failure."[6] On reflection, though, the best example of this so-called market failure seemed to be democratic *government.* As the economics of politics developed, appeals to rational ignorance grew alongside it. Rational ignorance became the root of an intellectual orthodoxy—an orthodoxy I call *Classical Public Choice.*

Rational Ignorance: Evidence and Alleged Consequences

Although political scientists classify about one-third of the public as "know-nothings,"[7] it is hard to find people whose political knowledge is *literally* nonexistent. There are a handful of facts—like the name of the president—that nearly everyone knows. Incentives are a little more complex than they seem on the surface. Ubiquitous and entertaining facts are easier to absorb than avoid, and recall than forget. Political knowledge also has "off-label" benefits: good grades in impractical subjects still help your career prospects, and your friends or a date might scoff at full-fledged political cluelessness.

So Classical Public Choice's stories about rational ignorance prove too much. But not *much too much.* By any absolute measure, average levels of political knowledge are low.[8] Less than 40% of American adults know both of their senators' names.[9] Slightly *fewer* know both senators' parties—a particularly significant finding given its oft-cited informational role.[10] Much of the public has forgotten—or never learned—the elementary and unchanging facts taught in every civics class. About half knows that each state has two senators, and only a quarter knows the length of their terms in office.[11] Familiarity with politicians' voting records and policy positions is predictably close to nil even on high-profile issues, but amazingly good on fun topics irrelevant to policy. As Delli Carpini and Keeter remark:

> During the 1992 presidential campaign 89 percent of the public knew that Vice President Quayle was feuding with the television character Murphy Brown, but only 19 percent could characterize Bill Clinton's record on the environment . . . 86 percent of the public knew that the Bushes' dog was named Millie, yet only 15 percent knew that both presidential candidates supported the death penalty. Judge Wapner (host of the television series "People's Court") was identified by more people than were Chief Justices Burger or Rehnquist.[12]

This is precisely what the logic of rational ignorance would lead one to suspect. When people decide whether to devote mental effort to the dry facts vital for intelligent political choice, or to irrelevant fluff, they choose the latter.[13]

Rational ignorance's intuitive and empirical appeal would have guaranteed it academic airtime. Yet it took an extra selling point to turn rational ignorance into the keystone of Classical Public Choice: its apparent ability to explain the failures of democracy. Imagine that a single voter is sealed in a room for life, cut off from any contact with the world outside his tiny cell. He has a lifetime supply of food and water, but no windows. The cell has a one-way intercom; the voter can tell politicians his preferences, but they are unable to speak to him. Once every four years, the voter gets to voice his support for one of two candidates. The voter knows that he determines the winner, but he has no way to find out what the candidates did in the past or intend to do in the future.

It would be astonishing if democracy worked in this story, because neither candidate can improve his chance of winning. The voter inside the cell neither sees politicians' actions nor hears their words. So the winner can do whatever he likes without the slightest fear of losing office *as a result* of his decisions. This does not mean the officeholder has no worries. He can be voted out of office in the next election. The point is that he is *equally likely* to be thrown out of office if he follows the voter's intercom instructions to the letter, or does the opposite.

Little changes if there are millions of voters in isolation chambers. As long as none know what goes on outside his cell, leaders can ignore the expressed wishes of the majority—*even though the majority has complete control over electoral outcomes*. If candidate behavior is unobservable, voters cannot condition their votes on candidate behavior. If voters cannot condition their votes on candidate behavior, candidates have no incentive to heed them.

Voters do not live in physical isolation chambers, but they could be comparably ignorant by choice. If they were, the perceived failings of democracy seem easy to explain. Why can special interest groups turn legislatures against majority interests? Voters' rational ignorance: many fail to realize that tobacco farmers get subsidies, and few know where their representative stands. Why can politicians defy public opinion? Voters' rational ignorance: few pay attention to politicians' position on unpopular programs like foreign aid, and fewer remember at the next election. Why are inefficient policies like the minimum wage popular? Voters' rational ignorance: few bother to learn enough economics to understand the policies' drawbacks.[14]

The flip side of public ignorance is insider expertise. While the voters sleep, special interests fine-tune their lobbying strategy. Just as voters know little because it doesn't pay, interest groups know a lot because—for them—it *does*; hence the mantra of "concentrated benefits, dispersed costs." As Mancur Olson proclaims, "There is a systematic tendency for exploitation of the great by the small!"[15] The orange tariff costs me, the orange consumer, a few pennies, but it means millions for orange growers.

When economists stopped theorizing long enough to peruse the political landscape, special interests seemed to lurk behind practically every government policy. Like an old civics text, the professors grumbled, "If only the voters knew . . . " Unlike the civics text, however, they could not offer the consolation that "one day the electorate is bound to wake up and put the nation's house in order." The social harm of rational ignorance does not make it individually advantageous to crusade against it.

In sum, according to Classical Public Choice, voter ignorance transforms politics from a puzzling anomaly into a textbook example of the explanatory power of information economics. Voter ignorance opens the door to severe government failure. Interest groups—not to mention bureaucrats and politicians themselves—walk straight in.

Resisting Irrationality

Ordinary language has many words for disparaging false beliefs and the people who hold them. In spite of subtle shades of meaning, most fall into one of two categories: words that blame the *mind of the agent*—like "irrational," "stupid," "delusional," and "dogmatic"—and words that blame the *information available to the agent*—like "ignorant," "uninformed," "misled," and "uneducated."

The truth could easily be mixed. But most economists resist mixed accounts of human error that give irrationality *any* share of the responsibility. You might expect the ones who study politics to be less rigid, but if anything the opposite is true.[16] Downs made rationality a foundation of his analysis, and his successors have been true to his vision. Still, at least Downs *defends* his decision to ignore irrationality:

> Our desire to by-pass political irrationality springs from (1) the complexity of the subject, (2) its incompatibility with our model of purely rational behavior, and (3) the fact that it is an empirical phenomenon which cannot be dealt with by deductive logic alone but also requires actual investigation beyond the scope of this study.[17]

In contrast, the orthodoxy Downs inspired often forgets that an alternative exists. Any popular error, no matter how bizarre, supposedly confirms that voters are rationally ignorant. After perusing the empirical evidence of systematically biased beliefs about economics, many in the tradition of Classical Public Choice interpret it as evidence of rational ignorance. Indeed, the economists *most* willing to accept the empirics are often *least* willing to interpret them as the very thing that Downs "bypassed" 50 years ago: political irrationality.

Why are economists so hostile towards theories rooted in "stupidity" or "irrationality," and so friendly towards the extreme "ignorance only" take on human error? One defense is tautologous: equating all error with "ignorance," then equivocating between the standard and catchall definitions. Yet whatever words you prefer, two distinct causes of error remain: Either you lack sufficient data, or you fail to take full advantage of the data you have. A mystery might remain unsolved by a detective because he needs more clues, or because he lacks the desire or wit to piece his clues together.

When proponents of the ignorance-only view tire of semantic debate, the next defense is to appeal to the difficulty of empirically distinguishing the two sources of error. Who is to say what is or is not "irrational"?[18] This objection is puzzling because modern economic theorists *have* a simple and appealing benchmark: "rational expectations," which essentially equates rationality with the absence of systematic error.[19] The intuition is that mere ignorance produces nothing worse than random mistakes. If you overestimate the level of traffic one morning, and underestimate it the day after, no one impugns your rationality. How are you supposed to know if a car will break down at rush hour and block two lanes? In contrast, if you underestimate the severity of traffic every day, "How was I supposed to know?" is a hollow excuse. There was not enough information to predict perfectly; but that hardly explains why predictions consistently fail the same way.

As formalizations go, rational expectations makes a lot of sense. Its violation is close to the everyday meaning of "irrationality." Furthermore, an assumption akin to rational expectations is hard to do without. Who has not said something like "As price goes up, sellers increase their production"? Yet this elementary claim assumes that *objective facts* and *subjective beliefs* about price move in the same direction. If sellers systematically mistook rising prices for falling prices, their response would be the reverse of the standard prediction.

It is not surprising, then, that informal substitutes for rational expectations predate the formal literature. Years before Muth or Lucas, economists routinely affirmed that one can judge the "rationality" of actors' *means*. For Downs, "The term *rational* is never applied to an agent's ends, but only to his means. This follows from the definition of *rational* as efficient, i.e., maximizing output for a given input."[20] Like rational expectations, Downs's benchmark measures agents' beliefs against objective reality:

> If a theorist knows the ends of some decision-maker, he can predict which actions will be taken to achieve them as follows: (1) he calculates the most reasonable way for the decision-maker to reach his goals, and (2) he assumes this way will actually be chosen because the decision-maker is rational.[21]

The "rational expectations *revolution*" is a misnomer. It did triumph quickly as an analytical approach. But—with the exception of Keynesian macroeconomics—the change was usually cosmetic. Rational expectations primarily gave older styles of economics a more definite shape, leaving their spirit intact.

Still, economists often lose their enthusiasm for rational expectations once evidence of systematic errors starts to pour in. If you equate rationality with the absence of systematic errors, hard empirical evidence of their presence is an open-and-shut case for irrationality. Rather than accept this unpalatable conclusion, lots of economists throw the rational expectations benchmark to the wolves.

Then a third defense springs up: a looser definition of rationality that allows for systematic mistakes. Bayesianism is one alternative. As long as people update their beliefs according to Bayes' Rule, they qualify as "rational," even if they are grossly in error. However, this weak standard too has been experimentally tested and found wanting.[22]

A still weaker definition of rationality equates it with "truth-seeking."[23] As long as a person sincerely *tries* to understand the world, he is rational in this sense, no matter what he believes. The only irrational people are those who fail to try; everyone else gets an A for effort.

It is important to notice that systematic errors like those in the SAEE are *constitutive* of irrationality in the rational expectations sense of the term, but remain a *symptom* of irrationality in its weaker senses. The sillier errors get, the more likely it is that the cause is lack of mental discipline, not lack of information.

The deepest problem with substitutes for rational expectations is that they give only a semantic victory. A lower threshold for "rationality" makes it easier to vouch for an individual's rationality, but there is a high cost. Most models assume that individuals' beliefs are unbiased, not merely that they are rational in some sense. So once you lower the threshold of rationality, you can no longer safely build on standard "rational actor" theorems. You have to go back to square one to save a word.

What's Wrong with Rational Ignorance, I

The phrase "*rational* ignorance" functions as a disclaimer. Stamping "rationally ignorant" on a person certifies that "the aforementioned ignorance of the subject does not impugn his rationality, which continues to enjoy a full warranty." When people mention "irrationality," economists dismiss them with the truism, "There is a difference between irrationality and ignorance."[24] But this cuts both ways: if ignorance can be mistaken for irrationality, irrationality can be mistaken for ignorance. Maybe failing students in introductory econ could excel if they attended class and read the textbook. Then again, *maybe not.*

Still, I do not want to dismiss the "ignorance only" view too hastily. What is wrong with it? This section and the next ask two critical questions of the "ignorance only" view:

First: *Is the ignorance-only view consistent with introspection and personal testimony?*
Second: *Can the ignorance-only view explain democratic failure?*

The connection between error and lack of information is obvious. But is lack of information the root of *all* error? Introspection and personal testimony advance another candidate: emotional commitment.[25] Holding fast to beloved opinions increases subjective well-being. When the typical person defends the claims of his religion, to take the clearest example, he *cares* about the answer, and meets pertinent information with hostility if it goes against his convictions. To a large degree, we expect religious discussions to be "dogmatic," with believers on all sides refusing to give rival sects a fair hearing. Cynics might call this posturing, but it is usually hard to doubt devotees' sincerity. By and large, people are not *pretending* to be closed-minded on matters of faith.

In a secular age, politics and economics have displaced religion itself as the focal point for passionate conviction and dogmatism. As McCloskey says, "The man in the street cherishes his erroneous ideas about free trade. . . . He regards his ideas as part of his character, like his personality or his body type, and takes very unkindly to critical remarks about them."[26] When liberals and conservatives quarrel about the effect of tax cuts, they have emotional investments in the answer. Conservatives like arguments that support tax cuts even if they are factually dubious; liberals dislike arguments that support tax cuts even if they make perfect sense.

Undoubtedly this is partly strategic, but it strains credulity to claim that the confidence of the typical ideologue is "just an act." Listen to Arthur Koestler describe his conversion to Communism:

> To say that one has "seen the light" is a poor description of the mental rapture which only the convert knows (regardless of what faith he has been converted to). The new light seems to pour from all directions across the skull; the whole universe falls into pattern like the stray pieces of a jigsaw puzzle assembled by magic at one stroke. There is now an answer to every question, doubts and conflicts are a matter of the tortured past—a past already remote, when one had lived in dismal ignorance in the tasteless, colorless world of those who *don't know*. Nothing henceforth can disturb the convert's inner peace and serenity—except the occasional fear of losing faith again, losing thereby what alone makes life worth living, and falling back into the outer darkness, where there is wailing and gnashing of teeth.[27]

Whittaker Chambers makes the same point more succinctly:

> I was willing to accept Communism in whatever terms it presented itself, to follow the logic of its course wherever it might lead me, and to suffer the penalties without which nothing in life can be achieved. For it offered me what nothing else in the dying world had power to offer at the same intensity—faith and a vision, something for which to live and something for which to die.[28]

The fanaticism of Koestler or Chambers is obviously rare, but I submit that in politics, disinterested objectivity is just as scarce.

Introspection also uncovers mixed cognitive motives. Recall the last argument you had on a topic you feel strongly about. You probably made an effort to give the other side a fair hearing. Why was it necessary, though, to *make an effort*? Because you knew that your emotions might carry you away; you might heatedly proclaim yourself the victor even if the evidence was against you. Whether or not *you* give in to temptation, there are always many who will. Irrationality is therefore all around us, and not just according to a demanding test like rational expectations. Drop the standard of rationality down to "truth-seeking" if you like. You can grade people for effort, and they still flunk.

If ignorance were the sole cause of error, sufficiently large doses of information would be a cognitive panacea. You could fix *any* misconception with enough facts. A few thought experiments show how implausible this is. Imagine trying to convert an audience of creationists to Darwinism. You might change some minds with patient lectures on genetics, fossil evidence, or fruit fly experiments.[29] But it would be miraculous if you convinced half. Similarly, envision John Lott addressing the Million Mom March on "more guns, less crime."[30] Even if his empirical work were impeccable, it is hard to see more than a handful of crusaders for gun control exclaiming, "Oops, who would have guessed?" Indeed, few would concede, "This issue is more complicated than I thought; I'll stop protesting until I get a better grip." Or consider explaining the benefits of free trade to globalization protestors. A few might gain new insight into comparative advantage and economic development. Yet is anyone naive enough to suppose that he could convince a majority?

My point is not that real-world evidence is one-sided (though it often is!). Rather, my point is that if the evidence *were* one-sided, the fraction convinced would not rise to 100% with *all* the relevant information. Their emotional attachment to their beliefs is too intense: "Don't confuse me with the facts."

Almost every interesting topic in economics fits this description. Think about the SAEE. What would it take to convince everyone that supply-and-demand typically governs price? That excessive foreign aid is not a major problem? That downsizing is good in the long run? That living standards are rising? In each case, emotional commitment to the wrong answer—and hostility to naysayers—is widespread. A good teacher could change some minds, but the best teacher in the world would be lucky to convince half.

Aristotle says that "all men by nature desire to know,"[31] but that is not the whole story. It is also true that all men by nature desire *not* to know unpleasant facts. Much of the time, *both* motives are at work. The human mind has mixed motives: people want to learn about the world *without sacrificing their worldview.*[32] Investigating only the first motive yields a distorted picture of the way we use our heads.

What's Wrong with Rational Ignorance, II

Many detractors reject Classical Public Choice on aesthetic grounds.[33] The civics textbook presents a beautiful picture of democracy. Its flaws should never be depicted as more than transient aberrations. Information economics adds insult to injury. It not only unveils deep flaws in democracy; it paints its flaws as *inherent.* Voters are ignorant due to inborn human selfishness, not an epidemic of apathy induced by "insufficient democracy." Other critics, however, have substantive objections to Classical Public Choice. Taken together, they seriously undermine it.

The Miracle of Aggregation and the Irrelevance of Biased Information

Chapter 1 already worked through the deepest objection to Classical Public Choice's account of political failure: Ignorant voters choose randomly, so with a reasonably large electorate they balance each other out, leaving the well informed in the driver's seat.[34] A natural objection to this Miracle of Aggregation is that it takes on a straw man. The problem, one might say, is not that the ignorant vote randomly, but that the ignorant are easily *misled* by propaganda. The trouble is not the shortage of information, but its bias, which fills the heads of the ignorant with lies.[35]

While this story sounds good, it is theoretically wobbly. Ignorant does not mean *impressionable*. When you walk onto a used car lot, you may be highly ignorant, but you can still *discount* or ignore the words of the salesmen who shout, "You won't get a better deal anywhere else!" As Wittman critically remarks:

> I have never met anyone who believes that the defense department does not exaggerate the need for defense procurement. But if everyone knows the defense department will exaggerate the importance of its contribution to human welfare, then, on average, voters will sufficiently discount defense department claims. Even when the ruling class has a virtual domestic monopoly on the instruments of information, as was the case in the former Soviet Union, we observe people discounting the information contained in their papers and trusting foreign sources.[36]

At minimum, why wouldn't highly ignorant voters *tune out* unreliable sources? They do not have to fact-check political ads, just greet them with blanket skepticism. That is the commonsense response to unverified assertions from sources with questionable motives.

Popular metaphors are partly to blame for the confusion. Writers often compare the ignorant to empty vessels, clean sheets of paper, or blank slates. Mao Zedong thought it fortunate that the Chinese peasantry was "poor and blank" because "a clean sheet of paper has no blotches and so the newest and most beautiful words can be written on it."[37] Such metaphors gloss over the distinction between being ignorant and being *receptive to new ideas*. One does not follow from the other. A blank slate can be difficult to write upon; an ignorant voter can be hard to persuade. If you hear only cheap talk by rival politicians, the rational course is to stay agnostic.

Thus, you can grant that (almost all) voters are morbidly ignorant yet remain optimistic about how well democracy works. There is nothing mystical about the Miracle of Aggregation—it is simple statistics. And as long as ignorance is circumscribed by common sense, the Miracle of Aggregation is sturdy enough to withstand floods of biased information.[38]

Optimal Punishment and Correlations between Information and Interests.   What happens if the more informed have predictably different interests than the less informed—in technical terms, if there is a *correlation* between information and interests? Political corruption is a clear example. Those who know the most about the corruption—the bribe-taker and the bribe-payer—profit from it; the people who suffer because of corruption do not know who is paying whom to do what.

You face the same problem if well-informed voters have different interests than the rest of the population. Suppose that 60% of voters are uninformed and poor, 20% are uninformed and rich, 5% are well informed and poor, and 15% are well informed and rich. If people vote their pocketbooks in a two-candidate race, the more prorich politician gets half the uninformed votes but three-quarters of the well-informed votes. The prorich candidate wins with 55% of the vote, though 65% of voters are poor.

Correlations between information and interests seem like a strong objection to the Miracle of Aggregation. The more informed have the power to manipulate the system, and there is nothing the less informed can do about it. But like biased information, there is less to this problem than meets the eye. One can circumvent its dangers with a little help from the economics of crime.

Suppose a robber has a 50% chance of being caught lifting $1,000 from a cash register. If the punishment is a $1,000 fine, crime pays: Heads, the thief wins; tails, he breaks even. Legal systems cope with this problem by making a convicted criminal *much* worse off than he would have been if he had obeyed the law. In economic jargon, the law imposes "probability multipliers"—making sentences tougher as the chance of being caught declines.[39] As Gary Becker originally put it, the idea is "to keep police and other expenditures relatively low and to compensate by meting out strong punishments to those convicted."[40]

An ignorant electorate can use the same strategy to control politicians. Voters do not need to pay much attention to politics; they only need to vow revenge if they catch their leaders misbehaving. You learn that a congressman uses the franking privilege to send personal

mail—give him a year of jail. A cabinet member mutters a racial epi-
thet on tape—demand his resignation. A convict on furlough commits a murder—vote against the incumbent governor in the next election. Finally, if a politician pays too much attention to the well
informed, declare him an elitist and throw the snob out. What appears to be an "overreaction" is an easy way for the ignorant to elicit
good behavior day in, day out.

Big Government: The Neglected Victim of Asymmetric Information.
Information is "asymmetric" when more-knowledgeable people interact with less-knowledgeable people. The classic example is the
used-car market: the dealer knows details that customers can only
guess.[41] Political corruption fits the same description: A politician
knows if he has been dishonest, but the public may not.

Harsh punishment is the simplest way for the ignorant to protect
their interests. But what if the harshest available punishment is too
mild to keep politicians in line? A used-car dealer who gets caught
lying to his customers might lose more than their goodwill; he risks
a fraud conviction as well. In contrast, after he irreversibly ruins his
public reputation, a politician can earn a comfortable living in a law
firm. A democratically elected leader can break all his campaign
promises without risking a day in jail or a one-dollar lawsuit. Heads
he wins, tails he breaks even: a recipe for constant abuse.

To many, unmitigated asymmetric information provides a clean account of how democracy fails.[42] It is the alleged mechanism that sus-
tains Big Government, letting politicians, bureaucrats, and lobbyists
waste taxpayers' money on one pointless program and regulation
after another. The insiders are the only ones who know what is going
on, and if they are caught red-handed, they get a slap on the wrist,
not harsh "optimal punishments."

This story is plausible but incomplete and easy to misinterpret. To
see why, return to the used-car market. Due to their informational
disadvantage, as Akerlof explained,[43] prospective purchasers of used
cars are wary. Salesmen must demonstrate the quality of their product
to consumers' satisfaction. If the demonstration is unconvincing,
buyers slash their bids to reflect uncertainty. If their doubts are strong
enough, they walk away. Thus, the greater sellers' informational advantage, the smaller the demand for their product. Asymmetric information is bad for sellers as well as buyers.

The same principle applies to politics. You do not need to follow
politics closely in order to realize that insiders *know more than you do.*
Armed with this epiphany, you have a straightforward countermove:
When in doubt, say no.[44] Voters can assign fewer responsibilities and

surrender less money to a government they do not trust by voting for politicians who share their doubts. So contrary to popular stories, asymmetric information leads to *less* government.[45]

To see why, suppose that there are 10 proposed government programs. Four of them make the typical voter $100 better off; the other six transfer $100 from the typical voter to an interest group. If voters know which programs are good and which are bad, four of the 10 will enjoy popular support. However, if there is asymmetric information, if voters cannot distinguish good programs from bad, they expect to lose $20 from any given program, and therefore oppose all 10.

If insiders lobbied harder for the bad programs, the effect of asymmetric information would be even stronger. There could be forty good proposals, and only six bad ones. If voters hear about all of the bad ones, but only 10% of the good ones, asymmetric information leads voters to oppose *every* new program that crosses their path. The whole barrel can go to waste because of a few bad apples.

Yes, in vital areas, voters might prefer corrupt government to none at all. But these are rare compared to the countless marginal functions that voters might assign to government if they knew it would do a good job.[46] Government transparency is bad for insiders with something to hide, but good for government overall.

Inarticulate Knowledge and Cognitive Shortcuts.   The preceding arguments are skeptical about the *consequences* of voter ignorance. None questions its severity. But some critics add that voters' ignorance is greatly exaggerated. Objective tests show that voters are bad at *articulating* what they know about politics. Perhaps, however, they hold the same positions they would have adopted after intensive study. How? By falling back on "cognitive shortcuts"—informal or subliminal cues.[47] Lupia and McCubbins use the example of a motorist crossing a busy intersection:

> Advocates of complete information might argue that successful automotive navigation requires as much information as you can gather about the intentions of other drivers and the speed, acceleration, direction, and mass of their cars. At many intersections, however, there is a simple substitute for *all* of this information—a traffic signal.[48]

Brand names help shoppers far more than *Consumer Reports* ever will. Perhaps party labels play an analogous role in politics. Or consider word of mouth. You often buy on a friend's recommendation. You would look foolish if you were quizzed about the pros and cons of your decision. But it was ultimately well informed. The same could hold for political stances—a person who slavishly follows friends' advice might flunk a test of political knowledge despite the fact that his decision indirectly draws from a well of careful deliberation. As Lupia and McCubbins wryly observe: "Asserting that limited information precludes reasoned choice is equivalent to requiring that people who want to brush their teeth recall the ingredients of their toothpaste."[49]

The leading version of this approach is the theory of *retrospective voting*.[50] The intuition: Instead of second-guessing your leader's decisions, look at the country during his tenure. If it enjoyed prosperity and peace, reelect the incumbent or his anointed successor. If it suffered from depression and war, throw the bum out. This cognitive shortcut rewards smart decisions, and in turn spurs politicians to make smart decisions—even if you have no idea what the smart decision is.

In my view, appeals to inarticulate knowledge are far less compelling than other objections to Classical Public Choice. Inarticulate knowledge clearly exists, but you would expect articulate and inarticulate knowledge to positively correlate. Knowledge of anatomy does not make one a surgeon, but most trained surgeons can still describe in detail how the human body works. Low objective test scores are not sure proof of incompetence, but they point in that direction.

Shoppers rely on brand names and word of mouth, but that is not the limit of their knowledge. They also have a lot of articulate knowledge, without which their cognitive shortcuts would be far less useful. If you do not grasp the difference between orange juice and detergent, brand names will at best help you drink the finest detergent on the market, and wash your dishes with the right amount of pulp. What protects shoppers from making this mistake is their *conscious* ability to identify and explain the pros and cons, the uses and limitations, of hundreds of products.

In contrast, a voter unable to describe his representative's policies, demarcate his areas of authority—or name him—is not out of the ordinary. This puts a serious damper on retrospective voting. If voters do not know term lengths, incumbent politicians will be punished for the sins of their predecessor, and share credit for their achievements with their successors. If voters pay no attention to policy, "prosperity and peace" voting heavily discourages the adoption of policies with long-run gains but short-term costs—such as a preemptive war against a rising menace.

Furthermore, what good does retrospective voting do if voters do not know which branch—or branches—of government are responsible for what?[51] Reelecting incumbent presidents during periods of prosperity is a silly shortcut if economic performance primarily depends on the independent central bank. Correctly assigning credit and blame is especially important under divided government, when retrospective voting could create truly perverse incentives. If voters punish presidents for high unemployment, a Republican Congress could defeat a Democratic president by fighting against recovery.

Someone unschooled in physics can be a great pool player. Researchers who emphasize inarticulate knowledge correctly point out that tests of articulate knowledge understate functional know-how.[52] But they do not show that tests of political knowledge understate functional voter know-how to a *larger than normal* degree, still less that articulate knowledge and voter know-how are unrelated. Indeed, as Althaus observes, research on enlightened preferences shows the opposite. Articulate knowledge usually predicts systematically different policy views:

> While many respondents may use heuristics, on-line processing, and information shortcuts to arrive at the political opinions they express in surveys, these substitutes for political knowledge do not necessarily help ill-informed people express policy preferences similar to those of well-informed people. If they did, surveyed opinion across the board should closely resemble fully informed opinion.[53]

Wittman's Fork

The most compelling objections to Classical Public Choice *accommodate* rational ignorance. Instead of disputing its theoretical coherence or empirical accuracy, they quarrel with conventional beliefs about its *consequences*:

- Contrary to Classical Public Choice, the level of voter ignorance has little effect on policy. More careful analysis, guided by the law of large numbers, shows that the influence of well-informed voters is disproportionate to their head count.
- Ignorance does not turn voters into easy marks for propaganda and deceit. Lack of information is not equivalent to folly, and only a fool would take unverified, self-serving political advertising at face value.
- Voter ignorance does not imply corruption and insider manipulation. True, if the severity of formal and informal punishment stays constant, voter inattention implies lower expected penalties for misbehavior. But there is an obvious cure: compensate for lax monitoring with unforgiving punishment.

- Finally, if harsh punishments cannot be imposed, the sensible voter response to insider manipulation is skepticism. They can reject so-called government "solutions" until the day—and that day may never come to pass—when there is solid proof of their efficacy.

The implications for Classical Public Choice are radical. Rational ignorance, long since convicted by a vast literature of subverting democracy, lacks the means to commit the crime of which is stands accused. The defendant has a solid alibi. Appeals to the self-evidence of the premise or the conclusion are beside the point. The issue is the *link*, or lack thereof, between rational ignorance and inefficiently large government.

Once we understand how rational ignorance does and does not matter, there is a temptation to "close the case" against democracy. Yet it would be premature to infer that the *conclusions* of Classical Public Choice are false. The fact that the prime suspect in a murder investigation is innocent does not mean that the victim died of natural causes. Logic texts are full of examples of invalid arguments from true premises to true conclusions. The premises "Some men are mortal" and "I am a man" are true, and so is the conclusion, "I am mortal." But "Some men are mortal; I am a man; therefore I am mortal" is not a valid argument. (Consider the logically parallel "Some men have red hair; I am a man; therefore I have red hair.") The failure of rational ignorance implies that democracy's critics must find an alternative mechanism.

This is not as easy as it sounds. The maverick economist Donald Wittman of UC Santa Cruz persuasively contends that there are essentially three routes: "Behind every model of government failure is an assumption of extreme voter stupidity, serious lack of competition, or excessively high negotiation/transfer costs."[54] Wittman adds that economists ordinarily treat all three sorts of explanations as dubious. I call this *Wittman's Fork*: there are but three paths to democratic failure (fig. 4.1).[55]

Building on the preceding critique of rational ignorance, Wittman deliberately says "extreme stupidity," not "ignorance." This is a bit harsh: Wittman might make you wear a dunce cap for having a mediocre grasp of advanced game theory.[56] His point, though, is that ignorance cannot carry the weight the critics of democracy assign to it. If voters are to blame for the failures of democracy, their flaw has to be deeper than "lack of information."

What about Wittman's two other options? Despite its focus on the rational ignorance of the electorate, Classical Public Choice leaves

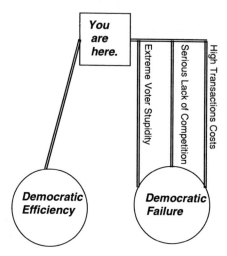

Figure 4.1 Wittman's Fork

room for fully informed political failure. A market monopoly can fleece fully informed consumers; a political monopoly could do the same to fully informed voters. But in recent decades economists have met charges of "monopoly" with suspicion.[57] How do you become a "monopoly"—business, political, or other—in the first place? Wittman aptly encapsulates modern thinking:

> Incumbents tend to be reelected for the same reason that the winner of the last footrace is likely to win the next one and the head of a corporation is likely to maintain his position tomorrow. They are the best. That is why they won in the first place and why they are likely to win again.[58]

If market monopoly worries you, then probably so should political monopoly. But before you rush to "restore competition," in either arena, reflect on the long-term dangers of penalizing success.

A parallel story holds for the remaining refuge of Classical Public Choice: "excessively high negotiation/transfer costs." Markets fail to execute some otherwise beneficial trades because of transaction costs. Political logrolling has the same problem.[59] Yet it is hard to get excited about these missed opportunities. Will it not be the marginal deals, of little consequence, that remain undone? On top of this, democracy is *designed* to shear the transactions costs of ordinary contract law.[60] In markets, you need participants' unanimous consent to strike a bargain; under democracy, majorities often suffice to reach a decision.

It is tempting to reply that Wittman's sanguine views on political competition and transactions costs have been empirically refuted during the past decade.[61] Direct democracy yields different outcomes than indirect democracy. Senators from the same state often disagree. Open primaries, redistricting, campaign finance rules, and the degree of party competition affect political outcomes.[62] Besley and Case feel comfortable stating, "At a general level, the median voter model, the workhorse of so much political economy modeling for more than a generation, receives little empirical support."[63]

I suspect, however, that Wittman would be unfazed by these findings. In the grand scheme of things, he would probably say, the reported effects are small. Perhaps Besley and Case are right, for example, that "a ten percentage point increase in the fraction of seats held by Democrats in both the lower and upper houses is associated with an increase in overall state spending per capita of $10 in 1982 dollars."[64] Does that refute the claim that government basically gives voters what they want? Even the fact that senators from the same state often disagree is not so troubling. Maybe voters deliberately elect senators from different parties to dilute the effect of ideological shirking.[65] And if new legislation *slightly* adjusts a status quo that is *close* to constituents' preferences to begin with, senators from the same state only need a little slack in order to vote differently.

Wittman would also probably argue that other researchers misinterpret their findings. If lopsided legislatures really pushed policy away from voters' preferences, they would stop voting for them. A more plausible story, for Wittman, would be that researchers do not correctly *measure* voter preferences. Voters elect lopsided legislatures *in order* to get the policies lopsided legislatures typically deliver. Surely, he might inquire, you are not suggesting that people systematically underestimate the effects of giving one party the lion's share of power?

Wittman's aim is to drive Classical Public Choice in his preferred direction by blocking every option but his own. Then all serious students of politics will have to concede that democracy works well. In fact, however, Wittman leaves the route of "extreme voter stupidity" wide open. He provides little empirical evidence of voters' mental prowess.[66] Instead, he tries to dissuade us with scary rhetoric. Faced with a choice between the implausible view that "democracy works well" and the embarrassing view that "voters are extremely stupid," Wittman bets that democracy's detractors will endorse the former.

Rethinking "Extreme Voter Stupidity"

Efforts to minimize the effect of voter ignorance may have struck you as far-fetched. Errors harmlessly cancel out? The average voter seamlessly adjusts for media bias, and imposes probability multipliers to discipline misbehavior? Government shrinks because voters do not know how well its programs work? To escape such odd conclusions, all you have to do is stop talking about voter *ignorance*, and start talking about voter *irrationality*.[67]

Take the Miracle of Aggregation. The mistakes of ignorant voters cancel each other out, leaving informed voters in charge. If you find this conclusion fantastic, relief is at hand. Admit that voters have systematic biases, that they are, in technical terms, somewhat irrational. Then instead of canceling, the electorate's errors tilt policy in the expected direction.

The same goes for biased information. Rationally ignorant individuals would not be swayed, but that does not mean no swaying occurs. If individuals fall short of full rationality, they might inadequately adjust for the credibility of the source. They might embrace propaganda because they like the way that a speaker sounds or smiles or dresses— or the movies he starred in. Irrationality does not imply impressionability, but—unlike rational ignorance—it does not rule it out.

Irrational voters' punishment strategies may be equally inept. Just because they *possess* the right tools for keeping politicians honest does not mean they will *deploy* them. Optimal punishment rises as the probability of detection falls and the benefit of breaking the rules goes up. Irrational voters may flout these vital principles. They might bemoan politicians' dishonesty, then turn around and forgive flagrant promise-breaking. Irrational voters could make the reputational fallout for minor offenses higher than major ones with the same probability of detection. In the real world, which is more likely to incur the public's wrath: an off-color joke, or a broken campaign promise? A sex scandal, or failure to prevent a terrorist attack?

Along the same lines, irrational voters may respond to asymmetric information with blind faith rather than cautious skepticism. Rationally ignorant voters employ a "When in doubt, say no" strategy, giving politicians and activists with good ideas a strong incentive to prove their case. But irrational voters might take the naive stance, "If they say we need a program, we must!"—tempting insiders to concoct one scary story after another.[68]

Conclusion

Unlike ignorance, irrationality allows a wide range of outcomes. Many see the absence of a unique prediction as a defect, or a sign of intellectual sloth. I do not. As Richard Thaler pointedly asks, "Would you rather be elegant and precisely wrong, or messy and vaguely right?"[69] Recognizing that objective facts do not nail down political beliefs shows us how to spend our time more wisely. *Theories of irrationality need discipline from the empirics of public opinion.* We should focus on this vital task—as the last chapter did—instead of making tortured arguments about how voters' beliefs flow logically from the facts.

Unfortunately, many economists have trouble getting over the conflict between voter irrationality and economic theory. One is tempted to say "So what?" but this is a flippant response. In all fairness, the economic approach to human behavior has been extremely fruitful. Basic economic theory cannot be lightly cast aside.

Fortunately, there is no need to do so. With a slight conceptual twist, voter irrationality becomes a natural extension of basic economic theory, not a deviation from it. The next chapter develops and explores a new model of cognition to show how one and the same individual can be both a "rational consumer" and an "irrational voter." From this standpoint, the evidence of systematic error ceases to be anomalous. Economists should have expected it all along. With this new groundwork laid, a disquieting yet intuitive vision of political economy falls naturally into place.

Chapter 5

RATIONAL IRRATIONALITY

> For it seemed to me that I could find much more truth in
> the reasonings that each person makes concerning mat-
> ters that are important to him, and whose outcome ought
> to cost him dearly later on if he judged badly, than in
> those reasonings engaged in by a man of letters in his
> study, which touch on speculations that produce no effect
> and are of no other consequence to him except perhaps
> that, the more they are removed from common sense, the
> more pride he will take in them.
> —*Rene Descartes*, Discourse on Method[1]

SUPPOSE you grant that voters are irrational. Can you stop there? Voters are people. If they are highly irrational on election day, one would
expect them to be equally irrational the rest of the year. Do individuals
magically transform into a lower form of life when they enter the
voting booth, then revert to their normal state upon exit?

The thesis of global human rationality is internally consistent. So
is the opposite thesis that humans are irrational through and through.
Is there a coherent intermediate position? Without one, the practical
relevance of voters' folly shrinks or vanishes. If people are rational on
Monday and irrational on Tuesday, it is a good idea to shift decision-
making to Monday. But if people are irrational twenty-four seven, you
just have to live with the fact that *all* decisions will be worse. By the
same reasoning, if people are rational as consumers but irrational as
voters, it is a good idea to rely more on markets and less on politics.
But if people are irrational across the board, we should expect less of
every form of human organization. The relative merits of alternative
systems stay roughly the same.[2]

Even if an intermediate position is coherent, is it consistent with
what we already know? One could postulate voter irrationality as an
ad hoc exception to the laws of human behavior. But ad hoc exceptions to well-established principles understandably provoke skepticism.[3] Is there any way to subsume established patterns and anomalies under a single rule?

This chapter meets these theoretical challenges. Though initially jarring, it is coherent to assert that people are rational in some areas but not others. Irrational beliefs probably play a role in all human activities, but politics makes the "short list" of areas where irrationality is exceptionally pronounced. Furthermore, basic economic theory—properly interpreted—helps define the boundaries of rationality. Political irrationality is not an ad hoc anomaly, but a predictable response to unusual incentives.

Preferences over Beliefs

> "I ca'n't believe that!" said Alice.
> "Ca'n't you?" the Queen said in a pitying tone.
> "Try again: draw a long breath, and shut your eyes."
> Alice laughed. "There's no use trying," she said.
> "One *ca'n't* believe impossible things."
> "I dare say you haven't had much practice," said
> the Queen. "When I was your age, I always did it for half-
> an-hour a day. Why, sometimes I've believed as many as
> six impossible things before breakfast."
> —*Lewis Carroll,* Through the Looking-Glass[4]

The desire for truth can clash with other motives. Material self-interest is the leading suspect. We distrust salesmen because they make more money if they shade the truth. In markets for ideas, similarly, people often accuse their opponents of being "bought," their judgment corrupted by a flow of income that would dry up if they changed their minds. Dasgupta and Stiglitz deride the free-market critique of antitrust policy as "well-funded" but "not well-founded."[5] Some accept funding from interested parties, then bluntly speak their minds anyway. The temptation, however, is to balance being right and being rich.

Social pressure for conformity is another force that conflicts with truth-seeking.[6] Espousing unpopular views often transforms you into an unpopular person. Few want to be pariahs, so they self-censor. If pariahs are less likely to be hired, conformity blends into conflict of interest. However, even bereft of financial consequences, who wants to be hated? The temptation is to balance being right and being liked.

But greed and conformism are not the only forces at war with truth. Human beings also have mixed *cognitive* motives.[7] One of our goals is to reach correct answers in order to take appropriate action, but that is not the *only* goal of our thought. On many topics, one position is more comforting, flattering, or exciting, raising the danger that our judgment will be corrupted not by money or social approval, but by our own passions.

Even on a desert isle, some beliefs make us feel better about ourselves. Gustave Le Bon refers to "that portion of hope and illusion without which [men] cannot live."[8] Religion is the most obvious example.[9] Since it is often considered rude to call attention to the fact, let Gaetano Mosca make the point for me:

> The Christian must be enabled to think with complacency that everybody not of the Christian faith will be damned. The Brahman must be given grounds for rejoicing that he alone is descended from the head of Brahma and has the exalted honor of reading the sacred books. The Buddhist must be taught highly to prize the privilege he has of attaining Nirvana soonest. The Mohammedan must recall with satisfaction that he alone is a true believer, and that all others are infidel dogs in this life and tormented dogs in the next. The radical socialist must be convinced that all who do not think as he does are either selfish, money-spoiled bourgeois or ignorant and servile simpletons. These are all examples of arguments that provide for one's need of esteeming one's self and one's own religion or convictions and at the same time for the need of despising and hating others.[10]

Worldviews are more a mental security blanket than a serious effort to understand the world: "Illusions endure because illusion is a need for almost all men, a need they feel no less strongly than their material needs."[11] Modern empirical work suggests that Mosca was on to something: The religious consistently enjoy greater life satisfaction.[12] No wonder human beings shield their beliefs from criticism, and cling to them if counterevidence seeps through their defenses.

Most people find the existence of mixed cognitive motives so obvious that "proof" is superfluous. Jost and his coauthors casually remark in the *Psychological Bulletin* that "Nearly everyone is aware of the possibility that people are capable of believing what they want to believe, at least within certain limits."[13] But my fellow economists are unlikely to sign off so easily. If one economist tells another, "Your economics is just a religion," the allegedly religious economist normally takes the distinction between "emotional ideologue" and "dispassionate scholar" for granted, and paints himself as the latter. But when I assert the generic existence of preferences over beliefs, many economists challenge the whole category. How do I know preferences over beliefs exist? Some eminent economists imply that this is *impossible* to know because preferences are unobservable.[14]

They are mistaken. I observe one person's preferences every day—mine. Within its sphere I trust my introspection more than I could ever trust the work of another economist.[15] Introspection tells me that I am getting hungry, and would be happy to pay a dollar for an ice cream bar. If anything qualifies as "raw data," this does. Indeed, it is harder to doubt than "raw data" that economists routinely accept—like self-reported earnings.

One thing my introspection tells me is that some beliefs are more emotionally appealing than their opposites. For example, I like to believe that I am right. It is worse to *admit* error, or lose money because of error, but error is disturbing all by itself. Having these feelings does not imply that I indulge them—no more than accepting money from a source with an agenda implies that my writings are insincere. But the temptation is there.

Introspection is a fine way to learn about your own preferences. But what about the preferences of others? Perhaps you are so abnormal that it is utterly misleading to extrapolate from yourself to the rest of humanity. The simplest way to check is to *listen* to what other people say about their preferences.

I was once at a dinner with Gary Becker where he scoffed at this idea. His position, roughly, was, "You can't believe what people *say,*" though he still paid attention when the waiter named the house specialties. Yes, there is a sound core to Becker's position. People fail to reflect carefully. People deceive.[16] But contrary to Becker, these are not reasons to *ignore* their words. We should put less weight on testimony when people speak in haste, or have an incentive to lie. But listening remains more informative than plugging your ears. After all, human beings can detect lies as well as tell them. Experimental psychology documents that liars sometimes gives themselves away with demeanor or inconsistencies in their stories.[17]

Once we take the testimony of mankind seriously, evidence of preferences over beliefs abounds. People can't shut up about them. Consider the words of philosopher George Berkeley:

> I can easily overlook any present momentary sorrow when I reflect that it is in my power to be happy a thousand years hence. If it were not for this thought I had rather be an oyster than a man.[18]

Paul Samuelson himself revels in the Keynesian revelation, approvingly quoting Wordsworth to capture the joy of the *General Theory:*

Bliss was it in that dawn to be alive,
But to be young was very heaven![19]

Many autobiographies describe the pain of abandoning the ideas that once gave meaning to the author's life. As Whittaker Chambers puts it:

> So great an effort, quite apart from its physical and practical hazards, cannot occur without a profound upheaval of the spirit. No man lightly reverses the faith of an adult lifetime, held implacably to the point of criminality. He reverses it only with a violence greater than the faith he is repudiating.[20]

No wonder that—in his own words—Chambers broke with Communism "slowly, reluctantly, in agony."[21] For Arthur Koestler, deconversion was "emotional harakiri." He adds, "Those who have been caught by the great illusion of our time, and have lived through its moral and intellectual debauch, either give themselves up to a new addiction of the opposite type, or are condemned to pay with a lifelong hangover." Richard Wright laments, "I knew in my heart that I should never be able to feel with that simple sharpness about life, should never again express such passionate hope, should never again make so total a commitment of faith."[22]

The desire for "hope and illusion" plays a role even in mental illness.[23] According to his biographer, Nobel Prize winner and paranoid schizophrenic John Nash often preferred his fantasy world—where he was a "Messianic godlike figure"[24] —to harsh reality:

> For Nash, the recovery of everyday thought processes produced a sense of diminution and loss. . . . He refers to his remissions not as joyful returns to a healthy state, but as "interludes, as it were, of enforced rationality."[25]

Historians of thought also frequently document enthusiastic support for dubious dogmas. Listen to Böhm-Bawerk trace the psychological appeal of Marxian exploitation theory:

> It drew up the line of battle on a field where the heart, as well as the head is wont to speak. What people wish to believe, they believe very readily. . . . When the implications of a theory point toward raising the claims of the poor and lowering those of the rich, many a man who finds himself faced with that theory will be biased from the outset. And so he will in large measure *neglect to apply that critical acuity which he ordinarily would devote to an examination of scientific justification.* Naturally it goes without saying that the great masses will become devotees of such doctrines. Critical delib-

eration is of course no concern of theirs, nor can it be; they simply follow the bent of their wishes. They believe in the exploitation theory because of its conformity to their preferences, and despite its fallaciousness. And they would still believe in it, if its scientific foundations were even less stable than they actually are.[26]

If neither way of verifying the existence of preferences over beliefs appeals to you, a final one remains. Reverse the direction of reasoning. Smoke usually means fire. The more bizarre a mistake is, the harder it is to attribute to lack of information. Suppose your friend thinks he is Napoleon. It is conceivable that he got an improbable coincidence of misleading signals sufficient to convince any of us. But it is awfully suspicious that he embraces the pleasant view that he is a world-historic figure, rather than, say, Napoleon's dishwasher. Similarly, suppose an adult sees trade as a zero-sum game. Since he experiences the opposite every day, it is hard to blame his mistake on "lack of information." More plausibly, like blaming your team's defeat on cheaters, seeing trade as disguised exploitation soothes those who dislike the market's outcome.

The Material Costs of Error

> The human being . . . very rarely fails to keep two great aspirations before his eyes, two sentiments that ennoble, uplift, and purify him. He seeks the truth, he loves justice; and sometimes he is able to sacrifice to those two ideals some part of the satisfaction he would otherwise give to his passions and his material interests.
> —*Gaetano Mosca*, The Ruling Class[27]

In extreme cases, mistaken beliefs are fatal. A baby-proofed house illustrates many errors that adults cannot afford to make. It is dangerous to think that poisonous substances are candy. It is dangerous to reject the theory of gravity at the top of the stairs. It is dangerous to hold that sticking forks in electrical sockets is harmless fun.

But false beliefs do not have to be deadly to be costly. If the price of oranges is 50 cents each, but you mistakenly believe it is a dollar, you buy too few oranges. If bottled water is, contrary to your impression, neither healthier nor better-tasting than tap water, you may throw hundreds of dollars down the drain. If your chance of getting an academic job is lower than you guess, you could waste your twenties in a dead-end Ph.D. program.

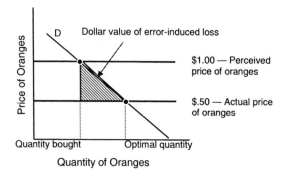

Figure 5.1 The Material Costs of Error

More fancifully, suppose you think the world ends tomorrow. You would probably decide you had more important tasks than going to work. Maybe you would loudly quit your job, then spend all the money in your bank account. If you awake the next morning to find that reports of the earth's demise were exaggerated, you will be happy to be alive but chagrined to realize that you are unemployed and broke.

It is amusing when the deluded triumph because of dumb luck: "I started with wrong directions, but I took a wrong turn, so I got to the right place on time." The story works because it cuts against our expectations. Ordinarily, false beliefs lead individuals to take actions that would be optimal *if the world were different.* For example, figure 5.1 contrasts the number of oranges a person buys with the number he *would* buy conditional on correctly perceiving the market price. The larger his misperception, the larger the triangle representing the dollar cost of the error.

The cost of error varies with the belief and the believer's situation. For some people, the belief that the American Civil War came before the American Revolution would be a costly mistake. A history student might fail his exam, a history professor ruin his professional reputation, a Civil War reenactor lose his friends' respect, a public figure face damaging ridicule.

Normally, however, a firewall stands between this mistake and "real life." Historical errors are rarely an obstacle to wealth, happiness, descendants, or any standard metric of success. The same goes for philosophy, religion, astronomy, geology, and other "impractical" subjects. The point is not that there is no objectively true answer in these fields. The Revolution *really did* precede the Civil War. But your optimal course of action if the Revolution came first is identical to your optimal course if the Revolution came second.

To take another example: Think about your average day. What would you *do* differently if you believed that the earth began in 4004 B.C., as Bishop Ussher infamously maintained?[28] You would still get out of bed, drive to work, eat lunch, go home, have dinner, watch TV, and go to sleep. Ussher's mistake is cheap.

Virtually the only way that mistakes on these questions injure you is via their *social* consequences. A lone man on a desert island could maintain practically any historical view with perfect safety. When another person washes up, however, there is a small chance that odd historical views will reduce his respect for his fellow islander, impeding cooperation. Notice, however, that the danger is deviance, not error. If everyone else has sensible historical views, and you do not, your status may fall. But the same holds if everyone else has bizarre historical views and they catch you scoffing.[29]

Mistakes on more practical questions also often fail to ricochet back with dire consequences. Some errors are costly for the person who commits them only under special circumstances that *hardly ever arise.* The belief that you can outrun a cheetah would prove fatal at the wrong place and the wrong time. But given the chance of cheetah encounters, it is usually a safe mistake. More interestingly, errors with *drastic* real-world repercussions can be cheap for the individual who makes them. How? When most or all of the cost of the mistake falls upon strangers. One person messes up, but other people live with the aftermath.

To use economic jargon, the *private cost* of an action can be negligible, though its *social cost* is high.[30] Air pollution is the textbook example. When you drive, you make the air you breathe worse. But the effect is barely perceptible. Your willingness to pay to eliminate your own emissions might be a tenth of a cent. That is the private cost of your pollution. But suppose that you had the same impact on the air of 999,999 strangers. Each disvalues your emissions by a tenth of a cent too. The social cost of your activity—the harm to *everyone* including yourself—is $1,000, a million times the private cost.

Notice that in the pollution story, you are not—selfishly speaking—making a mistake. But the distinction between social and private costs also applies to erroneous beliefs. A mad scientist, convinced he is too brilliant to fail, might unleash a virus on the world. If he is immune—and if no one catches him—the private cost of his inflated ego is zero, even though millions pay with their lives.

Stories with a lone polluter or a mad scientist are an unthreatening way to illustrate the distinction between private and social costs. In the real world, the roles of hero and villain are seldom so discrete. Practically everyone is a victim and a perpetrator; most of the people who breathe my auto emissions are drivers themselves. Returning to the pollution example, suppose that all of the million people drive and pollute, bringing the total social cost of pollution to a *billion* dollars.[31] Commonsense morality brands anyone who complains as a hypocrite, but the pollution level is still inefficiently high.

Gulfs between the private and social costs of error permeate group decision-making. Take a hiring committee. Its members deliberate between candidates A and B. The committee as a group has absolute power over the decision, and all members are worse off if the committee makes the inferior choice. Nevertheless, the most that any member can do is slightly tilt the scales, implying a gap between the private and social costs of mistaken beliefs about A and B.[32] When I tilt the scales the wrong way, I hurt everyone on the committee, not myself alone.

Rational Irrationality

> Thus the typical citizen drops down to a lower level of mental performance as soon as he enters the political field. He argues and analyzes in a way which he would readily recognize as infantile within the sphere of his real interests. He becomes a primitive again.
> —*Joseph Schumpeter,* Capitalism, Socialism, and Democracy[33]

Two forces lie at the heart of economic models of choice: preferences and prices. A consumer's preferences determine the shape of his demand curve for oranges; the market price he faces determines where along that demand curve he resides. What makes this insight deep is its generality. Economists use it to analyze everything from having babies to robbing banks.

Irrationality is a glaring exception. Recognizing irrationality is typically equated with rejecting economics.[34] A "logic of the irrational" sounds self-contradictory. This chapter's central message is that this reaction is premature. Economics can handle irrationality the same way it handles everything: preferences and prices. As I have already pointed out:

- People have preferences over beliefs: A nationalist enjoys the belief that foreign-made products are overpriced junk; a surgeon takes pride in the belief that he operates well while drunk.

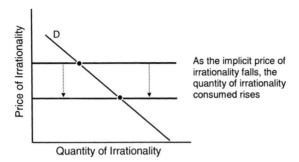

Figure 5.2 The Demand for Irrationality

- False beliefs range in material cost from free to enormous: Acting on his beliefs would lead the nationalist to overpay for inferior domestic goods, and the surgeon to destroy his career.

Snapping these two building blocks together leads to a simple model of irrational conviction. If agents care about both material wealth and irrational beliefs, then as the price of casting reason aside rises, agents consume less irrationality.[35] I might like to hold comforting beliefs across the board, but it costs too much. Living in a Pollyanna dreamworld would stop me from coping with my problems, like that dead tree in my backyard that looks like it is going to fall on my house.

I refer to this approach as *rational irrationality* to emphasize both its kinship with and divergence from, rational ignorance.[36] Both treat cognitive inadequacy as a choice, responsive to incentives. The difference is that rational ignorance assumes that people tire of the search for truth, while rational irrationality says that people actively avoid the truth.[37]

Rational irrationality implies that people have "demand for irrationality" curves (fig. 5.2). As usual, quantity is on the x-axis and price on the y-axis, but with an interpretive twist. The "quantity" is a degree of irrationality—the magnitude of the agent's *departure* from the unbiased, rational belief. To consume zero irrationality is to be fully rational. The "price of irrationality" is the amount of wealth an agent implicitly sacrifices by consuming another unit of irrationality.[38]

Economic theory says little about the shape of demand curves.[39] As the price of irrationality falls, quantity demanded rises. But demand for irrationality (fig. 5.3) could be relatively flat—like D_1—with a small increase in price leading to a large reduction in quantity, or relatively

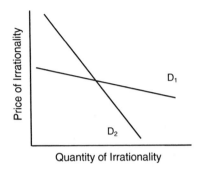

Figure 5.3 Varying Price-Sensitivity of Demand for Irrationality

steep—like D_2—requiring large price increases to curtail consumption. Demand could in fact be a vertical line overlapping the y-axis, indicating an agent who has no desire to be irrational at any price. I call this a *neoclassical* demand-for-irrationality curve because it is the assumption that most economists adopt by default (fig. 5.4).

One interesting prediction of rational irrationality is that *fluctuating* incentives make people bounce between contradictory viewpoints.[40] As a consumer, for instance, the protectionist usually casts bad economic theory aside. Suddenly, products' price and quality become more important, and national origin is lucky to have any influence. Similarly, most people reject the view that pushing up wages increases unemployment. When I teach intro econ, linking unemployment and excessive wages frequently elicits not only students' disbelief, but anger: How could I be so *callous*? But irrationality about labor demand is selective. What happens when my outraged students reach the "Salary Requirements" line on job applications? They could ask for a million dollars a year, but they don't. When their future rides on it, students honor the economic truism that labor demand slopes down.

The cynical explanation is that my students understood labor demand curves all along. But why would you get angry at a professor for saying what you believe yourself? They are more likely in denial. When they fill out the application, though, their standby rationality kicks in, telling them: "This is no time to get angry." It does not take an A student to reflect: "I do not want to lowball it, but I am an entry-level worker, and the only way I am going to land a job is by asking for an entry-level salary. The more I ask for, the less likely they are to hire me."

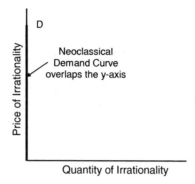

Figure 5.4 Neoclassical Demand for Irrationality

Psychological Plausibility

> The bulk of available evidence suggests that people in all
> societies tend to be relatively rational when it comes to
> the beliefs and practices that directly involve their
> subsistence. . . . The more remote these beliefs and
> practices are from subsistence activities, the more likely
> they are to involve nonrational characteristics.
> —*Robert Edgerton,* Sick Societies[41]

Arguably the main reason why economists have not long since
adopted an approach like mine is that it seems psychologically
implausible.[42] Rational irrationality appears to map an odd route to
delusion:

Step 1: Figure out the truth to the best of your ability.

Step 2: Weigh the psychological benefits of rejecting the truth
against its material costs.

Step 3: If the psychological benefits outweigh the material costs,
purge the truth from your mind and embrace error.

The psychological plausibility of this stilted story is underrated. It
coheres well with George Orwell's chilling account of "doublethink"
in *1984*:

Doublethink means the power of holding two contradictory beliefs
in one's mind simultaneously, and accepting both of them. The
Party intellectual knows in which direction his memories must be
altered; he therefore knows he is playing tricks with reality; but by

the exercise of *doublethink* he also satisfies himself that reality is not violated. The process has to be conscious, or it would not be carried out with sufficient precision, but it also has to be unconscious, or it would bring with it a feeling of falsity and hence of guilt. . . . Even in using the word *doublethink* it is necessary to exercise *doublethink*. For by using the word one admits that one is tampering with reality; by a fresh act of *doublethink* one erases this knowledge; and so on indefinitely, with the lie always one step ahead of the truth.[43]

But rational irrationality does not require Orwellian underpinnings. The psychological interpretation can be seriously toned down without changing the model. Above all, *the steps should be conceived as tacit*. To get in your car and drive away entails a long series of steps— take out your keys, unlock and open the door, sit down, put the key in the ignition, and so on. The thought processes behind these steps are rarely explicit. Yet we know the steps on some level, because when we observe a would-be driver who fails to take one—by, say, trying to open a locked door without using his key—it is easy to state which step he skipped.

Once we recognize that cognitive "steps" are usually tacit, we can enhance the introspective credibility of the steps themselves. The process of irrationality can be recast:

Step 1: Be rational on topics where you have no emotional attachment to a particular answer.

Step 2: On topics where you have an emotional attachment to a particular answer, keep a "lookout" for questions where false beliefs imply a substantial material cost for you.

Step 3: If you pay no substantial material costs of error, go with the flow; believe whatever makes you feel best.

Step 4: If there are substantial material costs of error, raise your level of intellectual self-discipline in order to become more objective.

Step 5: Balance the emotional trauma of heightened objectivity— the progressive shattering of your comforting illusions—against the material costs of error.

There is no need to posit that people start with a clear perception of the truth, then throw it away. The only requirement is that rationality remain on "standby," ready to engage when error is dangerous.

What does this mean in practice? To help convince readers of the psychological plausibility of rational irrationality, this section illustrates my thesis using case studies from a wide variety of fields. Obviously, a series of examples will not prove me correct. The point, rather, is to get readers to look at different fact patterns, and see what the lens of rational irrationality brings into focus.

Nudity and the Jains. John Noss's comparative religion textbook, *Man's Religions,* summarizes an amusing doctrinal dispute between two branches of the Jain religion:

> Early in the history of the faith the Jains divided on the question of wearing clothes. The Shvetambaras or the "white-clad" were the liberals who took their stand on wearing at least one garment, whereas the stricter and more conservative Digambaras got their name from their insistence on going about, whenever religious duty demanded it, "clad in atmosphere." Mahavira [the last of the founding prophets of Jainism] did not wear clothes, they pointed out, so why, when there is a religious reason for not wearing clothes, should they? The Shvetambaras were in the north and yielded a bit both to the cold winds and to the social and cultural influences of the Ganges River plain. The Digambaras, not looked at askance by the Dravidian residents of their southland, have more easily maintained the earlier, sterner attitudes down the years.[44]

How could these suspiciously convenient doctrinal differences emerge? A plausible story: The default of members of both branches is to accept the teachings of their religion. But their beliefs about permissible clothing affect their bodily comfort—especially in colder climates. So northern Jains apply stricter intellectual scrutiny to their doctrines than southern Jains: "How do we really know that Mahavira wanted it this way?" The northerners are therefore less likely to accept their religion's more extreme teachings.

Mosca and Jihad. In the Jain example, stubborn belief leads to discomfort. Gaetano Mosca presents a case where stubborn belief leads to death.

> Mohammed, for instance, promises paradise to all who fall in a holy war. Now if every believer were to guide his conduct by that assurance in the Koran, every time a Mohammedan army found itself faced by unbelievers it ought either to conquer or to fall to the last man. It cannot be denied that a certain number of individuals do live up to the letter of the Prophet's word, but as between defeat and death followed by eternal bliss, the majority of Mohammedans normally elect defeat.[45]

Economists' knee-jerk reading is that Mosca describes a Prisoners' Dilemma. Soldiers who run away improve their own chances of sur-

vival at the expense of their compatriots; though widespread deser-
tion ensures defeat of the group, deserters act in their individual interest. But this misses the heart of Mosca's story. If a soldier believes that
death in battle sends him to paradise, running away is imprudent,
not cowardly. He is literally *better off dead*. As danger approaches,
then, the Muslim warrior does not act *more* selfishly; he revises his
beliefs about *how* to pursue his self-interest.

Rational irrationality makes sense of Mosca's example. Muslim soldiers' "default belief" is that their religion's teachings are true. As long
as they are at peace or militarily have the upper hand, the belief that
Allah brings the fallen to paradise gives psychological comfort with
little risk. When they are losing, however, soldiers' "standby" rationality kicks in. The devil on their shoulders whispers: "What makes you
think that paradise even exists?" Some would rather die than doubt.
But, confronting the choice between fidelity and death, most quietly
put on their thinking caps and abandon their fatal belief.

The reader may be tempted to throw the World Trade Center sui-
cide attacks in his face, but Mosca does not forget heterogeneity. He
presciently adds that "a certain number of individuals do live up to
the letter of the Prophet's word." A handful of people climb Mount
Everest in spite of risks that scare off the rest of the human race. A
few Muslims sacrifice their lives for their faith, but a billion do not.[46]

Sati. On some interpretations of Hinduism, a widow must join her
deceased husband on his funeral pyre, a practice known as *sati*. Fulfilling this duty supposedly has great rewards in the afterlife. On the
surface, sati looks like a clear case of persistent irrationality despite
deadly incentives. But the reality, explains anthropologist Robert Edgerton, is different. Few Hindu widows ever complied with their puta-
tive duty: "Even in Bengal where sati was most common, only a small
minority of widows—less than 10 percent—chose sati although the
prospect of widowhood was dismal at best."[47] Some of these were
frankly murdered by their husband's relatives. When the widow refused the pyre, she was not allowed to resume a normal life. She could
not remarry, and had to spend the rest of her years in fasting and
prayer. Overall, one of the world's most shocking religious practices
coheres well with rational irrationality:

> Despite the wretched conditions of widowhood, the promised re-
> wards of sati, and the often relentless pressure exerted by the de-
> ceased husband's relatives on the widow to choose their supreme
> act of devotion, the great majority of widows preferred to live.[48]

Genetics, relativity, and Stalin. Marxist philosophers have dogmatic objections to modern biology and physics. Genetics is "a bourgeois fabrication designed to undermine the true materialist theory of biological development," and relativity theory and quantum mechanics are "idealist positions" that "contravene[d] the materialism espoused by Lenin in *Materialism and Empirio-Criticism.*"[49] But Marxist regimes—and Stalin in particular—treated biology and physics asymmetrically.

In biology, Stalin and other prominent Marxist leaders elevated the views of the quack antigeneticist Trofim Lysenko to state-supported orthodoxy, leading to the dismissal of thousands of geneticists and plant biologists.[50] Lysenkoism hurt Soviet agriculture, and helped trigger the deadliest famine in human history during China's Great Leap Forward.[51]

In physics, on the other hand, leading scientists enjoyed more intellectual autonomy than any other segment of Soviet society. Internationally respected physicists ran the Soviet atomic project, not Marxist ideologues. When their rivals tried to copy Lysenko's tactics, Stalin balked. A conference intended to start a witch hunt in Soviet physics was abruptly canceled, a decision that had to originate with Stalin. Holloway recounts a telling conversation between Beria, the political leader of the Soviet atomic project, and Kurchatov, its scientific leader:

> Beria asked Kurchatov whether it was true that quantum mechanics and relativity theory were idealist, in the sense of antimaterialist. Kurchatov replied that if relativity theory and quantum mechanics were rejected, the bomb would have to be rejected too. Beria was worried by this reply, and may have asked Stalin to call off the conference.[52]

The "Lysenkoization" of Soviet physics never came.

The best explanation for the difference is that modern physics had a practical payoff that Stalin and other Communist leaders highly valued: nuclear weapons. "The Soviet Union wanted the bomb as soon as possible, and was prepared to pay virtually any price to obtain it."[53] Lysenkoist biology, in contrast, injured the low-priority agricultural sector. Stalin had already presided over decades of hunger, and knew that it posed little threat to the Soviet state.

Most of Stalin's biographers view him as power-hungry but fairly sincere.[54] His default was to embrace the secular religion of Marxism-Leninism, but he retained a good helping of "standby" rationality. When he sensed that strict adherence to Leninist dogma put his power at risk, he set ideology aside:

Stalin was not so concerned about the condition of agriculture—
he tolerated, after all, a desperate famine in the Ukraine in 1947—
and so it may not have mattered very much to him whether Lysenko
was a charlatan or not. The nuclear project was more important,
however, than the lives of Soviet citizens, so it was crucial to be sure
that the scientists in the nuclear project were not frauds.[55]

Indeed, not only did Stalin squelch philosophical attacks on modern
physics; he also embraced other commonsensical "bourgeois" here-
sies to accelerate his atomic program. Soviet economic failures were
routinely blamed not on inadequate resources, but on "Trotskyite
wrecking" and other bizarre conspiracies. For the atomic project,
though, Stalin recognized the realities of scarcity: "He told Kurchatov
that 'it was not worth engaging in small-scale work, but necessary to
conduct the work broadly, with Russian scope, that in that connection
the broadest all-round help would be provided. Comrade Stalin said
it was not necessary to seek cheaper paths.' "[56]

Similarly, in many other areas of the Soviet economy, Marxism fos-
tered reluctance to motivate workers with material rewards for success. In the atomic project, however, Stalin dumped Marxist dogma
in favor of bourgeois horse sense:

> Stalin said also that he was anxious to improve the scientists' living
> conditions, and to provide prizes for major achievements—"for ex-
> ample, for the solution of our problem," Kurchatov wrote. Stalin
> "said that our scientists were very modest and they sometimes did
> not notice that they live poorly . . . our state has suffered very
> much, yet it is surely possible to ensure that several thousand
> people can live very well, and several thousand people better than
> very well, with their own *dachas*, so that they can relax, and with
> their own cars."[57]

He kept his promises, tripling the science budget, giving scientists
large pay raises in 1946, and dachas and cars to the leading nuclear
scientists after the successful nuclear test in 1949.[58]

Maybe Stalin covertly scoffed at the inanities of Marxism, but a
more plausible interpretation is that he was rationally irrational.
Marxism-Leninism was important to his sense of identity, but his
preference was not absolute. As the price of illusion went up, he chose
to be less fanatical and more objective.

Want to bet? We encounter the price-sensitivity of irrationality whenever someone unexpectedly offers us a bet based on our professed
beliefs.[59] Suppose you insist that poverty in the Third World is sure to
get worse in the next decade. A challenger immediately retorts, "Want

to bet? If you're really 'sure,' you won't mind giving me ten-to-one odds." Why are you are unlikely to accept this wager? Perhaps you never believed your own words; your statements were poetry—or lies. But it is implausible to tar all reluctance to bet with insincerity. People often believe that their assertions are true until you make them "put up or shut up." A bet moderates their views—that is, *changes their minds*—whether or not they retract their words.[60]

How does this process work? Your default is to believe what makes you feel best. But an offer to bet triggers standby rationality. Two facts then come into focus. First, being wrong endangers your net worth. Second, your belief received little scrutiny before it was adopted. Now you have to ask yourself which is worse: Financial loss in a bet, or psychological loss of self-worth? A few prefer financial loss, but most covertly rethink their views. Almost no one "bets the farm" even if—pre-wager—he felt sure.

Rational Irrationality and Politics

> Merchants eagerly grasp all philosophic generalizations presented to them without looking closely into them, and the same is true about politics, science, and the arts. But only after examination will they accept those concerning trade, and even then they do so with reserve.
> —*Alexis de Tocqueville*, Democracy in America[61]

Suppose a referendum determines whether we have policy A or policy B. A is $10,000 better for you. What is the material cost of believing the opposite and voting accordingly? The naive answer of $10,000 is wrong *unless* your vote is "decisive"; that is, if it reverses or *flips* the electoral outcome. This is possible only if the choices of all other voters exactly balance. Thus, in elections with millions of voters, the probability that your erroneous policy beliefs cause unwanted policies is approximately zero.[62] The infamous Florida recounts of 2000 do not undermine this analysis.[63] Losing by a few hundred votes is a far cry from losing by one vote.

Critics of polling say it hurts democracy. The leading complaint is that polls provide no incentive to seriously weigh policy consequences.[64] Unlike elections, polls do not change policy, right? Wrong. Politicians frequently take action based on polls, and your response might push them over the edge. Survey respondents have about as much—or as little—incentive to think seriously as voters do. Indeed, elections *are* surveys. Responses to both are cheap talk bundled with a remote chance of swaying policy.

If you listen to your fellow citizens, you get the impression that they disagree. How many times have you heard, "Every vote matters"? But people are less credulous than they sound. The infamous poll tax—which restricted the vote to those willing to pay for it—provides a clean illustration. If individuals acted on the belief that one vote makes a big difference, they would be willing to pay a lot to participate. Few are. Historically, poll taxes significantly reduced turnout.[65] There is little reason to think that matters are different today. Imagine setting a poll tax to reduce presidential turnout from 50% to 5%. How high would it have to be? A couple hundred dollars? What makes the poll tax alarming is that most of us subconsciously know that most of us subconsciously know that one vote does not count.

Citizens often talk as if they personally have power over electoral outcomes. They deliberate about their options as if they were ordering dinner. But their actions tell a different tale: They expect to be served the same meal no matter what they "order."

What does this imply about the material price a voter pays for political irrationality? Let D be the difference between a voter's willingness to pay for policy A instead of policy B. Then the expected cost of voting the wrong way is not D, but the probability of decisiveness p times D. If $p = 0$, $pD = 0$ as well. Intuitively, if one vote cannot change policy outcomes, the price of irrationality is zero.

This *zero* makes rational irrationality a politically pregnant idea. The institutional structure of democracy makes political irrationality a free good for its ultimate decision-makers, the electorate.[66] So we should *expect* voters to be on their worst cognitive behavior; in the words of Le Bon, to "display in particular but slight aptitude for reasoning, the absence of the critical spirit, irritability, credulity, and simplicity."[67]

A diner at an all-you-can-eat buffet stuffs himself until he cannot bear another bite. In economic jargon, he consumes up to his "satiation point," where his demand curve and the x-axis intersect (fig. 5.5). Voter irrationality works the same way. Since delusional political beliefs are free, the voter consumes until he reaches his "satiation point," believing whatever makes him feel best. When a person puts on his voting hat, he does not have to give up practical efficacy in exchange for self-image, *because he has no practical efficacy to give up in the first place.*

Consider how the typical person forms beliefs about the deterrent effect of the death penalty. Ordinary intellectual self-discipline requires you to look at the evidence before you form a strong opinion. In practice, though, most people with definite views on the effective-

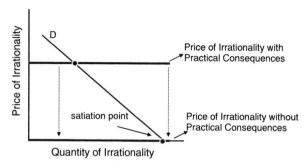

Figure 5.5 Voters' Demand for Irrationality

ness of the death penalty *never* feel the need to examine the extensive empirical literature. Instead, they start with strong emotions about the death penalty, and heatedly "infer" its effect.[68]

The death penalty is an unusually emotional issue, but its template fits most politically relevant beliefs. How many people can take sides in a military conflict and still have the detachment of George Orwell?

> I have little direct evidence about the atrocities in the Spanish civil war. I know that some were committed by the Republicans, and far more (they are still continuing) by the Fascists. But what impressed me then, and has impressed me ever since, is that atrocities are believed in or disbelieved in solely on grounds of political predilection. Everyone believes in the atrocities of the enemy and disbelieves in those of his own side, without ever bothering to examine the evidence.[69]

The same people who practice intellectual self-discipline when they figure out how to commute to work, repair a car, buy a house, or land a job "let themselves go" when they contemplate the effects of protectionism, gun control, or pharmaceutical regulation. Who ever made an enemy by contradicting someone's belief about what is wrong with his car? For practical questions, standard procedure is to acquire evidence before you form a strong opinion, match your confidence to the quality and quantity of your evidence, and remain open to criticism. For political questions, we routinely override these procedural safeguards.

The contrast between markets and politics is sharpest when voters have what I call *near-neoclassical* demand for irrationality.[70] Under normal market conditions, an agent with these preferences appears fully rational. He is willing and able to live without irrationality. Under normal political conditions, however, he pulls off the mask of objec-

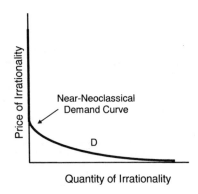

Figure 5.6 Near-Neoclassical Demand for Irrationality

tivity. His reasonableness in one sphere fails to carry over to the other; or to be more precise, he *chooses* not to carry it over because the market has a "user fee" for irrationality, and democracy does not.

When Joseph Schumpeter compares rationality in politics and the market, he seems to have near-neoclassical demand for irrationality in mind.[71] Alongside his famous complaints about voters' illogic in *Capitalism, Socialism, and Democracy,* Schumpeter affirms that "Neither the intention to act as rationally as possible nor the steady pressure toward rationality can seriously be called into question at whatever level of industrial or commercial activity we choose to look."[72] He adds:

> And so it is with most of the decisions of daily life that lie within the little field which the individual citizen's mind encompasses with a full sense of its reality. Roughly, it consists of the things that directly concern himself, his family, his business dealings, his hobbies, his friends and enemies, his township or ward, his class, church, trade union or any other social group of which he is an active member—the things under his personal observation, the things which are familiar to him independently of what his newspaper tells him, which he can directly influence or manage and for which he develops the kind of responsibility that is induced by a direct relation to the favorable or unfavorable effects of a course of action.[73]

Bastiat similarly states that make-work bias has zero effect on private action:

> No one has ever seen, and no one will ever see, any person who works, whether he be farmer, manufacturer, merchant, artisan, soldier, writer, or scholar, who does not devote all the powers of his

mind to working better, more quickly, and more economically—in short, *to doing more with less.*[74]

Whether or not Schumpeter and Bastiat are right, the near-neoclassical demand curve is analytically useful. It is a microscopic departure from standard economic assumptions, so economists would have to be awfully dogmatic to rule it out.[75]

Rational Irrationality and Experimental Evidence

Rational irrationality is a modest refinement of existing models of human behavior. Assuming that all people are fully rational all the time is bad economics. It makes more sense to assume that people tailor their degree of rationality to the costs of error.[76]

Researchers at the intersection of psychology and economics often take a more radical position: Not only are people irrational, but their irrationality stays the same or *increases* as its cost rises. The eminent Richard Thaler said so at the 2004 American Economic Association Meetings.[77] The abstract of a well-known survey article by Colin Camerer and Robin Hogarth on the experimental effects of financial incentives seems to back Thaler up:

> We review 74 experiments with no, low, or high performance-based financial incentives. The modal result is no effect on mean performance (though variance is usually reduced by higher payment). . . . We also note that *no* replicated study has made rationality violations disappear purely by raising incentives.[78]

On closer reading, however, Camerer and Hogarth reach a nuanced conclusion. First, they emphasize that experimental findings are heterogeneous. Incentives often improve performance on tasks of judgment and decision. People "spend" hypothetical money more freely than actual money; they are much more likely to *say* they will buy something than to actually do so.[79] Incentives also lead subjects away from "favorable self-presentation behavior toward more realistic choices."[80] Furthermore, a recent paper finds that people get less overconfident when they have to bet real money on their beliefs.[81]

Second, and more importantly, Camerer and Hogarth recognize experiments' limitations:

> Our view is that experiments measure only short-run effects, essentially holding capital fixed. The fact that incentives often do not induce different (or better) performance in the lab may understate

the effect of incentives in natural settings, particularly if agents faced with incentive changes have a chance to build up capital—take classes, seek advice, or practice.[82]

Think about any skilled worker. Would he have his specialized knowledge if there were no market demand for what he does? To answer no is to admit that incentives massively improve human judgment in the real world. It just takes time for incentives to work their magic. Camerer and Hogarth concur: "Useful cognitive capital probably builds up slowly, over days of mental fermentation or years of education rather than in the short-run of an experiment (1–3 hours) ... [I]ncentives surely *do* play an important role in inducing long-run capital formation."[83] This claim is consistent with the growing literature on field experiments: Economic actors in their "natural habitat" look considerably more rational than they do in the lab.[84]

Camerer and Hogarth also admit that experiments slight the power of incentives by relying on volunteers, whose "intrinsic motivation"—desire to do well for its own sake—is unusually high.[85] Money cannot spur greater effort in those who are already trying their best. A related point that Camerer and Hogarth do not make is that most experiments avoid touchy subjects like religion and politics, where participants have "intrinsic motivation" to reach *incorrect* answers. Once there is a trade-off between psychological and material well-being, incentives have more room to operate.

A common summary of the experimental literature is that incentives improve performance on easy problems but hurt performance on hard problems.[86] As Einhorn and Hogarth argue:

Performance ... depends on both cognition and motivation. Thus, if incentive size can be thought of as analogous to the speed with which one travels in a given direction, cognition determines the direction. Therefore, if incentives are high but cognition is faulty, one gets to the wrong place faster.[87]

What Camerer and Hogarth highlight, however, is that the difficulty of a problem falls if you have more time and flexibility to solve it. Hard problems naturally decay into easier problems. Once they are easy enough, incentives work like they are "supposed to."

The moral is that we should take experimental evidence seriously, but not be intimidated when experimentalists announce that "there is little or no experimental evidence that stronger incentives make people more rational." As Camerer and Hogarth observe, few experiments on human beings last more than a few hours. It would be too expensive to continue for days or years. If rationality gradually responds to incentives, existing experiments will not detect it.

Fortunately, experiments are not our only information. Everyday experience is relevant. The typical person faces both practical questions—doing his job, buying groceries, or driving—and impractical ones—like politics and religion. It is hard to deny that both intellectual effort and accuracy are much higher for practical questions. How many people believe they can catch bullets in their teeth—or fly without mechanical assistance? Furthermore, when previously impractical questions suddenly become practical—perhaps due to a change in occupation—intellectual effort plainly rises, and accuracy eventually along with it. In a world without water, there would be no demand for ships, so few would know how to design and build them. To me, these are ubiquitous facts; I leave it to readers to judge whether they agree.

Even if we trust only experimental evidence, rational irrationality is a credible explanation for the public's biased beliefs about economics. Experimentalists admit that incentives help for relatively easy questions. Antimarket, antiforeign, make-work, and pessimistic bias all qualify. These are not subtle errors, but knee-jerk reactions. In nonpolitical contexts, people routinely overcome them. How many refrain from buying appliances because it "destroys jobs"? Experimentalists also emphasize that incentives help less when there is intrinsic motivation to get things right. In economics, there is intrinsic motivation to get things *wrong*. If you *think* the right answer, you feel insensitive and unpatriotic; if you *say* the right answer, you feel like a pariah. There is about as much intrinsic motivation to understand economics as there is to take out the garbage.

Rational Irrationality and Expressive Voting

My work owes a great deal to Geoffrey Brennan and Loren Lomasky's expressive voting model, best articulated in their *Democracy and Decision: The Pure Theory of Electoral Preference*.[88] Though complementary, our accounts differ in several key respects.

Since the work of Brennan and Lomasky has enjoyed less attention than it deserves, let me begin with a summary. Nearly all economists assume that people vote *instrumentally*; that is, they vote to get the policies they prefer. What else would they do?

Brennan and Lomasky point to the *expressive* function of voting. Fans at a football game cheer not to help the home team win, but to express their loyalty. Similarly, citizens might vote not to help policies win, but to express their patriotism, their compassion, or their devotion to the environment. This is not hair-splitting. One implication is that inefficient policies like tariffs or the minimum wage might win because expressing support for them makes people feel good about themselves.

The same holds to some degree for consumer products. Even if generic perfume smelled as good as Calvin Klein, some shoppers would pay extra for the glamorous image of the name brand. In politics, though, Brennan and Lomasky point out that voters' low probability of decisiveness drastically distorts the trade-off. If your vote does not change the outcome, you can safely vote for "feel good" policies even if you know they will be disastrous in practice.

Case in point: When economists analyze discrimination, they emphasize the financial burden of being a bigot.[89] In politics, the social cost of prejudice remains, but the private cost vanishes due to voters' low probability of decisiveness:

> The bigot who refuses to serve blacks in his shop foregoes the profit he might have made from their custom; the anti-Semite who will not work with Jews is constrained in his choice of jobs and may well have to knock back one she would otherwise have accepted. To express such antipathy at the ballot box involves neither threat of retaliation nor any significant personal cost.[90]

Brennan and Lomasky do *not* merely draw the moderate conclusion that political decisions, like market decisions, depend on expressive as well as instrumental concerns. Their conclusion is instead the radical one that—unlike market decisions—political decisions depend *primarily* on expressive concerns:

> Private interests in the electoral context will be *heavily muted* and the purely expressive or symbolic *greatly magnified*. This is simply a matter of relative prices. We should, moreover, emphasize that the relative price change at stake is of an order of magnitude that is enormous in comparison with those with which economists normally deal.[91]

The parallels with rational irrationality are clear. Both views focus on the *psychological* benefits voters enjoy, not their microscopic effect on policy. Both argue that voters' low probability of decisiveness bifurcates economic and political behavior; as Brennan and Lomasky put it, "Considerations dormant in market behavior become significant in the polling booth."[92] Both explain how ineffective and counterproductive policies can be politically popular.

The key difference is the mechanism. In expressive voting theory, voters *know* that feel-good policies are ineffective. Expressive voters do not embrace dubious or absurd beliefs about the world. They simply care more about how policies *sound* than how they *work*. The expressive protectionist thinks: "Sure, protectionism makes Americans poorer. But who cares, as long as I can wave the flag and chant 'U.S.A.! U.S.A.!'" In contrast, rationally irrational voters believe that feel-good policies work. The rationally irrational protectionist genuinely holds that protectionism makes Americans richer. If he must deny comparative advantage, so be it.

To repeat, expressive voting and rational irrationality are not mutually exclusive. A person might simultaneously think, "Protectionism leads to prosperity" and, "I do not care if protectionism leads to prosperity." But in most cases, the rational irrationality account is more credible. False descriptive views usually accompany support for feel good policies. Few protectionists see their policies as economically harmful.[93] If they realistically assessed the effect of this "feel-good" policy, supporting the policy would no longer make its friends feel good.

The best way to illustrate the contrast between the two approaches is with one of Brennan and Lomasky's own examples. Suppose an electorate chooses between a cataclysmic war with honor, or peace and prosperity with dishonor. The majority pragmatically prefers the latter: "Just as individuals, in situations of interpersonal strain, will often swallow their pride, shrug their shoulders, and stroll off rather than commit to an all-out fight (particularly one that might imply someone's death), so the interests of most voters would be better served by drawing back from the belligerent course."[94] But by the logic of expressive voting, a war referendum could easily prevail. "Individual voters may, each of them, be *entirely rational* in voting for war—even where no one of them would, if decisive, take that course."[95]

Brennan and Lomasky's story is logically possible. But unless we relax the rationality assumption, it comes off as odd. How many vocal hawks would admit to themselves that war leads to devastation and appeasement to prosperity? They would more likely insist, against all evidence, "The boys will be out of the trenches by Christmas"—and add that no matter how bad war looks, appeasement is the true threat to our well-being. And most of the people who took this position would sincerely believe it! Consider this famous scene from *Gone with the Wind*:[96]

> MR. O'HARA: The situation is very simple. The Yankees can't fight and we can.
> CHORUS: You're right!
> MAN: There won't even be a battle, that's what I think! They'll just turn and run every time.

MAN: One Southerner can lick twenty Yankees.

MAN: We'll finish them in one battle. Gentlemen can always fight better than rabble.

Rhett Butler enrages the crowd by taking the contrary position:

RHETT BUTLER: I think it's hard winning a war with words, gentlemen.

CHARLES: What do you mean, sir?

RHETT: I mean, Mr. Hamilton, there's not a cannon factory in the whole South.

MAN: What difference does that make, sir, to a gentleman?

RHETT: I'm afraid it's going to make a great deal of difference to a great many gentlemen, sir.

CHARLES: Are you hinting, Mr. Butler, that the Yankees can lick us?

RHETT: No, I'm not hinting. I'm saying very plainly that the Yankees are better equipped than we. They've got factories, shipyards, coal mines . . . and a fleet to bottle up our harbors and starve us to death. All we've got is cotton, and slaves and . . . arrogance.

MAN: That's treacherous!

CHARLES: I refuse to listen to any renegade talk!

RHETT: I'm sorry if the truth offends you.

The Southerners are not *pretending* to overestimate their military strength. They really do overestimate it. If they had as accurate an assessment of their side's military prospects as Rhett Butler, their war fervor would be hard to sustain. The lesson: Support for counterproductive policies and mistaken beliefs about how the world works normally come as a package. Rational irrationality emphasizes this link; expressive voting theory—despite its strengths—neglects it.

Conclusion

Rational irrationality does not imply that political views are *invariably* senseless. You will not gorge on all-you-can-eat pizza if you hate Italian food. But rational irrationality does put political beliefs under suspicion—and yes, that includes mine.

Democracy asks voters to make choices, but gives each only an infinitesimal influence. From the standpoint of the lone voter, what happens is independent of his choice. Practically every economist admits this. But after their admission, most economists minimize the broader implications.[97]

I take the opposite approach: Voters' lack of decisiveness changes everything. Voting is not a slight variation on shopping. Shoppers have incentives to be rational. Voters do not. The naive view of democracy, which paints it as a public forum for solving social problems, ignores more than a few frictions. It overlooks the big story inches beneath the surface. When voters talk about solving social problems, they primary aim is to boost their self-worth by casting off the workaday shackles of objectivity.

Many escape my conclusion by redefining the word *rational.* If silly beliefs make you feel better, maybe the stickler for objectivity is the real fool. But this is why the term *rational irrationality* is apt: Beliefs that are irrational from the standpoint of truth-seeking are rational from the standpoint of individual utility maximization. More importantly—whatever *words* you prefer—a world where voters are happily foolish is unlike one where they are calmly logical. We shall soon see how.

Political behavior seems weird because the incentives that voters face are weird. Economists have often been criticized for evading the differences between political and market behavior.[98] But this is a failure of *economists* rather than a failure of *economics.* Economists should never have expected political behavior to parallel market behavior in the first place. Irrationality in politics is not a puzzle. It is precisely what an economic theory of irrationality predicts.

Chapter 6

FROM IRRATIONALITY TO POLICY

> A jaded old statehouse reporter noticed my astonishment
> and offered some perspective on the unruly behavior of
> the elected representatives. "If you think these guys are
> bad," he said, "you should see their constituents."
> —*William Greider,* Who Will Tell the People?[1]

IRRATIONAL VOTERS open up novel ways for democracy to fail—counterintuitive to economists, but perhaps common sense to others. For example:

- People might blame all their troubles on harmless scapegoats, and rally to politicians who persecute them.[2]
- Irrational voters could "kill the messenger" of bad news, giving politicians an incentive to paper over problems instead of facing them. Histories of the savings-and-loan bailouts often appeal to this mechanism.[3]
- Citizens of a wealthy, well-fed nation may vote for a candidate who warns of imminent starvation unless the Fatherland acquires more *Lebensraum.*[4]

There are parallels with a classic philosophical paradox.[5] Recall the story of Oedipus. Oedipus wanted to marry Jocasta. Jocasta was Oedipus' mother. But Oedipus did *not* want to marry his mother: He put out his own eyes when he found he had. Similarly: The median voter wants protection. Protection makes the median voter worse off. But the median voter does *not* want to be worse off. The efforts of both Oedipus and the median voter backfire due to their false beliefs. For Oedipus, the false belief is that Jocasta is not his mother; for the median voter, the false belief is that protectionism is good for the economy.

Economists have spent more time criticizing the public's misconceptions than precisely explaining *how* they cause bad policies. They take the connection largely for granted. For Böhm-Bawerk, bad policies virtually imply public confusion: "The legal prohibitions of interest may, of course, be taken as evidence of a strong and widespread conviction that the taking of interest was, as a practical thing, to be condemned. . . . "[6] Donald Wittman himself casually grants that

> A model that assumes that voters or consumers are constantly fooled and there are no entrepreneurs to clear up their confusion will, not surprisingly, predict that the decision-making process will lead to inefficient results.[7]

Böhm-Bawerk and Wittman are too hasty. In theory, it is conceivable that the public's biases spin the wheels of democracy with little effect on policy.[8] In a variant of the Miracle of Aggregation, different delusions might mutually annihilate. Maybe each voter who overestimates the social benefits of protectionism also overestimates his ability to thrive under free trade. With selfish voters, free trade would still prevail, enriching a population convinced that "free trade hurts everyone but me."

The purpose of this chapter is to move from the microfoundations of individual voter irrationality to the macro outcome of democratic policy. I proceed in the economist's usual way: Start with a simple case, then gradually complicate it. The method is pedantic, but works better than any other. As Paul Krugman amusingly begins his essay "The Accidental Theorist":

> Imagine an economy that produces only two things: hot dogs and buns. Consumers in this economy insist that every hot dog come with a bun, and vice versa. And labor is the only input to production.
>
> OK, time out. Before we go any further, I need to ask what you think of an essay that begins this way. Does it sound silly to you?[9]

Krugman retorts:

> One of the points of this essay is to illustrate a paradox: You can't do serious economics unless you are willing to be playful. Economics . . . is a menagerie of thought experiments—parables, if you like—that are intended to capture the logic of economic processes in a simplified way. In the end, of course, ideas must be tested against the facts. But even to know what facts are relevant, you must play with those ideas in hypothetical settings.[10]

Because the real world is tricky, I start with a thought experiment that has a transparent link between irrational beliefs and inefficient policy outcomes. I then progressively add empirically relevant complications, which usually leave the connection between irrational public opinion and inefficient public policy intact.[11] Finally, in answer to the question, "Given public opinion, why isn't democracy far worse than it is?," I discuss forces that dilute the policy fallout of voter irrationality.

Thought Experiment 1: Irrationality with Identical Voters

Democracy *aggregates preferences.* Members of a group want things done. Democracy combines their wants and stirs to get a group decision. This process is terribly confusing because humans almost never completely agree. So what happens? On every issue, democracy must either impose a compromise, or favor one side over its rivals—which is another way of answering, "Who knows?"

In order to demystify democracy, we need to start small. Since ubiquitous disagreement makes the waters of democracy murky, let us temporarily forget about it. For the sake of argument, ask yourself: How would democracy work in the *absence* of disagreement?[12] How would democracy respond to a unanimous public demand? To be more precise, assume the following:

1. All voters have the same preferences and endowments.[13]
2. Two politicians compete for voter support by taking positions on a single issue.
3. People vote for the politician whose position is closer to their own. If both politicians take the same position, they flip a coin.
4. Politicians care only about winning, not how they play the game.
5. The politician with more votes wins the election and implements his promised position.

What happens? The politician closer to everyone's first choice captures 100% of the votes. Since both politicians want to prevail but only one can, they race to match the electorate's preferences, until both adopt the voters' most-preferred position. Voters get their first choice, and politicians settle for a fifty-fifty shot of holding office.

This democracy seems above reproach. Every voter gets his first choice. How many political decisions in the real world can claim half as much? It is easy to fault the outcome, however, if voters share a *taste for a relevant form of irrationality.*

Suppose the tariff rate is at issue. The conceivable positions range from complete free trade—0% tariff—to absolute embargo—infinite tariff. Since voters are identical, class conflict cannot be a motive for protectionism. If each member of the electorate votes for the policy most in his material self-interest, indifferent to the fate of everyone

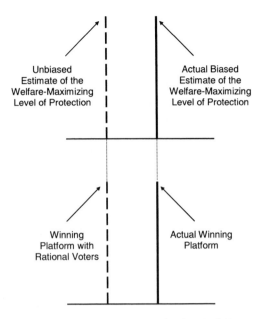

Figure 6.1 Electoral Impact of Irrationality with Identical Voters
Top: Distribution of Beliefs on Welfare-Maximizing Level of Protection
Bottom: Most-Preferred Degree of Protectionism

else, the Law of Comparative Advantage tells us that the unanimous first pick is a 0% tariff.[14]

But what if one of the voters' shared preferences is a mild fondness for antiforeign bias? To be more concrete, what happens if voters want to believe that the best tariff rate for people like themselves (i.e., everyone!) is not 0%, but 100%?

An inkling of this desire turns the election upside down. A 100% tariff could reduce per capita income by $10,000 a person, and each person could put a $1 value on fealty to antiforeign bias. As long as the probability of voter decisiveness is under 1 in 10,000, each voter sticks to his belief in the glory of the 100% tariff.[15] Voters unanimously prefer a protectionist over a free-trader, so rival politicians scramble to endorse the public's ideal. The 100% tariff wins hands down, inflicting a net loss of $9,999 per capita. A mild taste for *psychological* well-being precipitates a massive reduction in *material* well-being.

If individuals get a sense of meaning and identity from their worldview, cost-benefit analysis counts it a benefit. Nevertheless, because voters are not decisive, the social cost of irrationality exceeds its benefit. Think of it this way. Irrationality makes society as a whole better off as long as the psychological benefits minus the material costs are positive:

$$\text{Psychological Benefits} - \text{Material Costs} > 0.$$

Irrationality makes the individual better off under far less stringent conditions:

$$\text{Psychological Benefits} - p * \text{Material Costs} > 0.$$

where p is the probability of casting the decisive vote. If $p = 0$, irrationality is utility-maximizing as long as there are *any* psychological benefits:

$$\text{Psychological Benefits} > 0$$

The implications are especially stark if voters have what the last chapter dubbed *near-neoclassical* demand for irrationality (fig. 5.6). Under this assumption, Psychological Benefits—the area under the demand for irrationality curve—are negligible. Unless the Material Costs of acting on irrational beliefs are negligible, too, heeding irrational beliefs *always* makes society worse off. Yet everyone chooses to be irrational, because the private benefits ever so slightly exceed zero. With identical preferences, lots of voters, and near-neoclassical demand for irrationality, acting on irrational beliefs is invariably a bad idea for society, but society obeys these irrational beliefs without fail—indeed, without dissent.

With identical voters, most of the biases from the SAEE readily map into foolish policies. Antimarket bias boosts price controls and shortsighted redistribution. Antiforeign bias pushes for protectionism and immigration restrictions, and against trade agreements. Make-work bias recommends labor market regulation to "save jobs." The policy ramifications of pessimistic bias are less clear, but it is a catalyst for all sorts of ill-conceived crusades and scapegoating.[16] In this simple thought experiment, fallacies remain harmless primarily if they are irrelevant.

What about relevant errors that mutually cancel, leaving no net effect of irrationality on policy? Even if voters are identical, this cannot be completely ruled out. Especially on issues that engage the emotions, however, it seems more common for errors to *compound*, not cancel. When you dislike someone, you tend to see all his actions through a negative filter. When you dislike imports, similarly, it is only natural to overestimate the economic harm of imports, their quantity, the number of jobs they destroy, and the "unfairness" of other countries' trade policies.

As beliefs rise to higher levels of generality, the link between error and poor policy tightens. If voters underestimate the benefit of trade with Japan, maybe this is balanced by their overestimate of the benefit of trade with Great Britain, leaving the tariff rate at its optimal level.[17] But if voters underestimate the benefit of foreign trade *in general*— as they empirically do—what countervailing beliefs are left to undo the damage?

Thought Experiment 2: Irrationality with Belief Heterogeneity

In the real world, unanimity is an unmistakable sign of dictatorship, not democracy. An empirically relevant model of democracy must allow for disagreement. To get it takes only a small twist on the first thought experiment. Keep assumptions 2–5, but change assumption 1 to assumption 1′:

   1′. All voters have the same endowments. All voters have the same preferences with one exception: their preference over beliefs.

Since endowments remain the same, there is still no room for class conflict. The disagreement that emerges is ideological. The near-clones have diverse tastes over beliefs, and therefore choose to see the political world differently.

Returning to the trade policy example: voters no longer unanimously prefer to believe that a tariff of 100% is optimal. Some feel the right tax rate is 110%, or 200%. Others say 0%. What are politicians to do? Whatever stance they adopt, they make enemies. Fortunately, all the winner needs is a majority.

Since citizens vote for the politician closer to them, and both politicians want to win, thought experiment 2 has a simple outcome: Both politicians adopt the position of the median voter, offering a tariff rate that half the electorate sees as too high, and half sees as too low.[18] The only novelty: Since conflicting beliefs are the source of voter disagreement, executing the wishes of the median voter is equivalent to *acting as if the median belief about the optimal tariff were true.*

If the Miracle of Aggregation holds, then the median belief *is* true. There is no cause for alarm. Democracy listens to those who are "in the know" and ignores the deluded fanatics. Unfortunately, the Miracle of Aggregation is a hoax. It is both theoretically possible and empirically typical for the median voter to *be* one of the deluded fanatics, albeit a relatively moderate one.

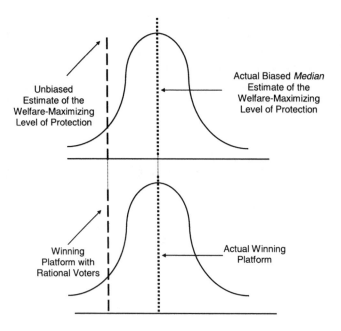

Figure 6.2 Electoral Impact of Irrationality of Otherwise Identical Voters with Heterogeneous Beliefs
Top: Distribution of Beliefs on Welfare-Maximizing Level of Protection
Bottom: Distribution of Most-Preferred Platforms on Protection

A Necessary Digression on the Self-Interested Voter Hypothesis

The link between irrationality and policy is plain in highly stylized thought experiments. But relaxing more assumptions seems to make matters painfully intractable. If voters have different endowments, then many may objectively benefit from socially harmful policies. Inequality of wealth is the simplest reason: Even if redistribution is an awfully leaky bucket, it might still enrich the majority.[19] But inequality is only the beginning. The owner of a textile mill may be just as rich as the owner of a clothing store, but tariffs affect their interests oppositely. With so much complexity, perhaps the people who overestimate the social benefits of protection *really do* lose out because of foreign competition. They might be protectionists because they correctly judge its effect on their personal well-being, not because they overestimate its effect on national well-being.

If people vote in a narrowly selfish way, there is no easy way to untangle the effect of misconceptions on policy. The problem seems insoluble. Fortunately, the problem does not need to be solved, because, contrary to *both* economists and the man in the street, voters are not selfishly motivated.[20] The *self-interested voter hypothesis*—or SIVH—is false. In the political arena, voters focus primarily on national well-being, not personal well-being. That makes it straightforward to move from systematic errors about the causes of national well-being to policies that are—from the standpoint of national well-being—counter-productive.

The SIVH is so embedded in both economics and popular culture that it has to be debunked before I can go on. Many economists find it peculiar even to speak of self-interested voting as a "hypothesis" in need of empirical support.[21] Political cynicism drives the general public to the same conclusion: If you still haven't noticed that people vote their pocketbooks, grow up!

Since economists and the public rarely agree on anything of substance, their shared sympathy for the SIVH has long made me uneasy. In graduate school, I rarely came across hard evidence one way or the other. Many economists took the SIVH for granted, but few bothered to defend it.[22] After completing my doctorate I read more outside my discipline, and discovered that political scientists have subjected the SIVH to extensive and diverse empirical tests.[23] Their results are impressively uniform: The SIVH fails.

Start with the easiest case: partisan identification.[24] Both economists and the public almost automatically accept the view that poor people are liberal Democrats and rich people are conservative Republicans. The data paint a quite different picture. At least in the United States, there is only a flimsy connection between individuals' incomes and their ideology or party. The sign fits the stereotype: As your income rises, you are more likely to be conservative and Republican. But the effect is small, and shrinks further after controlling for race. A black millionaire is more likely to be a Democrat than a white janitor.[25] The Republicans might be the party *for* the rich, but they are not the party *of* the rich.

We see the same pattern for specific policies.[26] The elderly are not more in favor of Social Security and Medicare than the rest of the population. Seniors strongly favor these programs, but so do the young.[27] Contrary to the SIVH-inspired bumper sticker "If men got pregnant, abortion would be a sacrament," men appear a little *more* pro-choice on abortion than women.[28] Compared to the overall population, the unemployed are at most a little more in favor of government-guaranteed jobs, and the uninsured at most a little more supportive of national health insurance.[29] Measures of self-interest predict little about beliefs about economic policy.[30] Even when the stakes are life and death, political self-interest rarely surfaces: Males vulnerable to the draft support it at normal levels, and families and friends of conscripts in Vietnam were in fact more opposed to withdrawal than average.[31]

The broken clock of the SIVH *is* right twice a day. It fails for party identification, Social Security, Medicare, abortion, job programs, national health insurance, Vietnam, and the draft. But it works tolerably well for a few scattered issues.[32] You might expect to see the exceptions on big questions with a lot of money at stake, but the truth is almost the reverse. The SIVH shines brightest on the banal issue of smoking. Donald Green and Ann Gerken find that smokers and nonsmokers are ideologically and demographically similar, but smokers are a lot more opposed to restrictions and taxes on their favorite vice.[33] Belief in "smokers' rights" cleanly rises with daily cigarette consumption: fully 61.5% of "heavy" smokers want laxer antismoking policies, but only 13.9% of people who "never smoked" agree. If the SIVH were true, comparable patterns of belief would be everywhere. They are not.

Most voters disown selfish motives. They *personally* back the policies that are best for the country, ethically right, and consistent with social justice. At the same time, they see *other* voters—not just their opponents, but often their allies too—as deeply selfish. The typical liberal Democrat says he votes his conscience, and impugns opponents for caring only about the rich. But he often ascribes selfish motives to fellow Democrats too: "Why do lower-income people vote Democratic? In order to better their own condition, of course." The typical voter's view of the motivation of the typical voter is schizophrenic: *I* do not vote selfishly, but most do.

When individuals contrast their own faultless motives to the selfishness of others, our natural impulse is to interpret it as self-serving bias. But the empirical evidence suggests that self-descriptions are accurate. People err not in overestimating their own altruism, but in underestimating the altruism of others. Indeed, "underestimate" is an understatement. Individuals are not just *less* politically selfish than usually thought. As voters, they scarcely appear selfish at all.

I suspect that the real reason most economists embrace the SIVH is not empirical evidence, but basic economic theory. If people are selfish consumers, workers, and investors, how can they fail to be selfish voters? It is tempting to respond, "If the theory fails empirically, so much the worse for the theory." But we should first verify that the theory has been correctly applied.

Consider. First, altruism and morality generally are consumption goods like any other, so we should expect people to buy more altruism when the price is low.[34] Second, due to the low probability of decisiveness, the price of altruism is drastically cheaper in politics than in markets.[35] Voting to raise your taxes by a thousand dollars when your probability of decisiveness is 1 in 100,000 has an expected cost of a penny.[36]

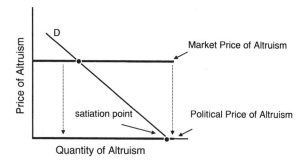

Figure 6.3 The Price of Altruism in Markets versus Politics

Now snap the pieces together. If people buy more altruism when the price is low, and altruistic voting is basically free, we should *expect* voters to consume a lot more altruism. It would cut against basic economics if the SIVH *did* work.[37]

Hollywood is famous for its leftist millionaires like Tim Robbins and Susan Sarandon. Clinton's victory over Bush in 1992 probably cost the respective stars of *The Shawshank Redemption* and *The Rocky Horror Picture Show* hundreds of thousands in extra taxes. But Robbins's and Sarandon's votes were not six-figure philanthropy. All they did was buy a negative lottery ticket: In the astronomically unlikely case that Clinton won *because of their actions*, they would have lost a large sum. With these incentives, you would expect Hollywood millionaires to "vote their conscience." If they pay hundreds of dollars for a trendy haircut, it would be odd if they refused to pay a few expectational pennies to enhance their self-image.

The case of Hollywood leftists is unusually vivid, but entirely typical. The average American has less money riding on the outcome of a presidential election. But given the tiny probability of decisiveness, any psychological benefit is almost sure to outweigh its expected financial cost.[38]

Summing up: Correctly interpreted, the simple economic model *specifically predicts* that people will be less selfish as voters than as consumers. Indeed, like diners at an all-you-can-eat buffet, we should expect voters to "stuff themselves" with moral rectitude. Once again, analogies between voting and shopping are deeply misleading.

Thought Experiment 3: Irrationality with Unselfish Voters

The empirical evidence against the SIVH points to our next thought experiment. Replace assumption 1 with 1″:

1″. All voters want to maximize social welfare, but they have different preferences over their beliefs about *how* to maximize it. Voters can have any endowments.

If voters' goal is to maximize social welfare, if their motivation is, as political scientists term it, *sociotropic*, the complex interaction between policy and individual endowments can be ignored.[39] Whether you are rich or poor, a landowner or a stockholder, a creditor or a debtor, does not change the answer to the question "Which policies are best for society overall?" If people have the common goal of maximizing social welfare, the only source of conflict is disagreement about *how* to maximize it. The only obstacle to maximum social welfare is false beliefs about what policies work best.

Suppose the polity is fighting over tariffs. According to thought experiment 3, this is a symptom of ideological struggle between those who think high tariffs are good for the nation, and those who do not. If the median voter has antiforeign bias, the system performs poorly. Even though everyone *wants* to maximize social welfare, even though democratic competition gives the people what they want, the outcome paradoxically disappoints.

Political theorists often allege that economists' belief in the SIVH leads them to underestimate democracy. According to Virginia Held, "There are good reasons to believe that a society resting on no more than bargains between self-interested or mutually disinterested individuals will not be able to withstand the forces of egoism and dissolution pulling such societies apart."[40] However, once you accept the reality of systematic biases, the SIVH fades in importance as a handicap for democracy. Voters who solemnly put their own interests aside still do a bad job. If voters are rational and selfish, at least the status quo benefits *somebody*.

Unselfishness *expands the range* of democratic performance.[41] Good gets better. With rational selfishness, you get socially optimal outcomes if and only if incentives align private interests and the public interest. With rational unselfishness, this alignment is superfluous: People pursue the public interest for its own sake.

But unselfishness also lets democratic performance fall from bad to worse. Irrational unselfish voters are probably more dangerous than irrational selfish ones. If unselfish voters misunderstand the world, they can easily reach a misguided consensus. Their irrationality points them in the wrong direction; their unselfishness keeps them in marching formation, enabling them to rapidly approach their destination. In contrast, if selfish voters misunderstand the world, dissension persists. They move less cohesively—or not at all.

Suppose voters overestimate the social benefits of price controls on petroleum. If they vote altruistically, then everyone—from owners of gas-guzzling Hummers to oil barons—supports price controls. The response of selfish voters would be less monolithic. Some—like those who own petroleum stock—would want to protect their "right to gouge" despite what they misperceive as its negative effect on society. Their selfishness helps mitigate the effect of antimarket bias on policy.

The upshot is that the failure of the SIVH makes democracy look worse. Voter irrationality is not tempered by the petty squabbling ordinarily guaranteed by human selfishness. Precisely because people put personal interests aside when they enter the political arena, intellectual errors readily blossom into foolish policies.

Multi-Issue Democracy and the Dimensionality of Public Opinion

All of the thought experiments so far assume that the public is only concerned about one issue, such as the tariff rate. In reality, there are hundreds or thousands of contentious topics, which means that the tidy results of the Median Voter Theorem cease to hold. The winning platform for N issues decided as a package differs from the winning platform for N issues decided one by one. Strange as it sounds, a "winning platform"—a platform able to defeat any other—may not exist. Theorists often expect democratic policies to "cycle," and wonder why real-world policies are so stable.[42]

In my view, this is another dilemma that can be sidestepped using existing research on public opinion. There are countless issues that people care about, from gun control and abortion to government spending and the environment. But on closer inspection, these superficially disparate topics contain a great deal of structure. If you know a person's position on one, you can predict his views on the rest to a surprising degree.[43]

In formal statistical terms, political opinions look *one-dimensional.* They boil down roughly to one big opinion, plus random noise. Numerical ratings of "how liberal" or "how conservative" a congressman is often accurately predict his votes.[44] Higher-powered statistical analyses reach the same conclusion.[45] The same is true for the general public. Partisan voting is prevalent, suggesting that the public and elites use a similar ideological framework.[46] Data on specific beliefs confirms this story. For economic beliefs, for instance, self-reported position on the liberal-conservative spectrum predicts a lot about respondents' specific views, and almost always confirms ideological stereotypes.[47]

Opinion is more clearly one-dimensional at some times and places than others.[48] Overall, though, one overriding fact about public opinion is that it is far less multi-dimensional than you might guess. The analytically tractable Median Voter Theorem stands on firmer empirical ground than usually thought.

But suppose you are not convinced by the empirical work on the dimensionality of public opinion.[49] What follows? It definitely gets harder to specify which policies will win out and stay on top. But that is no reason to expect *better* policies. Multi-dimensionality might undermine an especially foolish policy that the median voter favors, but it is equally able to sustain policies so silly even the median voter balks. In short, the policy consequences of one-dimensional opinion are more predictable—but not predictably worse—than those of multi-dimensional opinion.

Another Necessary Digression: What Makes People Think Like Economists?

The preceding thought experiments put a spotlight on a widely neglected variable: *the economic literacy of the median voter*. When the median voter suffers from strong systematic biases, foolish policies prevail; if the median voter sees clearly, democracy picks socially optimal policies.

This suggests a pressing question: What determines the median voter's economic literacy? Are all segments of the population equally in the dark? Or do some "think more like economists" than others? We know from chapter 3 that education reduces the lay-expert belief gap. But this is only one of several regularities in the data.[50] All else equal, the following predict greater agreement with economists:

- Education
- Income *growth*
- Job security
- Male gender

Consistent with the failure of self-serving bias and ideological bias to account for the lay-expert belief gap, income *level* and ideological conservatism do *not* make the list.

Figure 6.4 shows how much education, income growth, job security, and gender matter.[51] The top bar is the yardstick. It indicates how

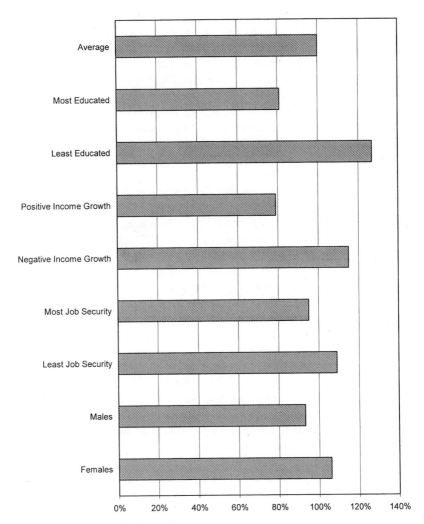

Figure 6.4 The Distribution of Economic Illiteracy
% Belief Gap Relative to Average

much two otherwise *average* people would disagree if one were a
Ph.D. economist and one were not. The lower bars show how much
larger or smaller the belief gap gets if the noneconomist is, in one
respect, *not* average. Bars smaller than 100% mean below-average levels of disagreement. Bars larger than 100% mean the opposite.

Education is the strongest predictor of economic literacy. The belief
gap of the least educated is 127% as large as average; the belief gap

of the most educated is only 81% as large as average. In other words, moving from the highest to the lowest education level expands disagreement by over 50%.

Income *growth* is a close runner-up. The SAEE asked respondents whether their income rose, fell, or stayed the same during the last five years, and asked them what they expect will happen to their income during the next five years. Individuals who both had and expect rising income think markedly more like economists than individuals who gave the opposite answers. The risers' belief gap was 79% of the usual size; the fallers' 115%. This is almost as large as five steps up the seven-step educational ladder.

Job security and male gender have smaller effects. Moving from being "very concerned" about losing your job to "not at all concerned" matters as much as two steps of education; being male rather than female matters slightly less.

What do all these results mean? The role of education is no surprise. Education predicts knowledge on a wide variety of subjects. Economics is no exception. Figuring out why is harder. Does education directly cause greater knowledge of economics in the classroom?[52] Does it do so indirectly by raising the economic knowledge of the people you socialize with? Or is education just a proxy for other traits—like intelligence or curiosity?[53] Given the limits of the data, this is an open question.

The gender gap is not out of the ordinary either. One gender often knows more about a field than the other. Economics is a field where men happen to have the advantage. Other researchers document similar disparities. Men also have more political knowledge than women, and think more like toxicologists.[54] There are many possible explanations, but the differences do exist.[55]

The link between income growth, job security, and economic literacy is the hardest to rationalize. Determined believers in self-serving bias will probably take comfort in these patterns: Upwardly mobile people with secure jobs can safely adopt economists' callous outlook. But then why does income *level* conspicuously fail to matter? A more plausible story is that personal and social optimism go together. Maybe some people are just optimists, or perhaps personal experience with progress makes it easier to spot on a larger scale.

Selective Participation

Failure to vote is a major leak in the pipeline between public opinion and public policy. Politicians only need the support of a majority of people who *exercise* their right to vote. If they can win the affection of one voter by alienating a thousand nonvoters, competition spurs them to do so.

This would not affect policy if voters and nonvoters had the same distribution of preferences and beliefs, but voters are not a random sample. The most visible difference is that voters are richer than non-voters. On closer examination, income is largely a proxy for education; education increases both income and the probability of voting. The other big predictor of turnout is age; the old vote more than the young.[56]

Most commentators treat disparate turnout as a grave social evil. If voters are out to promote their own interests, then groups that show up use and abuse groups that stay home.[57] Many blame the high turnout of the rich for policies that "make the rich richer and the poor poorer," and the high turnout of the elderly for the expense of Social Security and Medicare.

The weakness of these complaints is that they take the discredited SIVH for granted. Yes, the rich are more likely to vote. But since the rich are not *trying* to advance upper-class interests, it does not follow that the interests of the poor suffer. Similarly, just because the old vote in greater numbers, it does not follow that the young lose out. For that fear to be justified, the young would have to be less supportive of old-age programs than their seniors. They are not.[58]

Good intentions are ubiquitous in politics; what is scarce is accurate beliefs. The pertinent question about selective participation is whether voters are *more biased* than nonvoters, not whether voters *take advantage* of nonvoters.[59] Empirically, the opposite holds: The median voter is less biased than the median nonvoter. One of the main predictors of turnout, education, substantially *increases* economic literacy. The other two—age and income—have little effect on economic beliefs.

Though it sounds naive to count on the affluent to look out for the interests of the needy, that is roughly what the data advise. All kinds of voters hope to make society better off, but the well educated are more likely to get the job done.[60] Selective turnout widens the gap between what the public gets and what it wants. But it narrows the gap between what the public gets and what it needs.

In financial and betting markets, there are *intrinsic* reasons why clearer heads wield disproportionate influence.[61] People who know more can expect to earn higher profits, giving them a stronger to incentive to participate. Furthermore, past winners have more assets to influence the market price. In contrast, the disproportionate electoral influence of the well educated is a lucky surprise. Indeed, since the value of their time is greater, one would expect them to vote *less*. To be blunt, the problem with democracy is not that clearer heads have surplus influence. The problem is that, compared to financial and betting markets, the surplus is small.

If education *causes* better economic understanding, there is an argument for education subsidies—albeit not necessarily higher subsidies than we have now.[62] If the connection is not causal, however, throwing money at education treats a symptom of economic illiteracy, not the disease. You would get more bang for your buck by defunding efforts to "get out the vote."[63] One intriguing piece of evidence *against* the causal theory is that educational attainment rose substantially in the postwar era, but political knowledge stayed about the same.[64]

Education is the only variable that predicts *both* economic literacy and voter participation. But other predictors of economic literacy—particularly income growth and job security—interact with democratic politics in potentially interesting ways. For example, suppose income growth and job security *cause* higher economic literacy. Then given a negative economic shock, income growth and job security would decline, reducing the median voter's economic literacy, increasing the demand for foolish economic policies, which in turn hurts economic performance further. I refer to this downward spiral as "the idea trap."[65] Perhaps it can help solve the central puzzle of development economics: Why poor countries stay poor.[66]

Before studying public opinion, many wonder why democracy does not work better. After one becomes familiar with the public's systematic biases, however, one is struck by the opposite question: Why does democracy work as well as it does? How do the unpopular policies that sustain the prosperity of the West survive? Selective participation is probably one significant part of the answer. It is easy to criticize the beliefs of the median voter, but at least he is less deluded than the median nonvoter.

Thought Experiment 4: Mixed Policy/Outcome Preferences

Now let us see where one last empirically interesting complication leads. Suppose voters have systematically biased beliefs about the effectiveness of economic policies, but perceive the current state of the economy without bias. What happens if they hold politicians accountable for *both* their policy decisions *and* the state of the economy?[67]

With these incentives, politicians who want to retain power need to keep their eyes on two balls, not one. If voters' beliefs about effective policy were correct, this would be easy, because the two balls would be fused together. But in the real world, politicians face a visual challenge: keeping their eyes on two balls flying in different directions. If leaders ignore the public's policy preferences, they will be thrown out of office no matter how good economic conditions are. If they fully implement those preferences, though, leaders become scapegoats for poor economic performance.

This mechanism resembles what political scientists call "retrospective voting."[68] Its novel feature is the perverse trade-off between policies and outcomes. In most retrospective voting models, voters are agnostic about policy, and judge politicians purely for their observable success. Leaders' dominant strategy is therefore to implement the most effective policies.[69] This is no longer true, however, if voters "know what ain't so"—if they want specific policies but resent their predictable consequences.

These incentives interestingly lead politicians to supply better economic policies than the public wants. Take Clinton's support of NAFTA.[70] He knew both that NAFTA would raise American living standards, and that a majority of Americans thought the opposite. If Clinton's sole goal were to maximize his probability of reelection, what should he have done? Both options were unappealing. The first was to defy the public, lose face, and hope that the economic benefits of NAFTA undid the damage before the next election. The second was to go along with the public, retain its trust, and hope it would overlook the lackluster economy. Clinton took the first route, and it may well have been the prudent choice.

If voters are systematically mistaken about what policies work, there is a striking implication: They will not be satisfied by the politicians they elect. A politician who ignores the public's policy preferences looks like a corrupt tool of special interests. A politician who implements the public's policy preferences looks incompetent because of the bad consequences. Empirically, the shoe fits: In the GSS, only 25% agree that "people we elect to Congress try to keep the promises they have made during the election," and only 20% agree that "most government administrators can be trusted to do what is best for the country."[71] Why does democratic competition yield so few satisfied customers? Because politicians are damned if they do and damned if they don't. The public calls them venal for failing to deliver the impossible.

One problem with outcome-linked voting is that judgments about outcomes may be biased too. "Believing is seeing"—people may wear rose-colored glasses if and only if their preferred policies hold sway.[72] During the 1990s, employment rates reached peaks not seen in three

decades, but opponents of NAFTA announced that its dire consequences were plain for all to see.[73]

Another weakness of outcome-linked voting is that voters may
punish leaders for problems outside their control.[74] As Achen and
Bartels observe:

> If jobs have been lost in a recession, something is wrong, but is that
> the president's fault? If it is not, then voting on the basis of eco-
> nomic results may be no more rational than killing the pharaoh
> when the Nile does not flood.[75]

This is especially troublesome under divided government. If the public holds the president accountable for economic turmoil, then Congressmen from the other party might prevent his reelection by doing
a bad job. Alternately, Congress might push popular but counterproductive policies, forcing the president to either veto them (and lose
votes for being out of sync with public opinion) or sign them (and
lose votes for bad economic performance). Costly but popular social
legislation sponsored by the Democrats during the 1988–92 Bush
presidency has been interpreted this way.[76]

A final reason not to overrate outcome-linked voting is that many
people have a low threshold for what counts as a "result." Social scientists conceive of "results" as things like economic growth, life ex-
pectancy, crime rates, or peace. But politicians habitually equate "results" with passing legislation and spending money. How many
campaign ads cite "achievements" like a "tough new gun control
bill"? It would be odd to call this a "result" if gun control increases
the murder rate.

Despite these caveats, mixed policy/outcome preferences remain a
plausible explanation for why democracy is not worse. Respondents
in the SAEE have biased beliefs about outcomes, not just policies. Yet
their outcome judgments are less biased, and their perceptions about
the *current* state of the economy are fairly accurate.[77] Unless the costs
of economic policy are well in the future, politicians have to think
twice before caving in to popular misconceptions.

Bias beyond Economics: Systematically Biased Beliefs about Toxicology

Most of my examples come from economics, and with good reason:
Economics dominates the agenda of modern governments. But my
analysis can and should be applied to other politically relevant fields
where the general public's beliefs are systematically mistaken.

Table 6.1
The Public versus Toxicologists on Dosage

"For pesticides, it's not how much of the chemical you are exposed to that should worry you, but whether or not you are exposed at all."

	Strongly Disagree	Disagree	Agree	Strongly Agree	Don't Know
Public	11.9%	47.3%	29.2%	6.9%	4.6%
Toxicologists	61.5%	33.1%	1.8%	2.4%	1.2%

Source: Kraus et al (1992: 223)

Toxicology, with its obvious implications for environmental, health, and safety policy, is a compelling example. The public has numerous prejudices about this apparently dry, technical field.[78] For instance, Kraus, Malmfors, and Slovic ask people whether they agree with this statement: "For pesticides, it's not how much of the chemical you are exposed to that should worry you, but whether or not you are exposed at all."[79]

Toxicologists are far more likely to emphasize dosage. Nontoxicologists "tend to view chemicals as either safe or dangerous and they appear to equate even small exposures to toxic or carcinogenic chemicals with almost certain harm."[80]

As in economics, laymen reject the basics, not merely details. Toxicologists are vastly more likely than the public to affirm that "use of chemicals has improved our health more than it has harmed it," to deny that natural chemicals are less harmful than man-made chemicals, and to reject the view that "it can never be too expensive to reduce the risks associated with chemicals."[81] While critics might like to impugn the toxicologists' objectivity, it is hard to take such accusations seriously. The public's views are often patently silly, and toxicologists who work in industry, academia, and regulatory bureaus largely see eye to eye.[82]

How would the public's misconceptions about, say, dosage, affect policy? This chapter's thought experiments are a useful guide. *With identical voters*, failure to recognize the importance of dosage leads straight to misguided environmental regulations. Instead of focusing on quantitatively significant risks, the government wastes resources trying to eliminate minute dangers.[83] If *otherwise identical voters disagree* about the importance of dosage, but the median believer doubts the truism that "the poison is in the dosage," environmental regulations lean in a wasteful direction. Similarly wasteful policies can be expected if voters are *not identical but seek to maximize social welfare.*

Why then does environmental policy put as much emphasis on dosage as it does? Selective participation is probably part of the story. Mirroring my results, Kraus, Malmfors, and Slovic (1992) find that education makes people think like toxicologists.[84] The bulk of the explanation, though, is probably that *voters care about economic well-being as well as safety* from toxic substances. Moving from low dosage to zero is expensive. It might absorb all of GDP. This puts a democratic leader in a tight spot. If he embraces the public's doseless worldview and legislates accordingly, it would spark economic disaster. Over 60% of the public agrees that "it can never be too expensive to reduce the risks associated with chemicals,"[85] but the leader who complied would be a hated scapegoat once the economy fell to pieces. On the other hand, a leader who dismisses every low-dose scare as "unscientific" and "paranoid" would soon be a reviled symbol of pedantic insensitivity. Given their incentives, politicians cannot disregard the public's misconceptions, but they often drag their feet.

Conclusion

The proposition that irrational beliefs lead to foolish policies is largely correct. Under realistic assumptions, irrational thought leads to foolish action. Recognizing the empirical weakness of the SIVH sweeps away needless complexity. If voters aim to advance the public interest rather than their own, there is no need to build a rickety bridge from the public interest to each individual's private interests. We can walk straight from misperceptions about the public interest to support for misguided policy.

The main caveat is that if the public got exactly what it asked for, policy would be a lot worse. The United States is more market-oriented and open to international competition than you would expect after studying the economic beliefs of its inhabitants, whose aspirations seem more in tune with those of Latin American populists like Perón.

On further consideration, this disparity should be expected. Selective participation, so often maligned as a source of class bias, leaves the median voter more economically literate than the median citizen. More importantly, the public's ungracious tendency to scapegoat its most faithful agents encourages felicitous hypocrisy. Politicians face an uneasy predicament: "Unabashed populism plays well at first, but once the negative consequences hit, voters will blame me, not themselves." This hardly implies that it never pays to take the populist route. But leaders have to strike a balance between doing what the public thinks works, and what actually does.

TECHNICAL APPENDIX

What Makes People Think Like Economists

Qualitatively, there are five main variables in the SAEE that make people "think like economists": education, male gender, past income growth, expected income growth, and job security.[86] They frequently push beliefs in the same direction as economic training, and almost never push in the opposite direction. But how strong is the overall link between these variables and the economic way of thinking? My article in the *Journal of Law and Economics* quantified it using the following technique.[87]

Step 1 is to set up a system of 37 equations, one for each question in the SAEE:

$$(1) \quad TAXHIGH = c(1) + w(1)\left[\begin{array}{l} e(1)Education + e(2)Male + e(3)Yourlast5 + \\ e(4)Yournext5 + e(5)Jobsecurity + Econ \end{array} \right] + \varepsilon$$

$$(2) \quad DEFICIT = c(1) + w(2)\left[\begin{array}{l} e(1)Education + e(2)Male + e(3)Yourlast5 + \\ e(4)Yournext5 + e(5)Jobsecurity + Econ \end{array} \right] + \varepsilon$$

$$(3) \quad FORAID = c(3) + w(3)\left[\begin{array}{l} e(1)Education + e(2)Male + e(3)Yourlast5 + \\ e(4)Yournext5 + e(5)Jobsecurity + Econ \end{array} \right] + \varepsilon$$

and so on for equations (4)–(37). Each of the coefficients inside the brackets—the e's—*has to be* the same across all 37 equations. For instance, the coefficient on Education, $e(1)$, has the same value in equation (1), equation (2), equation (3), and so on. Conversely, the constants and the w coefficients freely vary in each equation. The impact of the set of economistic variables in a given equation can thus be positive, negative, or zero, because there is an equation-specific w coefficient in front of the brackets. Intuitively, the e coefficients capture "how economistic" an *independent* variable is, while the w coefficients capture "how economistic" a *dependent* variable is.

Step 2 is to estimate the whole system's coefficients using nonlinear least squares. The results are completely consistent with qualitative appearances. Despite the strong collinearity restrictions, the w coefficients are highly significant in both statistical and economic terms. Economistic variables are significant at the 5% level in 34 out of 37 equations.

Furthermore, all of the e coefficients are positive and overwhelmingly statistically significant, indicating that they really do march in formation with economic training.

Table 6.2
The *w* Coefficients

#	Variable	Coefficient	t-stat	#	Variable	Coefficient	t-stat
1	TAXHIGH	−0.51	−16.96	20	WOMENWORK	0.18	6.21
2	DEFICIT	−0.14	−9.58	21	TECHGOOD	0.31	10.38
3	FORAID	−0.88	−26.84	22	TRADEAG	0.43	14.15
4	IMMIG	−0.70	−22.34	23	DOWNGOOD	0.50	16.21
5	TAXBREAK	−0.52	−17.12	24	CHANGE20	0.56	18.15
6	INADEDUC	−0.01	−0.24	25	TRADEJOB	0.58	18.88
7	WELFARE	−0.58	−18.85	26	WHYGASSD	0.40	13.33
8	AA	−0.36	−12.29	27	GASPRICE	−0.69	−21.51
9	HARDWORK	−0.37	−12.48	28	PRES	0.01	0.20
10	REG	−0.18	−6.14	29	NEWJOB	0.47	15.04
11	SAVINGS	0.07	2.26	30	GAP20	0.06	2.21
12	PROFHIGH	−0.77	−23.94	31	INCOME20	0.49	16.24
13	EXECPAY	−0.63	−20.29	32	WAGE20	0.30	10.30
14	BUSPROD	0.11	3.95	33	NEED2EARN	−0.11	−3.63
15	TECH	−0.70	−22.14	34	STAN5	0.34	11.44
16	OVERSEAS	−0.71	−22.51	35	CHILDGEN	0.12	4.17
17	DOWNSIZE	−0.67	−21.37	36	CHILDSTAN	0.00	−0.04
18	COMPEDUC	−0.26	−8.71	37	CURECON	0.43	13.97
19	TAXCUT	−0.22	−7.32				

Using the information in table 6.3, one can express the economic literacy of various subgroups of the general public as a scalar. The estimated belief gap between (*a*) a noneconomist with average characteristics across the board and (*b*) the Enlightened Public equals: the coefficient on education, *e(1)*, times 2.46 (the amount by which the

Table 6.3
The *e* Coefficients

Variable	Coefficient	t-stat
Education	0.093	18.1
Male	0.157	11.3
Yourlast5	0.122	11.8
Yournext5	0.099	10.1
Jobsecurity	0.059	10.0

Enlightened Public exceeds the average education level) *plus* 1 (the implicit coefficient on Econ). This comes out to .093 * 2.46 + 1 = 1.229. The belief gaps of other segments of the population can then be compared to this benchmark, as shown in Figure 6.4.

Example 1. The belief gap between the Enlightened Public and otherwise average members of the public with the lowest education level is 6 * .093 + 1 = 1.558. In percentage terms, this means that the belief gap of the lowest-educated segment of the population is roughly 1.558/1.229 = 127% as large as the benchmark.

Example 2. The belief gap between the Enlightened Public and otherwise average members of the public with maximal job security is *e(5)* multiplied by −1.12 (the difference between the average level of job security and the highest possible level) plus 1.229 (the normal gap). This simplifies to 1.163, roughly 95% the size of the benchmark.

Chapter 7

IRRATIONALITY AND THE SUPPLY
SIDE OF POLITICS

> First, even if there were no political groups trying to
> influence him, the typical citizen would in political
> matters tend to yield to extra-rational or irrational
> prejudice and impulse. . . .
> Second, however, the weaker the logical element in the
> processes of the public mind and the more complete
> the absence of rational criticism . . . the greater are the
> opportunities for groups with an ax to grind.
> —*Joseph Schumpeter,* Capitalism, Socialism,
> and Democracy[1]

MY JAUNDICED VIEW of the average voter is the most distinctive feature
of my political economy, but it is not the only distinctive feature.
Competing for the affection of irrational voters calls for different tactics and talents than competing for the affection of rational voters.[2]
Voter irrationality reshapes the whole political landscape, from lead-
ership and delegation to propaganda and lobbying.

The Rationality of Politicians

> The successful politician instinctively feels what the vot-
> ers feel, regardless of what facts and logic say. His guiding
> principle is neither efficiency nor equity but electability—
> about which he knows a good deal.
> —*Alan Blinder,* Hard Heads, Soft Hearts[3]

What happens if *fully rational* politicians compete for the support of
irrational voters—specifically, voters with irrational beliefs about the
effects of various policies? It is a recipe for mendacity. If politicians
understand the benefits of free trade, but the public is dogmatically
protectionist, honest politicians do not get far. Every serious con-
tender must not only keep his economic understanding to himself,

but "pander"—zealously advocate the protectionist views he knows to be false.

Machiavelli infamously advises his readers to break promises when it enhances their political careers: "A prudent ruler ought not to keep faith when by so doing it would be against his interest. . . . If all men were good, this precept would not be a good one; but as they are bad, and would not observe their faith with you, so you are not bound to keep faith with them."[4] Machiavelli is saying that—morally objectionable or not—lying is equilibrium behavior. In a modern democratic milieu, he could as easily written, "A prudent ruler ought not to promote socially beneficial policies when by so doing he would lose votes. . . . If all men were rational, this precept would not be a good one; but as they are irrational, and prone to kill the bearers of bad tidings, so you are not bound to challenge their misconceptions."

But are politicians likely to be paragons of rationality, a breed apart? It depends on the topic.[5] Sometimes politicians—unlike ordinary voters—have strong incentives for rationality. Above all, it pays a politician to understand how his policy positions and other actions *change his electoral prospects.* Politicians have as strong an incentive to think rationally about their popularity as capitalists have to think rationally about their profits.

For example, it is valuable for politicians to accurately estimate the effect of political advertising and the "rate of exchange" between campaign contributions and votes. If they overestimate the vote-benefit of money, they allocate too much time to raising money, and make too many damaging compromises. If they underestimate the vote-benefit, they allocate too little time to fund-raising, and are overly squeamish about repaying donors' favors.

Or consider incentives to think rationally about the media. Politicians often have skeletons in their closet, and face daily temptations to add to their collection. Unbiased beliefs about the probability of getting caught and the severity of the backlash are useful tools of political survival. This does not mean that politicians put zero value on illicit fun, but we should expect them to make intelligent trade-offs. Clinton's relations with "that woman, Miss Lewinsky" ultimately drew massive media attention, but he took many measures along the way to protect himself.[6]

In sum, politicians, unlike average voters, make some political choices where their cost of systematic error is high. In these cases, we should expect leaders to be shrewd and clear-eyed. Selection pressure reinforces this point. Politicians who alienate voters soon cease to be politicians at all.[7]

However, there is one important area where matters are less clear: *Beliefs about policy effectiveness.* Does it pay politicians to correctly diagnose how well policies work? If all that voters care about is adherence to their policy preferences, the answer is no. For the vote-maximizing politician, the majority is always right. Thomas Sowell explains:

> When most voters do not think beyond stage one, many elected officials have no incentive to weigh what the consequences would be in later stages—and considerable incentives to avoid getting beyond what their constituents think and understand, for fear that rival politicians can drive a wedge between them and their constituents by catering to public misconceptions.[8]

If voters are committed protectionists, politicians do not win their friendship with patient lectures on comparative advantage. Instead of trying to correct popular errors, they indulge them. As Alexander Hamilton put it in *The Federalist Papers,* they "flatter their prejudices to betray their interests."[9]

Unusually talented politicians do more than cater to current misconceptions. They steer the grateful public toward the "new and improved" misconceptions of tomorrow. A good politician tells the public what it wants to hear; a better one tells the public what it is *going* to want to hear. After a sudden rise in oil prices, the public would probably blame the greed of the oil companies on its own initiative, but lack the imagination to propose price controls. A skillful politician capitalizes on the crisis by alerting his constituents to an attractive solution: "Price controls! Why didn't *we* think of that?"

Leaders' incentive to rationally assess the effects of policy might be perverse, not just weak. Machiavelli counsels the prince "to do evil if constrained" but at the same time "take great care that nothing goes out of his mouth which is not full of" "mercy, faith, integrity, humanity and religion." One can freely play the hypocrite because "everybody sees what you appear to be, few feel what you are, and those few will not dare oppose themselves to the many."[10] Yet, contra Machiavelli, psychologists have documented humans' real if modest ability to detect dishonesty from body language, tone of voice, and more.[11] George Costanza memorably counseled Jerry Seinfeld, "Just remember, it's not a lie if you believe it."[12] The honestly mistaken politician appears more genuine because he *is* more genuine. This gives leaders who sincerely share their constituents' policy views a competitive advantage over Machiavellian rivals.[13]

As discussed in the previous chapter, there is a countervailing force. If voters care about *both* policies and outcomes, the pandering cynic has a fighting chance against the deluded idealist. The cynic suffers from voters' uneasy sense that, deep down, he is not one of them. But the cynic is more equipped to avoid disaster than the idealist, because he independently weighs the cost of the public's favorite policies. The true child of Machiavelli undermines and soft-pedals the public's worst ideas, paying them lip service the whole time.

To get ahead in politics, leaders need a blend of naive populism and realistic cynicism. No wonder the modal politician has a law degree. Dye and Zeigler report that "70 percent of the presidents, vice presidents, and cabinet officers of the United States and more than 50 percent of the U.S. senators and House members" have been lawyers.[14] The economic role of government has greatly expanded since the New Deal, but the percentage of congressmen with economic training remains negligible.[15] Economic issues are important to voters, but they do not want politicians with economic expertise—especially not ones who lecture them and point out their confusions.

Instead, the electoral process selects people who are professionally trained to plead cases persuasively and *sincerely* regardless of their merits.[16] Many politicians keep economists around to advise them. But the masters of rhetoric call the shots because they possess the most valuable political skill: Knowing how to strike the optimal balance between being right and being popular.

The Political Economy of Faith

Leaders have been known to inspire blind faith. Michels refers to "the belief so frequent among the people that their leaders belong to a higher order of humanity than themselves" evidenced by "the tone of veneration in which the idol's name is pronounced, the perfect docility with which the least of his signs is obeyed, and the indignation which is aroused by any critical attack on his personality."[17] Many totalitarian movements insist upon their leaders' *infallibility*. "The Duce is always right," was a popular Fascist slogan.[18] Rudolf Hess waxed poetic about the perfection of Hitler's judgment:

> With pride we see that one man remains beyond all criticism, that is the Führer. This is because everyone feels and knows: he is always right, and he will always be right. The National Socialism of all of us is anchored in uncritical loyalty, in the surrender to the Führer that does not ask for the why in individual cases, in the silent execution of his orders. We believe that the Führer is obeying a higher call to fashion German history. There can be no criticism of this belief.[19]

Democratically elected leaders rarely claim anything so outrageous. But they seem to enjoy a milder form of unreasoning deference.[20] The most charismatic president may not radiate infallibility to anyone, but that does not stop people from choosing to believe that he is honest in the absence of rock solid evidence to the contrary. As an exasperated Paul Krugman writes:

> Mr. Bush has made an important political discovery. Really big misstatements, it turns out, cannot be effectively challenged, because voters can't believe that a man who seems so likable would do that sort of thing.[21]

Even a colorless politician might find that his *title* makes his words credible. It works for the pope. Why not the president?

One striking instance of unreasoning deference: Shortly after 9/11, polls strangely found that the nation's citizens suddenly had *more* faith in their government.[22] How often can you "trust the government in Washington to do what is right"? In 2000, only 30% of Americans said "just about always" or "most of the time." Two weeks after 9/11, that number more than doubled to 64%. It is hard to see consumers trusting GM more after a major accident forces a recall. The public's reaction is akin to that of religious sects who mispredict the end of the world: "We believe now more than ever."

A close relative of blind faith is the ability to change men's minds with mere rhetoric. Think about it: People modify their view of the world because a current or aspiring leader *redescribes* the facts. With normal faith, the audience says, "I believe because *he* said it." Faith inspired by verbal ability is a slight variation: "I believe because he said it *so well.*" Perhaps the most extreme illustration is the political influence of great poets like Pablo Neruda. Common sense snaps, "What does he know? He's a *poet*," but many would rather listen and be swayed by the beautiful words.

What happens to democracy if the public puts a degree of irrational faith in its leaders? The most obvious effect is to give leaders slack or "wiggle room." Though they have to conform to public opinion, public opinion becomes partly a function of the politicians' own choices. If doing A gives the public faith in the wisdom of A, and doing B gives the public faith in the wisdom of B, then a politician may safely choose either one. It is arrogant for a leader to snicker that "the people will think what I tell them to think," but that does not make him wrong.

Faith helps explain politicians' tendency to dodge pointed questions with vague answers.[23] How can *refusing* to take a position (or changing the subject) be strategically better than candidly endorsing a moderate position?[24] Put yourself in the shoes of a voter who opposes the moderate view but has a degree of faith in a candidate's good intentions. If the candidate announces his allegiance to the moderate view, faith in him dissolves. But as long as the candidate is silent or vague, it does not tax your faith to maintain, "He's a decent man, he must agree with me." From politicians' point of view, the critical fact is that voters on *both sides* of the issue can "reason" in the same fashion.

The downside of quasi-religious faith in the powers-that-be (or want-to-be) is plain. Cushioned by the masses' credulity, an elected official could shirk to their detriment.[25] Recall that the simplest way to keep politicians in line is to harshly punish them when you catch them misbehaving. An electorate with faith in its leaders spares the rod and spoils the child.

Machiavelli notoriously urges leaders to take full advantage of leader worship: "But it is necessary . . . to be a great feigner and dissembler; and men are so simple and so ready to obey present necessities, that one who deceives will always find those who allow themselves to be deceived."[26] A corrupt politician can use faith-based slack to cater to special interests, a ideologue to push his agenda. Regardless of what one thinks about the war on terror, it is hard to deny that George Bush would have enjoyed comparable support if he made fairly different choices. If he decided that invading Iraq was not worth the effort, how many of his supporters would have balked? Since some of Bush's options were better for his financial backers and cohered more with his ideology, he faced *temptations* to shirk. The only question is whether he gave into temptation.

Still, one should not ignore the upside of political faith: its ability to neutralize the public's irrationality. A leader who understands the benefits of free trade might ignore the public's protectionism if he knows that the public will stand behind *whatever* decision he makes. Since politicians are well educated, and education makes people think more like economists, there is a reason for hope. Blind faith does not create an incentive to choose wisely, but it can eliminate the *dis*incentive to do so. Whether this outweighs the dangers of political faith is an open question.

The same goes for faith in experts. It opens up a low road and a high road. The low road is for experts to take advantage of the public, promoting their personal finances or ideology. The high road is for experts to help the public in spite of itself. Suppose the public has faith in the FDA. Its drug policy experts could take the low road, telling the credulous public that it is "in the public interest" to test drugs for efficacy as well as safety, ignoring the lives lost from years of delay.[27]

But sometimes experts take the high road instead. The public might be sure that Thalidomide should be totally banned, but defer when the FDA approves it as a treatment for leprosy.[28]

Irrationality and Delegation

> Princes should let the carrying out of unpopular duties
> devolve on others, and bestow favors themselves.[29]
> —*Niccolò Machiavelli*, The Prince

In complex modern political systems, leaders can only make a handful of big decisions. The rest must be left in subordinates' hands. High-level subordinates face the same dilemma, pushing concrete decisions further down the bureaucratic food chain. This fosters the sense that elected leaders are not in charge. The real power, supposedly, is the "faceless bureaucracy."

The economics of principal-agent relations cuts against this inversion.[30] When a principal delegates a task to a subordinate, his tacit instruction is, "Do *what I myself would have done* if I had the time," not, "Do as you please." The former does not have to evolve into the latter. Common sense tells a principal to occasionally audit his subordinates to see how well they mimic the decisions he would have made himself.[31]

It makes little difference if there is one principal and one agent, or one principal at the top of a tall bureaucratic pyramid. The preferences of the apex trickle down to the base. Imagine the pyramid has 26 layers, from A at the top to Z at the bottom. If the Z's ask, "What is expected of me?" the answer is, "To do what the Y above you would have done." If the Y's in turn ask, "What is expected of *me*?" the answer is, "To do what the X above you would have done." For any given Z, serving the wishes of the Y above him is equivalent to serving the wishes of the X two levels up. This principle lets us ascend the entire pyramid.

In a deep sense, the leader of an organization is responsible for everything his organization does. Mistakes happen, but part of the job is keeping an eye on subordinates. That includes keeping an eye on whether *they* are keeping an eye on *their* subordinates. If the grocery bagger at a supermark is rude to you, it is more than a personal failing. It reflects poorly on the entire chain for failing to detect and correct the bagger's etiquette.

This argument remains relevant for tenured professors, Supreme Court justices, and others who cannot be fired. When you cannot punish insubordination, rely on reputation instead. Choose candidates with a long history of support for your approach. If a justice undercuts the president who appointed him, a rational electorate can and should blame the president for being a poor judge of character.

So at first pass, simple models seem able to capture the complexities of modern government. Those who have been a cog in the political machine frequently relay a different impression, but their objections are fairly superficial. The fact that you have some latitude over the cosmetics of a delegated decision hardly shows that you—not your nominal superior—control its substance. The fact that your boss rarely double-checks your work or second-guesses you does not show that *he* is really working for *you*. More plausibly, it means that your superior rationally trusts you to make the decision he would have made *without being asked*. If he thinks you are sound, he leaves you alone, conserving his scrutiny for more questionable underlings.

By itself, irrationality does not amplify the importance of delegation. If voters believe that protectionism promotes the general welfare, they want more than a leader who promotes protectionism when a chance to do so lands on his desk. They expect their leader to impose his protectionist aims on his underlings—to make it known throughout the hierarchy that all decisions should have a protectionist flavor.

However, the right *kind* of irrationality undermines the standard analysis. Suppose that voters underestimate the ability of politicians to control their subordinates. This creates strange new leeway for politicians. They can take the crowd-pleasing action themselves, but allow or encourage their subordinates to do the opposite.

In the United States, the president appoints Supreme Court justices and the Senate confirms them. Rationally speaking, a justice's rulings reflect on the officials who put him on the bench. If a justice defies public opinion by protecting flag-burning, his decision should diminish the popularity of the president who appointed him and the senators who confirmed him.[32] This assumes, however, that average voters correctly perceive the chain of responsibility. If they systematically underestimate the strength of its connections, delegation undermines the popular will. Politicians have to denounce flag-burning to win voter approval, but it stays legal as long as the decision is in the hands of subordinates who demur.

The ability to wash his hands of his underlings' actions gives a leader extra slack. If he wants something unpopular to happen, he does not have to become unpopular himself. Instead, he publicly stands with the majority, but privately leads his subordinates to undercut him. In its crassest form, he could tell his subordinates, off the record, that his public statements are the opposite of his true wishes. But it is easier to appoint people who *want* to do the unpopular thing, then look the other way.

When the popular view and the reasonable view overlap, systematically biased beliefs about ultimate political responsibility are all for the bad. Corruption and favoritism flower if politicians can wink at their underlings as they denounce "influence-peddling." On a classic episode of *The Simpsons*, Bart became famous for excusing his misbehavior with the catchphrase "I didn't do it."[33] No one believed Bart. But if the electorate believes politicians who use Bart's strategy, they have a license to steal. To be more precise, they can sell licenses to steal, hiding behind the fact that they personally stole nothing. Ideologically committed politicians could use the same means for putatively nobler ends: "Funds for the Contras? I didn't do it."

But equating the popular and the reasonable unfairly tilts the scales against political slack. Irrationality about political responsibility has the potential to defuse the effect of irrationality on policy, as Tullock shows in one of his little fables:

> Consider a professor of economics and the dullest student in his class. Let us assume that . . . the dull student becomes a king, and . . . the professor of economics becomes his principal advisor. . . . Such a minister has open to him three courses of action: he may resign; he can stop trying to improve the economic conditions of the kingdom and simply implement the king's stupid ideas on economic matters; or he can try to deceive the king into carrying out the policies that he, the minister, thinks wise while agreeing with the king in council.[34]

False beliefs about who is responsible for what are particularly potent if voters care about both policies and results. Then a leader could win on both metrics. He publicly backs the popular view to show his laudable intentions. Meanwhile, he nudges his underlings to ignore public opinion and shoot for prosperity, proving his competence.

Biased beliefs about political responsibility have arguably greased much of the progress toward free trade. Congress and the president have full authority over trade policy. They can leave the World Trade Organization any time they want. When the WTO overrules protectionist moves by the United States, however, our leaders blame the WTO, conveniently forgetting that it has only the power they gave it.[35] Has democracy been undermined by bureaucratic sleight of hand? Yes—and the electorate is better off as a result.

Admittedly, to say this plays right into the hands of detractors of the economics profession like William Greider:

Disparaging public opinion is, of course, a necessary prelude to ignoring it. The elites' language of despair over the commonweal is a vital element in their politics, for it creates another screen—a climate that encourages political leaders to be "responsible" by going against the obvious wishes of their constituents.[36]

But his lament dodges the hard question: What if public opinion deserves to be disparaged?

Another oddity that thrives on misconceptions about political responsibility: Leaders often feel public pressure to "do something" about a problem, but the world finds fault with every concrete solution. A way out is to pass legislation that is loudly well intentioned, but vague.[37] Practically speaking, this leaves the hard decisions to so-called independent agencies or judges. One might object, "If you created the agency and retain the power to alter or abolish it with a simple majority vote, in what sense is it 'independent'?" But tough questions are a weak obstacle. Assuming the public falls for their semantic trickery, politicians can rise in popular esteem for "doing something," but deflect inevitable disappointment onto the shoulders of others.

U.S. antitrust laws are a beautiful example. Try to decipher the meaning of "attempted monopolization" or "restraint of trade" with the help of a dictionary. Am I "attempting to monopolize" the market for books about economics right now? No matter. Though the written law verges on meaningless, sponsors like Senator Sherman and Representative Clayton won credit for "fighting the trusts." Only after judges and regulators "interpreted" the laws could their effects be seen. From the point of view of the Shermans and Claytons, this makes the deal sweeter still. *Someone else* makes the tough decisions and risks embarrassment. All it takes to see through this ruse is the common sense to ask, "Who passed the ambiguous law that allowed the bad decisions to happen in the first place?" The ruse works if common sense is not so common.

Economists of little faith in democracy emphasize how hard it is for constituents to control their "representatives."[38] Defenders of democracy like Donald Wittman downplay the role of political slack. On balance, Wittman gets the better of the theoretical debate: Voters have several easy ways to keep leaders on a short leash. But both sides tend to misjudge the broader implications of their stance on slack. Given everything else we know about democracy, agency "problems" may be agency *solutions*.

When a master does not know his own best interests, a disobedient servant can be a blessing. The more misguided the electorate is, the less desirable it is for politicians to unquestioningly grant its wishes.

If voters want price controls, a politician with slack can ignore them for their own good. Or he might take money from Big Oil to oppose controls, proverbially turning a private vice into a public virtue. The lesson is that agency "problems" temper majoritarian extremes. Good outcomes become less good, because corrupt politicians stand in the way of the public's grand design. Bad outcomes become less bad, because politicians have the wiggle room to tone them down.

Strangely, then, if Wittman is right about agency problems, democracy arguably looks worse. As explained in the previous chapter, unselfish motivation amplifies the risks of irrational cognition. So when the electorate is irrational and unselfish, perhaps you should *hope* for agency "problems" to open up a livable gap between what voters want and what voters get. If politicians have no choice but to carry out constituents' wishes, democracy loses one of its main safety valves.

Irrationality and Propaganda

> I believe that voter preferences are frequently not a crucial *independent* force in political behavior. These "preferences" can be manipulated and created through the information and misinformation provided by interested pressure groups, who raise their political influence partly by changing the revealed "preferences" of enough voters and politicians.
> —*Gary Becker, "A Theory of Competition Among Pressure Groups for Political Influence"*[39]

The media want to entertain citizens; politicians, to influence their votes. If informing voters achieves these ends, the media and politicians have an incentive to distribute free information. Many social scientists think these giveaways help democracy work, and if voters are rational, they are correct.[40] But what happens if voters fall short of this ideal?

Irrationality and the Media

Perhaps the most common reaction to evidence of the public's systematic biases is to blame the media. Conservatives point to liberal bias in the programming. Liberals are more likely to assail the biases of the advertisers. In both cases, the model is persuasion through repetition: If people on TV repeat themselves often enough, viewers eventually believe them.[41] Many successful propagandists subscribe to this model, though few are as blunt as Hitler:

The receptivity of the great masses is very limited, their intelligence is small, but their power of forgetting is enormous. In consequence of these facts, all effective propaganda must be limited to a very few points and must harp on these in slogans until the last member of the public understands what you want him to understand by your slogan.[42]

Blaming the media for biased beliefs has gut-level appeal. Journalists routinely endorse economic fallacies. Trade coverage paints imports as a cost. Business news equates jobs with prosperity, and greed with high prices and dishonesty. Blaming the media for pessimistic bias is easiest of all. As Julian Simon argues:

The only likely explanation is that newspapers and television—the main source of notions about matters which people do not experience directly—are systematically misleading the public, even if unintentionally. There is also a vicious circle here: The media carry stories about environmental scares, people become frightened, polls then reveal their worry, and the worry is then cited as support for policies to initiate action about the supposed scares, which then raise the level of public concern. The media proudly say "We do not create the 'news.' We are merely messengers who deliver it." The data show that the opposite is true in this case.[43]

But the "blame the media" hypothesis has serious flaws. First, the writings of the classical economists show that most economic biases were popular before newspapers and periodicals were widely read.[44] People are plainly able to form foolish beliefs about economics without journalists' assistance. Second, uninformative content does not sway rational voters. They discount biased information, and do not naively swallow whatever journalists tell them—especially if they flagrantly rely on logical fallacies like "proof by repetition." The media can therefore be no more than a *catalyst* for the public's preexisting cognitive flaws.

For pseudoinformation to work as intended, voters need to be not only irrational, but irrational in the right way. The simplest of these is *overconfidence in the reliability of the media*. Imagine an audience puts blind, unconditional faith in Bill O'Reilly. Its gullibility allows O'Reilly to remake his audience in his own image. If he wanted to transform their faith into personal riches, he could "rent out" the support of his drones to the highest bidder.[45] O'Reilly's influence naturally falls short of this extreme, but there is a continuum from full rationality to utter fanaticism.

Overconfidence in the media can rationalize complaints about ideological bias. If viewers have faith in journalists, and most journalists are committed liberals, they have slack to pull audiences in their direction. Especially in a competitive news industry, however, the crafty approach is to move along the margins of the audience's indifference. If there are two equally entertaining stories, but one has a more left-wing flavor, liberal media can emphasize it without hurting ratings. It may well be, moreover, that most of the entertainment value of the news comes from the charisma of the reporter, not the story. If "star power" is unequally distributed across the political spectrum—as Hollywood suggests—we should expect stories to have a liberal slant.

Media can also shape opinion if the public is overconfident in particular *kinds of content*, as opposed to media per se. Schumpeter fears that "Information and arguments in political matters will 'register' only if they link up with the citizen's preconceived ideas."[46] Paul Rubin makes the more specific claim that systematically biased beliefs about economics are an "innate property of the mind." We would not originate them in solitary confinement, but they are easy for our minds to digest. Otherwise

> it would be relatively easy to unlearn these beliefs. There is no reason to expect that cultural errors should persist for over 200 years (about ten human generations), the time since Adam Smith first pointed out the benefits of a market economy. We have easily learned to adapt to numerous new technologies in much shorter times, when these technologies did not conflict with innate mental modules.[47]

Maybe we are inherently receptive to messages about bad foreigners who want to hurt us. It could be a leftover from our evolutionary past, when intergroup violence made xenophobia a lifesaver.[48] Similarly, despite his complaints about the media's scare-mongering, Julian Simon co-indicts the minds of the audience for their pessimistic bias:

> We will always find grounds for worry. Apparently it is a built-in property of our mental systems that no matter how good things become, our aspiration levels ratchet up so that our anxiety levels decline hardly at all, and we focus on ever smaller actual dangers.[49]

If people are more susceptible to some messages than others, exposure to *balanced* media can bring out people's "inner protectionist" or "inner pessimist." Coverage consistent with our prejudices resonates, so even a neutral stream of messages propels us deeper into error. Left to their own devices, viewers overreact only to evidence that they personally stumble upon. If the media magically vanished, their former audience would have to search harder for reasons to fear foreigners, and might grow less antiforeign out of laziness. The news industry, no matter how balanced, stops this from happening. It ensures that the public gets a steady stream of antiforeign coverage to which it can overreact.[50] People who lack the initiative or creativity to reach misconceptions under their own steam can relax and let the media tow them there.

But if this is so, balanced journalism is the last thing to expect. Journalism is a business. If consumers prefer news that fits their prejudices, journalists have an incentive to cater to them.[51] Pessimistic bias is probably the strongest example. No one spontaneously worries about Alar; it takes coverage to launch a panic.[52] But this does not make the media an *independent* causal force. The media are not forcing pessimism down the public's throats; the public lines up to get its daily dose of pessimism.[53] The Web offers "good news every day" at PositivePress.com, but this is no match for traditionally negative CNN.com. If the public were not predisposed to pessimism, CNN's days would be numbered.

Irrationality, Political Advertising, and Special Interests

Perhaps the angriest complaint against modern democracy is the following: Special interests purchase antisocial favors from politicians; then politicians use the money to "buy elections" with abundant advertising, and the worst candidate wins. As Kuttner laments:

> Lately, money has become newly influential in political life. As campaigns become more expensive, money tends to drive out more civic forms of participation. . . . Money-driven elections feed into a brand of politics that leaves out ordinary voters, except as objects to be manipulated by polling, focus groups, mass mailings, and paid TV spots.[54]

Donald Wittman objects that a rational electorate would stop this perverse process cold.[55] Rational voters would wonder *how* a politician raised the money to purchase airtime. If candidates get money solely by selling socially harmful favors to special interests, then advertising would backfire. The populace would reason: The more a politician spends on advertising, the more money he must have; the more money he has, the more illicit favors he must have sold. Lots of ads equal lots of corruption. If the public thought like this, no politician would advertise in the first place. Better not to advertise and be thought corrupt than to advertise and remove all doubt.

Wittman's mechanism has some empirical relevance: Politicians love to "out" their rivals for accepting money from tobacco companies and other reviled donors. Furthermore, most empirical work finds weak effects of money in politics. The typical study reports little or no effect on how politicians vote, and relative to GDP, the total value of donations is small.[56]

Still, the strategy of responding *negatively* to well-funded campaigns seems artificial. Rational voters would do it, but real voters? All it takes to avoid Wittman's curious conclusion is the right kind of irrationality. Suppose voters underestimate the strength of the link between advertising and corruption. Then selling favors to special interests to pay for commercials works as long as naive voters who think *more* of you outnumber sophisticated voters who think *less* of you.

It helps to sell the right kind of favors. Like a journalist with an ax to grind, a shrewd politician moves along the margins of voter indifference. The public is protectionist, but rarely has strong opinions about *which* industries need help. This is a great opportunity for a politician and a struggling industry to make a deal. Steel manufacturers could pay a politician to take (*a*) a *popular* stand against foreigners combined with (*b*) a *not unpopular* stand for American steel. In maxim form: Do what the public wants when it cares; take bids from interested parties when its doesn't. Bear in mind, though, that the important thing is not how burdensome a concession is, but how burdensome voters *perceive* it to be.

Conclusion

After studying irrationality on the demand side of politics, it is only human to shift hope to the supply side. Unlike voters, individuals on the supply side—whether politicians, civil servants, the media, or lobbyists—are professionals. Are they standing by to clean up the amateurs' mess? Unfortunately, it is often more rewarding to exacerbate voter irrationality than defuse it.[57] Political expertise mainly consists in understanding what the public wants—or will want—and handing it to them. Demand for corrective pedantry is minimal. As Paul Krugman puts it, "Voters have a visceral dislike for candidates who seem intellectual, let alone try to make the electorate do arithmetic."[58] Neither do they want politicians to tell them that their complaints about downsizing are misplaced, or watch news about the long-run benefits of flexible labor markets.

Experts are not an antidote to voter irrationality. But for better and worse, they loosen the link between public opinion and policy. The electorate's blind spots open loopholes for politicians, bureaucrats, and the media to exploit. But if the public was working against its own interests in the first place, the welfare effect of "exploitation" is ambiguous.

Faith in leaders is the clearest example. Its dangers are obvious—picture a charismatic sociopath, or a "rally round the flag" effect that reelects an incompetent incumbent. But political faith also allows leaders—if they are so inclined—to circumvent their supporters' misconceptions. Faith creates slack, and slack *in the right hands* leads to better outcomes. All you need are leaders who are *somewhat* well intentioned and *less* irrational than their followers. Since leaders are well educated, and education dilutes sympathy for popular misconceptions, at least the second condition is not hard to satisfy.

Bureaucracy also has mixed effects. If the public lets them, politicians pass the buck, blaming their mistakes and misdeeds on subordinates. Before we condemn buck-passing, however, we should remember how many good ideas and socially beneficial actions the public classifies as "mistakes" and "misdeeds."

Last, consider propaganda. We tend to think that causes twist the facts and appeal to emotions when truth is not on their side. Nazism and Communism are obvious examples. But in theory, propaganda can be used to fight error as well. If a person clings to his mistakes despite the evidence, irrational persuasion is his only hope.

On balance, most economists underestimate the dangers of the supply side of politics, but orthodox provoter critics of democracy overestimate them. Economists correctly reason that as long as the general public is rational, the best servants of voter interests win elections. This makes economists reluctant to recognize political phenomena like blind faith, buck-passing, or propaganda. "Blind faith" becomes "reputation," "buck-passing" becomes "agency costs," and "propaganda" becomes "information." If voters fall short of full rationality, however, these concerns can no longer be dismissed.

Noneconomists, in contrast, are too quick to pin democracies' failings on suppliers. Supply-side problems usually need voter irrationality to get off the ground, and if you acknowledge voters' irrationality, you weaken the presumption against thwarting their will. If a principal does not know his own interests, his agent's shirking *may* benefit principal and agent alike. Supply-side chicanery is only unambiguously harmful given conditions—full voter rationality—under which it does not arise.

Chapter 8

"MARKET FUNDAMENTALISM" VERSUS THE RELIGION OF DEMOCRACY

> The trouble with the world is that the stupid are cocksure
> and the intelligent are full of doubt.
> —*Bertrand Russell*[1]

ECONOMISTS perennially debate each other about how well the free market works. They have to step outside their profession to remember how much—underneath it all—they agree.[2] For economists, greedy intentions establish no presumption of social harm. Indeed, their rule of thumb is to figure out who could get rich by solving a problem—and start worrying if no one comes to mind. Most noneconomists find this whole approach distasteful, even offensive. Disputes between economists are quibbles by comparison.

Out of all their contrarian views, nothing about economists aggravates other intellectuals more than their sympathy for markets. As Melvin Reder aptly states, comprehension of mainstream economics "tends to generate appreciation of the merits of laissez-faire even when that appreciation does not extend to acceptance."[3] Left to their own devices, "normal" intellectuals could spend their careers cataloging human greed and the evils that flow from it. But economists stand in their midst, a fifth column, using their mental gifts to defend the enemy.

The hostility that economists provoke is evident from all the name-calling. Karl Marx, the classic poison pen, accused Ricardo and his fellow classical economists of "miserable sophistry," of suffering from "the obsession that bourgeois production is production as such, just like a man who believes in a particular religion and sees it as *the* religion, and everything outside of it only as *false* religions." For Marx, economists are apologists for the bourgeoisie, who "set up that single, unconscionable freedom—Free Trade" and replaced the feudal era's "exploitation veiled by religious and political illusions" with "naked, shameless, direct, brutal exploitation."[4] Rosa Luxemburg, in her essay "What is Economics?" proclaims with disgust that

> The bourgeois professors serve up a tasteless stew made from the leftovers of a hodge-podge of scientific notions and intentional circumlocutions—not intending to explore the real tendencies of capitalism, at all. On the contrary, they try only to send up a smoke screen for the purpose of defending capitalism as the best of all possible orders, and the only possible one.[5]

Modern detractors continue to oscillate between calling economists hired intellectual guns of the rich and a coven of conservative ideologues. But the more sophisticated critics protest that they object to certain brands of economics, not the whole field. For instance, Robert Kuttner's "quarrel is with a utopian—really, a dystopian—view of markets, not with economists as a breed."[6] But he takes back with one hand what he gives with the other, accusing "self-described liberal" economists of "dismantling much of the case for a mixed economy." If liberal Democratic economists are beyond the pale, who is not?

The Charge of Market Fundamentalism

"Market fundamentalism" is probably the most popular insult against economics these days. The world listened when billionaire George Soros declared that "Market fundamentalism . . . has rendered the global capitalist system unsound and unsustainable."[7] Robert Kuttner has a handy summary of what market fundamentalism amounts to:

> There is at the core of the celebration of markets a relentless tautology. If we begin, by assumption, with the premise that nearly everything can be understood as a market and that markets optimize outcomes, then everything comes back to the same conclusion—marketize! If, in the event, a particular market doesn't optimize, there is only one possible inference: it must be insufficiently marketlike.[8]

He insists, moreover, that this fault is not limited to a right-wing fringe: "Today, the only difference between the utopian version and the mainstream version is degree." Indeed, "As economics has become more fundamentalist, *the most extreme version of the market model has carried the greatest political, intellectual, and professional weight.*"[9] Even worse, economists' fundamentalism overflows into the policy arena:

> American liberals and European social democrats often seem unable to offer more than a milder version of the conservative program—deregulation, privatization, globalization, fiscal discipline,

but at a less zealous extreme. *Few have been willing to challenge the premise that nearly everything should revert to a market.*[10]

Joseph Stiglitz joins the chorus against market fundamentalism, happily discarding the guarded professorial prose of his Nobel prize-winning research:

> The discontent with globalization arises not just from economics seeming to be pushed over everything else, but because a particular view of economics—market fundamentalism—is pushed over all other views. Opposition to globalization in many parts of the world is not to globalization per se . . . but to the particular set of doctrines, the Washington Consensus policies that the international financial institutions have imposed.[11]

Market fundamentalism is a harsh accusation. Christian fundamentalists are notorious for their strict biblical literalism, their unlimited willingness to ignore or twist the facts of geology and biology to match their prejudices. For the analogy to be apt, the typical economist would have to believe in the superiority of markets virtually without exception, regardless of the evidence, and dissenters would have to fear excommunication.

From this standpoint, the charge of "market fundamentalism" is silly, failing even as a caricature. If you ask the typical economist to name areas where markets work poorly, he gives you a list on the spot: Public goods, externalities, monopoly, imperfect information, and so on. More importantly, almost everything on the list can be traced back to other economists. Market failure is not a concept that has been forced upon a reluctant economics profession from the outside. It is an *internal* outgrowth of economists' self-criticism. After stating that markets usually work well, economists feel an urge to identify important counterexamples. Far from facing excommunication for sin against the sanctity of the market, discoverers of novel market failures reap professional rewards. Flip through the leading journals. A high fraction of their articles present theoretical or empirical evidence of market failure.

True market fundamentalists in the economics profession are few and far between. Not only are they absent from the center of the profession; they are rare at the "right-wing" extreme. Milton Friedman, a legendary libertarian, makes numerous exceptions, on everything from money to welfare to antitrust:

> Our principles offer no hard and fast line how far it is appropriate to use government to accomplish jointly what is difficult or impossible for us to accomplish separately through strictly voluntary ex-

change. In any particular case of proposed intervention, we must make up a balance sheet, listing separately the advantages and disadvantages.[12]

When Friedman prefers laissez-faire, he often openly acknowledges its defects. He has no quasi-religious need to defend the impeccability of the free market. For example, his discussion of natural monopoly states:

> [T]here are only three alternatives that seem available: private monopoly, public monopoly, or public regulation. All three are bad so we must choose among evils. . . . I reluctantly conclude that, if tolerable, private monopoly may be the least of the evils.[13]

Friedman is far more market-friendly than the average economist. But a "market fundamentalist"? Hardly. He recognizes numerous cases where market performance is poor, and does not excommunicate less promarket colleagues for heresy.

If neither the typical economist nor Milton Friedman himself qualifies as a market fundamentalist, who does? The only plausible candidates are the followers of Ludwig von Mises and especially his student Murray Rothbard. The latter does seem to categorically reject the notion of suboptimal market performance:

> Such a view completely misconceives the way in which economic science asserts that free-market action is *ever* optimal. It is optimal, not from the personal ethical views of an economist, but from the standpoint of the free, voluntary actions of all participants and in satisfying the freely expressed needs of the consumers. Government interference, therefore, will necessarily and always move *away* from such an optimum.[14]

Both Mises and Rothbard have passed away, but their outlook—including Ph.D.s who subscribe to it—lives on in the Ludwig von Mises Institute. But groups like these have basically given up on mainstream economics; members mostly talk to each other and publish in their own journals. The closest thing to market fundamentalists are not merely outside the mainstream of the economics profession. They are *way* outside.

Popular accusations of market fundamentalism are plain wrong. Yes, economists think that the market works better than other people admit. But they acknowledge exceptions to the rule. The range of these exceptions changes as new evidence comes in. And it is usually economists themselves who discover the exceptions in the first place.

Democratic Fundamentalism

> In wide areas of life majorities are entitled to rule, if
> they wish, simply because they are majorities.
> —*Robert Bork*, The Tempting of America[15]

The disparity between economists' open-mindedness and the charge of market fundamentalism is so vast that it is hard not to speculate about the motives behind it. I sense a strong element of projection: accusing others of the cognitive misdeeds one commits oneself. Take "creation scientists." Faculty and researchers of the Institute for Creation Research follow a party line: "The scriptures, both Old and New Testaments, are inerrant in relation to any subject with which they deal, and are to be accepted in their normal and intended sense."[16] You can hardly get less scientific. Yet a standard debating tactic of creation scientists is to insist that "evolutionary theory, along with its bedfellow, secular humanism, is really a religion."[17] Creationists' attacks on the objectivity of mainstream evolutionists seem to stem from their sense of scientific inferiority to their opponents.

Similarly, the most vocal opponents of "market fundamentalism" are themselves often believers in what can accurately be called "democratic fundamentalism." Its purest expression is the cliché, attributed to failed 1928 presidential candidate Al Smith, that "All the ills of democracy can be cured by more democracy."[18] In other words, *no matter what happens*, the case for democracy remains untouched. Victor Kamber has a book called *Giving Up on Democracy.*[19] The title's rhetorical power stems from the widespread belief that democracy has to be the answer. You can complain about democracy, but you cannot "give up" on it. Indeed, many admire its flaws. As Adam Michnik exclaims, "Democracy is gray," but "Gray is beautiful!"[20]

A person who said, "All the ills of markets can be cured by more markets" would be lampooned as the worst sort of market fundamentalist. Why the double standard? Because unlike market fundamentalism, democratic fundamentalism is widespread. In polite company, you can make fun of the worshippers of Zeus, but not Christians or Jews. Similarly, it is socially acceptable to make fun of market fundamentalism, but not democratic fundamentalism, because market fundamentalists are scarce, and democratic fundamentalists are all around us.

Everyone from journalists and politicians to empirical social scientists and academic philosophers is willing to publicly profess his democratic fundamentalism without embarrassment. At the end of a book

experts and questions with well-established answers get less coverage than cranks and controversy.

Shapiro is slightly more hesitant to make a sweeping dismissal of economics. But democratic fundamentalism triumphs in the end:

> It would be foolish not to recognize that economists, for instance, often have esoteric knowledge (perhaps less than they think they have) about the workings of the economy that is relevant to democratic deliberation about it. But because decisions about the limits of the market sphere and the structure of its governance are linked to the controversial exercise of power, they are inescapably political; thus economic policy making should never be ceded to professional economists. They must persuade lay representatives, in nontechnical terms, if we are to be bound by their advice.[29]

Perversely, then, the *more* irrational the electorate is, the *less* of a say economists have. If a lay audience will listen to reason, economists wield some influence. But a stubbornly wrongheaded lay audience is entitled to do whatever it likes: "Economic policy making should *never* be ceded to professional economists."[30] If this is not democratic fundamentalism, what is?

In his research on "sacred values," psychologist Philip Tetlock observes that "people often insist with apparently great conviction that certain relationships and commitments are sacred and that *even to contemplate* trade-offs with the secular values of money or convenience is anathema."[31] In the modern world, democracy is one of the best examples; the faithful equate minor deviations with total apostasy, and condemn sinful thoughts as harshly as wicked deeds.

A standard rhetorical tactic is to equate modest reductions in the role of government with the elimination of government regulation altogether. Robert Kuttner tells us that "in the emblematic case of airline regulation, what began under President Carter as 'regulatory reform' quickly evolved into a drive for complete deregulation."[32] Apparently, the Federal Aviation Administration's continuing regulation of safety does not count. A similar ploy is to equate mere *talk* of cutting government with doing it. Richard Leone of the Twentieth Century Fund alleges that "faith in idealized market structures also has spawned a political jihad intent upon stripping away the community and government safeguards against market abuses and imperfections. . . . Democrats and moderate Republicans are stumbling all over each other to prove their conversion to the one true faith of laissez-faire economics."[33] Strangely, the laissez-faire jihad failed to push federal spending as a percentage of GDP below 18%—and most of the decline during the 1990s clearly stemmed from the end of the Cold War.[34]

In the end, apologists for democracy often fall back on Winston Churchill's slogan, "Democracy is the worst form of government, except all those other forms that have been tried from time to time."[35] On the surface, this sounds like mature realism, not democratic fundamentalism. But Churchill's maxim is an all-or-nothing rhetorical trick. Imagine if an economist dismissed complaints about the free market by snapping: "The free market is the worst form of economic organization, except all the others." This is a fine objection to communism, but only a market fundamentalist would buy it as an argument against moderate government intervention. Churchill's slogan is every bit as weak. Just because dictatorship is disastrous, it hardly follows that democracy must have free rein. Like markets, democracy can be limited, regulated, or overruled. Contramajoritarian procedures like judicial review can operate alongside democratic ones. Supermajority rules allow minorities to thwart the will of the majority. Twisting a marginal trade-off into a binary choice is fundamentalism trying to sound reasonable.

Will the Real Fundamentalism Please Stand Up?
The Case of the Policy Analysis Market

A major story broke on July 28, 2003.[36] Senators Ron Wyden and Byron Dorgan demanded that the Department of Defense end funding for an obscure program, the Policy Analysis Market (henceforth PAM). Still in its preliminary stage, the program's aim was to create online betting markets for questions of national security. PAM traders could profit by—among other things—correctly predicting the number of Western terror casualties. Critics quickly labeled it the "Terror Market" scheme. Wyden and Dorgan condemned it without reservation:

> Spending taxpayer dollars to create terrorism betting parlors is as wasteful as it is repugnant. The American people want the Federal government to use its resources enhancing our security, not gambling on it.[37]

Television and newspaper coverage was almost entirely unfavorable—and so was public opinion. Could the PAM's backers be too blind to see that it gave a financial incentive for terrorism? Was there any more egregious case of market fundamentalism? The Secretary of Defense killed the program on July 29—*one day* after the publicity began. John Poindexter, head of the Information Awareness Office, had to offer his resignation the next day. After two months, all funding for the office was terminated. So much for bureaucratic inertia.

Then a funny thing happened. Other media—published less frequently and aimed at more sophisticated audiences—followed up on the Terror Market story. They delved into the rationale of the project, and talked to its creators about possible flaws in its design. Several lessons emerged.[38]

First, there is a large body of empirical evidence on the predictive accuracy of speculative markets, on everything from horse-racing to elections to invasions. "Put your money where your mouth is" turns out to be a great way to get the well informed to reveal what they know, and the poorly informed to quiet down. No system is perfect, but betting markets outperform other methods of prediction in a wide variety of circumstances. The PAM was inspired not by ivory tower theorizing, but by the proven success of betting markets in other areas.

Second, the amount of money on the PAM table was very small. Individual bets were limited to a few tens of dollars. The idea that these paltry sums would motivate additional terrorism is ludicrous. Terrorists who wanted to profit from their attacks could make a lot more money by manipulating normal financial markets—shorting airline stocks and such. Incidentally, the 9/11 Commission found that did not happen either.[39]

Third, the program was shut down so quickly that there was no time to verify the accusations. According to Robin Hanson, my colleague and one of the brains behind the PAM, "During that crucial day, no one from the government asked the PAM team if the accusations were correct, or if the more offending aspects could be cut from the project."[40] The creators had anticipated and already addressed the obvious objections, but opponents were too inflamed to listen. Constructive criticism was in short supply, to say the least; the goal was to kill the program, not improve it.

Last, the PAM experience raised a dilemma for those who embrace the "wisdom of crowds." Surowiecki forcefully defends the merits of decision markets like the PAM. But he also affirms that "there's no reason to believe that crowds would be wise in most situations but suddenly become doltish in the political arena." As long as there *is* a right answer, "Democracy's chances of adopting good policies are high."[41] How then can Surowiecki account for the public's extreme hostility to the PAM? If decision markets and democracy both work well, the PAM should be popular.[42]

If the critics studied the PAM more thoroughly, they would have been angrier still. A key feature was the ability to make *conditional* bets. You could wager, for example, on the number of Western terrorist casualties *if* the United States invades Iraq, and the number *if* it does not. Comparing the price of those two bets would reveal whether the market thinks an invasion will make us more or less safe from terrorist attacks. In short, betting markets could second-guess not only political leaders, but public opinion itself. This is bound to rub democratic fundamentalists the wrong way.

Overall, the creators of the PAM were far from market fundamentalists. They built on a solid body of evidence, thought carefully about potential problems, and were open to criticism. Their plan was to test the program out on a small scale, work out the bugs, and gradually expand it.

Almost the opposite holds for opponents. They did not question the track record of predictive betting markets. Apparently, they knew nothing about it and did not care to learn. Despite the obvious failures of traditional intelligence in recent years, they were convinced that the best policy was more of the same. Listen to Wyden and Dorgan:

> The example that you provide in your report would let participants gamble on the question, "Will terrorists attack Israel with bioweapons in the next year?" Surely, such a threat should be met with intelligence gathering of the highest quality—not by putting the question to individuals betting on an Internet website.[43]

Surely? How do they know? At minimum, the PAM would have raced betting markets against old-fashioned intelligence gathering. But democratic fundamentalists did not want to put their antimarket dogma to the test.

Private Choice as an Alternative to Democracy and Dictatorship

Undemocratic politics is not the only alternative to democratic politics. Many areas of life stand outside the realm of politics, of "collective choice." When the law is silent, decisions are "up to the individual" or "left to the market." If the term were not preempted, private choice could be called "the Third Way," the alternative to both democracy and dictatorship.

For most of human history, religion was a state responsibility. The idea that government could have no established religion was inconceivable. All that has changed; now individuals decide which religion, if any, to practice. Verbal gymnastics notwithstanding, this depoliticization is undemocratic. The majority now has as little say about my religion as it would under a dictatorship; in both cases, the law ignores public opinion. Before the 1930s, similarly, many areas of U.S. economic life were undemocratically shielded from federal and state regulation.[44] The market periodically trumped democracy, on everything from the minimum wage to the National Recovery Administration. And unless you are a democratic fundamentalist, you have to be open to the possibility that this was all for the good.

Fervent partisans of democracy often grant that democracy and the market are substitutes. As Kuttner puts it, "The democratic state remains the prime counterweight to the market."[45] Their complaint is that the public has less and less say over its destiny because corporations have more and more say over theirs. To "save democracy," the people must reassert its authority.

Fair enough. Though their opponents greatly overstate the extent of privatization and deregulation, these policies take decisions out of the hands of majorities and put them into the hands of business owners. But the critics rarely wonder if this transfer might be desirable. They treat less reliance on democracy as automatically objectionable.

This is another symptom of democratic fundamentalism. If all that an economist had to say against a government program were, "That's government intervention. Government is supplanting markets!" he would be pigeonholed, then marginalized, as a market fundamentalist. But when an equally simplistic cry goes up in the name of democracy, there is a sympathetic audience. It is logically possible that clear-eyed business greed makes better decisions than confused voter altruism. Why not at least compare their performance, instead of prejudging?

The complaint that we are "losing democracy" is especially weak when we bear in mind that this is not a binary choice between unlimited democracy and pure laissez-faire. Just because *some* democracy is beneficial or necessary, it scarcely follows that we should not have *less*. Consider deregulation of the television and radio spectrum. Democratic fundamentalists find the idea offensive because it ends democratic oversight.[46] But it is hard to see the value of democracy in the entertainment industry. Premium networks like HBO demonstrate that the profit motive, uninhibited by majority preferences, is a recipe for high-quality, creative programming. Democratic fundamentalism holds back the rest of the industry.

Most democratic enthusiasts recognize that free markets are a substitute—albeit a self-evidently undesirable one—for democracy. A few take the more extreme position that the notion of depoliticized choice is incoherent.[47] This position is best expressed in the work of Ian Shapiro, who criticizes the "implausible notion that a scheme of collective action is an alternative to a scheme of private action."[48] "Were it possible somehow for society to 'not undertake' collective action," defects in collective decision-making "might amount to a prima facie argument against all collective action."[49] But in fact, private action is "parasitic" on collective action:

> The institutions of private property, contract, and public monopoly of coercive force . . . were created and are sustained by the state, partly financed by implicit taxes on those who would prefer an alternative system. The real question, for democrats, is not "whether or not collective action?" but whether or not democratic modes of managing it are superior to the going alternatives.[50]

This argument is seriously flawed.

First, even if private action presupposes the existence of collective action, it remains feasible to eschew collective action *in some or most areas.* Just because a doctor's treatment keeps you alive hardly shows that you have to grant him absolute authority over your whole life. You can heed his advice if your survival depends on it, and otherwise do as you please. Similarly, suppose we grant that private action is a parasite on the body of government. It does not follow that the host must have final say across the board. Indeed, a presumption against collective action is compatible with the view that private action depends upon government: What better reason could there be to overrule the presumption than that private action could not otherwise survive?

Second, Shapiro's argument can be readily reversed. Collective decision-making is "parasitic" on the wealth created by the market economy. It would be hard to have an orderly vote if businesses had not fed, clothed, housed, and transported the electorate and candidates. Does this reveal an internal contradiction in every regulation? Hardly.

Last, it is not true that private action is inherently parasitic or dependent upon collective action. The existence of the black market proves that property rights and contracts are possible without government approval. That is why one drug dealer can meaningfully tell another, "You stole my crack" or, "We had a deal." Indeed, the black market shows not only that property and contract can persist without the government's support, but that they can survive in the face of its determined resistance.

Contrary to naysayers, there is no conceptual flaw in prescriptions to rely more on private choice and less on collective choice. The proposal is quite intelligible. In fact, the counterarguments are so weak that their popularity seems to be another symptom of democratic fundamentalism. People want to rule alternatives to democracy out of court, to avoid putting their faith to the test.

Voter Irrationality, Markets, and Democracy

Critics of the economics profession are right about one thing. Economists *really do* subscribe to a long list of views that are unpopular, even offensive. Perhaps most offensive is economists' judgment that markets work considerably better than the general public thinks. That judgment is the foundation of economists' promarket outlook, the so-called Washington Consensus.

While this book has debunked the main efforts to undermine the objectivity of the economics profession, it adds little to the debate on the virtues of markets. My book weighs on the other side of the scales. The optimal mix between markets and government depends not on the absolute virtues of markets, but on their virtues *compared* to those of government. No matter how well you think markets work, it makes sense to rely on markets *more* when you grow more pessimistic about democracy. If you use two car mechanics and discover that mechanic A drinks on the job, the natural response is to shift some of your business over to mechanic B, whatever your preexisting complaints about B.

Should my book push you toward democratic pessimism? Yes. Above all, I emphasize that voters are irrational. But I also accept two views common among democratic enthusiasts: That voters are largely unselfish, and politicians usually comply with public opinion. Counterintuitively, this threefold combination—irrational cognition, selfless motivation, and modest slack—is "as bad as it gets."[51]

If public opinion is sensible, selfishness and slack prevent democracy from fulfilling its full promise. But if public opinion is senseless, selfishness and slack prevent democracy from carrying out its full threat. Selfishness and slack are like water rather than poison. They are not intrinsically injurious; they *dilute* the properties of the systems they affect. Thus, when the public systematically misunderstands how to maximize social welfare—as it often does—it ignites a quick-burning fuse attached to correspondingly misguided policies. This should make almost anyone more pessimistic about democracy.

The striking implication is that even economists, widely charged with market fundamentalism, should be more promarket than they already are. What economists currently see as the optimal balance between markets and government *rests upon an overestimate of the virtues of democracy.* In many cases, economists should embrace the free market in spite of its defects, because it still outshines the democratic alternative.

Consider the insurance market failure known as "adverse selection." If people who want insurance know their own riskiness, but insurers only know average riskiness, the market tends to shrink. Low-risk people drop out, which raises consumers' average riskiness, which raises prices, which leads more low-risk customers to drop out.[52] In the worst-case scenario, the market "unravels." Prices get so high that no one buys insurance, and consumers get so risky that firms cannot afford to sell for less.

Economists often take the presence of adverse selection as a solid reason to deviate from their laissez-faire presumption.[53] But given the way that democracy really works, the shift in presumption is premature. Given public opinion, what kind of regulation is democracy likely to implement? The essence of the adverse selection problem is that insurers do not know enough to charge the riskiest consumers the highest premiums. But how would a person with antimarket bias see things? The last thought on his mind would be, "If only insurance companies could identify the riskiest consumers and charge them accordingly." Reflected in the fun-house mirror of antimarket bias, the "obvious" problem to fix is *higher rates for riskier people*, not the imperfect match between risks and rates.

The fact that regulation *could* help correct the adverse selection problem—for example, by making everyone buy insurance—is therefore a weak argument for regulation. Given the public's antimarket bias, democracy will probably force companies to charge high-risk clients the same as everyone else. The basic economics of insurance tells us that this makes the adverse selection problem worse by encouraging low-risk consumers to opt out. But basic economics is what the public refuses to accept. It does not take a market fundamentalist to recognize that it may be prudent to muddle through with the imperfections of the free market, instead of asking the electorate for its opinion.

Even among economists, market-oriented policy prescriptions are often seen as too dogmatic, too unwilling to take the flaws of the free market into account.[54] Many prefer a more "sophisticated" position: Since we have already belabored the advantages of markets, let us not forget to emphasize the benefits of government intervention. I claim that the qualification needs qualification: Before we emphasize the benefits of government intervention, let us distinguish intervention designed by a well-intentioned economist from intervention that appeals to noneconomists, and reflect that the latter predominate. You do not have to be dogmatic to take a staunchly promarket position. You just have to notice that the "sophisticated" emphasis on the benefits of intervention mistakes theoretical possibility for empirical likelihood.

In the 1970s, the Chicago school became notorious for its "markets good, government bad" outlook. One could interpret my work as an attempt to revive that tradition. Many of its arguments were flawed, even contradictory. If people were as uniformly rational as Chicago economists assumed, government policy could not stay bad for long. George Stigler eventually pulled the rug out from under Milton Friedman by saying so.[55] But flawed arguments can still lead to a true conclusion; Stigler was a better logician, but Friedman had greater insight. Placed on a foundation of rational irrationality, perhaps the Chicago research program that Friedman inspired can live again.

Correcting Democracy?

The main upshot of my analysis of democracy is that it is a good idea to rely more on private choice and the free market. But what—if anything—can be done to improve outcomes, *taking the supremacy of democracy over the market as fixed*? The answer depends on how flexibly you define "democracy." Would we still have a "democracy" if you needed to pass a test of economic literacy to vote? If you needed a college degree? Both of these measures raise the economic understanding of the median voter, leading to more sensible policies. Franchise restrictions were historically used for discriminatory ends, but that hardly implies that they should never be used again for any reason. A test of voter competence is no more objectionable than a driving test. Both bad driving and bad voting are dangerous not merely to the individual who practices them, but to innocent bystanders. As Frédéric Bastiat argues, "The right to suffrage rests on the presumption of capacity":

> And why is incapacity a cause of exclusion? Because it is not the voter alone who must bear the consequences of his vote; because each vote involves and affects the whole community; because the community clearly has the right to require some guarantee as to the acts on which its welfare and existence depend.[56]

A more palatable way to raise the economic literacy of the median voter is by giving *extra* votes to individuals or groups with greater economic literacy. Remarkably, until the passage of the Representation of the People Act of 1949, Britain retained plural voting for graduates of elite universities and business owners. As Speck explains, "Graduates had been able to vote for candidates in twelve universities in addition to those in their own constituencies, and businessmen with premises in a constituency other than their own domicile could

vote in both."[57] Since more educated voters think more like economists, there is much to be said for such weighting schemes. I leave it
to the reader to decide whether 1948 Britain counts as a democracy.

A moderate reform suggested by my analysis is to reduce or eliminate efforts to increase voter turnout. Education and age are the two
best predictors of turnout. Since the former is the strongest predictor
of economic literacy, and the latter has little connection with it, the
median voter's economic literacy exceeds the median citizen's. If "get
out the vote" campaigns led to 100% participation, politicians would
have to compete for the affection of noticeably more biased voters
than they do today.[58]

Most worries about de jure or de facto changes in participation
take the empirically discredited self-interested voter hypothesis for
granted.[59] If voters' goal were to promote their individual interests,
nonvoters would be sitting ducks. People entitled to vote would intel-
ligently select policies to help themselves, ignoring the interests of
everyone else. There is so much evidence against the SIVH, however,
that these fears can be discounted. The voters who know the most do
not want to expropriate their less clear-headed countrymen. Like
other voters, their goal is, by and large, to maximize social welfare.
They just happen to know more about how to do it.

Since well-educated people are better voters, another tempting way
to improve democracy is to give voters more education. Maybe it
would work. But it would be expensive, and as mentioned in the previous chapter, education may be a proxy for intelligence or curiosity.
A cheaper strategy, and one where a causal effect is more credible, is
changing the curriculum. Steven Pinker argues that schools should
try to "provide students with the cognitive skills that are most important for grasping the modern world and that are most unlike the
cognitive tools they are born with," by emphasizing "economics, evolutionary biology, and probability and statistics."[60] Pinker essentially
wants to give schools a new mission: rooting out the biased beliefs
that students arrive with, especially beliefs that impinge on government policy.[61] What should be cut to make room for the new material?

> There are only twenty-four hours in a day, and a decision to teach
> one subject is also a decision not to teach another one. The ques-
> tion is not whether trigonometry is important, but whether it is
> more important than statistics; not whether an educated person
> should know the classics, but whether it is more important for an
> educated person to know the classics than elementary economics.[62]

Last but not least on the list of ways to make democracy work better
is for economically literate individuals who enjoy some political slack

to *take advantage of it* to improve policy.[63] If you work at a regulatory bureau, draft legislation, advise politicians, or hold office, figure out how much latitude you possess, and use it to make policy better. Subvert bad ideas, and lend a helping hand to good ones. As Ronald Coase says, "An economist who, by his efforts, is able to postpone by a week a government program which wastes $100 million a year . . . has, by his action, earned his salary for the whole of his life."[64] As Bastiat emphasizes, the voter who acts on his biased judgments is not just hurting himself. If you employ your political wiggle room to improve policy, you are doing your part to tame a public nuisance.

Economics: What Is It Good For?

> Our primary mission should be to vaccinate the minds of
> our undergraduates against the misconceptions that are
> so predominant in what passes for educated discussion
> about international trade.
> —*Paul Krugman, "What Do Undergrads*
> *Need to Know About Trade?"* [65]

Most of the preceding remedies suffer from a catch-22. Once you use up your political slack, the only way to curtail the political influence of the economically illiterate to is convince them it is a good idea. However, if you were persuasive enough to do *that*, you could "cut out the middleman" and directly convince them to start voting more sensibly. Persuasive resources are scarce. Is there anything that can be done, holding constant the persuasive resources of the economics discipline and "allied forces"?[66] Is there any way to make better use of their time? I believe there is.

Economists have a reputation for being unwilling to give definite answers and unable to reach a consensus. Harry Truman famously longed for a "one-handed economist," who could not say "on the one hand, on the other hand." Paul Samuelson added, "According to legend, economists are supposed never to agree among themselves. If Parliament were to ask six economists for an opinion, seven answers would come back—two, no doubt, from the volatile Mr. Keynes!"[67]

Both economists and their detractors know these stereotypes are dead wrong. But for once, however, economists themselves are largely to blame for the misunderstanding. When economists choose between communicating (*a*) nothing, or (*b*) simplified but roughly accurate conclusions, they strangely seem to prefer (*a*). When you have an *entire semester* with a group of students, they forget all but the main points. If you fail to hammer a few fundamental principles into your students, odds are they will take away nothing at all. Yet in the dozens of economics courses I have taken, the professors rarely took their constraint seriously. Many preferred to dwell on the details of national income accounting, or mathematical subtleties, or the latest academic fad.

I know from experience that professors have an enormous amount of slack. They can drastically change the content and style of their courses at low cost. So to the question, "How can teachers of economics make better use of their time?" I answer that they should strive to channel the spirit of the original one-handed economist, Frédéric Bastiat.

It makes no difference if "teacher of economics" is your official job description. Everyone who knows some economics—professors, policy wonks, journalists, students, and concerned citizens—has opportunities to teach. Each of us should begin, like Bastiat, by contrasting the popular view of a topic with the economic view. Make it obvious that economists think one thing and noneconomists think something else. Select a few conclusions with profound policy implications—like comparative advantage, the effect of price controls, and the long-run benefits of labor-saving innovation—and exhaust them. As Bastiat advises, "We must . . . present our conclusions in so clear a light that truth and error will show themselves plainly; so that once and for all victory will go either to protectionism or free trade."[68]

Economists who follow Bastiat's advice help their colleagues as well. A stereotype—that they fail to offer definite conclusions—handicaps economists. Being *counterstereotypical* not only makes you more persuasive and influential as an individual. It also undermines the stereotype, making economists more persuasive and influential as a profession.

At first, many feel uncomfortable being a one-handed economist. But anyone can do it. Spend less time qualifying general principles. Except at the best schools, introductory classes should be almost qualification free—there is too much nonsense to unlearn to waste time on rare conditions where standard conclusions fail. Most of the exceptions taught in introductory classes can be profitably deferred to intermediate courses; most of the exceptions taught in intermediate courses can be profitably deferred to graduate school. The best students will understand if you tell them, "Those questions will be addressed in more advanced courses." For the rest, you must respect the Laffer Curve of learning: They retain less if you try to teach them more.

To take an example that is likely to be controversial, economists do a bad job teaching students about competition.[69] Textbooks usually say, "Competition works *as long as* . . . " and then list the many strong assumptions of perfect competition. Many texts are wrong on technical grounds: Perfectly competitive assumptions are *sufficient* conditions of efficiency, not necessary ones.[70] But they also deserve censure for failing to emphasize that even imperfect competition defies the cliché that "businesses charge whatever they like." Indeed, students' casual equation of greedy motives and bad outcomes is overstated for *monopolies*. Like competitive firms, monopolies have an incentive to reduce costs, cut their prices when costs fall, and look over their shoulder for potential competition. It is more important for students to understand that self-interest often encourages socially beneficial behavior, than to understand that this mechanism falls short of perfection. Antimarket bias almost ensures that they will not forget the market's shortcomings.

At this point, a fair challenge to pose is: If people's views about economics are so irrational, how is persuasion possible? My answer is that irrationality is not a barrier to persuasion, but *an invitation to alternative rhetorical techniques*. Think of it this way: If beliefs are, in part, "consumed" for their direct psychological benefits, then to compete in the marketplace of ideas, you need to bundle them with the right emotional content. There is more than one way to make economics "cool," but I like to package it with an undertone of rebellious discovery, of brash common sense. Who does not side with the child in the Hans Christian Andersen fable who exclaims, "The Emperor is naked!"? You might be afraid of alienating your audience, but it depends on how you frame it. "I'm right, you're wrong," falls flat, but "I'm right, the people outside this classroom are wrong, and you don't want to be like *them*, do you?" is, in my experience, fairly effective.

Yes, these techniques can be used to inculcate fallacies as well as insight. But there is no intrinsic conflict with truth. You can actually get students *excited* about thinking for themselves on topics where society disapproves, as Ralph Waldo Emerson does in his essay "Self-Reliance." He paints truth-seeking as not merely responsible, but heroic:

> The nonchalance of boys who are sure of a dinner, and would disdain as much as a lord to do or say aught to conciliate one, is the healthy attitude of human nature. How is a boy the master of society; independent, irresponsible, looking out from his corner on such people and facts as pass by, he tries and sentences them on

their merits, in the swift, summary way of boys, as good, bad, interesting, silly, eloquent, troublesome. He cumbers himself never about consequences, about interests; he gives an independent, genuine verdict.[71]

Bastiat, similarly, makes logic and common sense appealing by ridiculing those who lack them. Take his famous Candlemakers' Petition:

We are suffering from the ruinous competition of a foreign rival who apparently works under conditions so far superior to our own for the production of light that he is *flooding the domestic market* with it at an incredibly low price; for the moment he appears, our sales cease, all the consumers turn to him. . . . This rival . . . is none other than the sun.

[I]f you shut off as much as possible all access to natural light, and thereby create a need for artificial light, what industry in France will not ultimately be encouraged?[72]

The petition does more than teach economics. It turns protectionism into a joke. In the process, Bastiat depicts economists not as pedants, but as the life of the intellectual party. Without compromising his intellectual integrity, Bastiat makes readers' desire to think well of themselves work in his favor.

If you do not have a full semester to enlighten your audience, my advice becomes more relevant still. The less time you have, the more important it is to (1) highlight the contrast between the popular view and basic economics in stark terms; (2) explain why the latter is true and the former is false; and (3) make it fun.

When the media spotlight gives other experts a few seconds to speak their mind, they usually strive to forcefully communicate one or two simplified conclusions. They know that is the best they can do with the time allotted to them. But economists are reluctant to use this strategy. Though the forum demands it, they think it unseemly to express a definite judgment. This is a recipe for being utterly ignored.[73] If you are one voice in a sea of self-promotion, you had better speak up clearly when you finally get your chance to talk.

Admittedly, economists have less latitude on television than in class. If a reporter interviews you about the trade deficit, but you keep changing the subject to comparative advantage, the interview might not be aired, and you reduce your chance of being interviewed again. But it is worth testing the limits of the media's tolerance. It is not so off-putting to preface any mention of the trade deficit with a short disclaimer: "Trade deficits, contrary to popular opinion, are not a bad thing. Whenever the trade deficit goes up, people always want to 'do something' about it, but they're wrong—like all trade, international trade is mutually beneficial, whether or not there is a trade deficit." Maybe you could tack on an amusing example too: "I run a huge trade deficit with Wegmans Supermarket—I buy thousands of dollars of its groceries, but Wegmans buys nothing from me—and it is nothing to worry about." If you cannot steer the conversation away from the latest numbers, at least steal a little time to put the numbers in perspective.

Outlets like newspaper columns and blogs lie somewhere between television sound bites and semester-long courses. You have more slack in print or online than on TV. But you still have to heavily simplify. I know one economist who intentionally writes columns with fewer words than the editor requests. That way, he explains, it is hard for newspapers to cut his favorite parts—which he evidently suspects copy editors are likeliest to hate.

There is much to learn from Bastiat's approach to economic education. But that is only the beginning.[74] Bastiat puts economic education in a broader context. Economists study the world, but are also a part of it. Where do they fit in? Bastiat's answer is "the refutation of commonplace prejudices." To use modern terminology, economists supply the public good of correcting systematically biased beliefs. Their main task: "clearing the way for truth . . . preparing men's minds to understand it . . . correcting public opinion . . . breaking dangerous weapons in the hands of those who misuse them."[75]

Economists already do some of this by instinct. It is hard to be sure, but in the absence of generations of economic education, changes like falling tariffs and privatization would probably have happened on a smaller scale, or not at all.[76] But economists are in a peculiar situation: They correct public opinion not because market forces *drive* them to, but because market forces *grant* them the wiggle room to perform this function, if they are so inclined. This means that a great deal depends on the profession's morale—how enthusiastically it accepts its responsibility.

One of the main factors that has undermined the profession's morale in recent decades is the marginalization of the idea of systematically biased beliefs about economics. If it really is the case that voters on average correctly understand economics before they hear word one, *who needs economists*? What social function do they serve?

This is not an impossible question to answer. Professional economists could devote themselves to reducing the variance of public opinion, to narrowing dispersion due to random errors. In so doing, they would attain Keynes's ambition: for economists to become "humble, competent people on a level with dentists."[77]

Such professional humility is dangerous. Economists who compare themselves to dentists will basically accept their society as it is. This would be fine if reducing variance were the only task for economists to perform. But in the real world, economists are the main defense against the systematic errors that are the foundation for numerous bad policies. If they look the other way, these mistakes go largely unchecked. Nothing is more likely to make economists desert their posts, to deter them from performing their vital function, than a misguided humility.

Economists should not forget that they have made mistakes in the past, and will again. We should all admit our limitations. But there are two kinds of errors to avoid. Hubris is one; self-abasement is the other. The first leads experts to overreach themselves; the second leads experts to stand idly by while error reigns.

Conclusion

Along with market fundamentalism, economists are often accused of arrogance. In a way, then, I am playing into the critics' hands. I advocate neither market fundamentalism nor arrogance, but we should quit trying so hard to avoid the impression of either. There is no reason to be defensive. Economists have created and popularized many of the most socially beneficial ideas in human history, and combated many of the most virulent. If they were self-conscious of their role in the world, they could do much more.

Conclusion

IN PRAISE OF THE STUDY OF FOLLY

> It is hard . . . to claim that the same individuals act in
> a rational and forward-looking way as economic agents
> but become fools when casting their vote.
> —*Torsten Persson and Guido Tabellini,*
> Political Economics[1]

DEMOCRACIES have a lot of apparently counterproductive policies.
Economists emphasize the folly of protection and price controls. Experts in other fields have their own bones to pick. How are these policies possible? There are three basic responses.

Response 1: Defend the accused policies on their merits.
Response 2: Argue that politicians and special interests have subverted democracy.
Response 3: Explain how policies can be *both* popular *and* counterproductive.

Response 1 is rarely convincing. We would laugh if a professor spent hours poring over a failing exam scrawled in crayon, searching for its elusive wisdom. Why should we take the effort to rationalize misguided policies any more seriously? Their typical proponent has no subtle counterarguments. Most cannot *state the experts' main objections,* much less answer them.

Response 2 is more intellectually satisfying.[2] A policy with negative overall effects can still have big benefits for a small minority. But in spite of the academic attention this explanation has accumulated in recent decades, it suffers from two great flaws. First: Theoretically, there are many ways for the majority to cheaply reassert its dominance.[3] Second: Empirical public opinion research shows that the status quo—including and perhaps especially its counterproductive policies—enjoys broad popular support, and that politicians respond to changes in public opinion.[4]

These facts have led me to response 3. Yes, it seems paradoxical for policies to be popular yet counterproductive. Common sense tells us that people like the policies that work the best.[5] Economic training reinforces this presumption by analogizing democratic participation to market consumption: If the policy is so bad, why do voters keep putting it in their shopping cart?

But on closer examination, the paradox fades away. The analogy between voting and shopping is false: *Democracy is a commons, not a market.* Individual voters do not "buy" policies with votes. Rather they toss their vote into a big common pool. The social outcome depends on the pool's average content.

In common-pool situations, economists usually fear the worst. Heedless of the aggregate effect, people will foul the waters. The main reason that they are complacent about democracy, I suspect, is that the pollution is hard to visualize. It is not run-of-the-mill *physical* pollution. Democracy suffers from a more abstract externality: the *mental* pollution of systematically biased beliefs.

While economists rarely discuss the consumption value of beliefs, the idea is intuitively plausible and theoretically unobjectionable. Anything can be a "good," as far as economic theory is concerned. Daily experience tells us that one of the goods people care about is their worldview. Few of us relish finding out that our religious or political convictions are in error.

Once you grant this point, you only need to combine it with elementary consumer theory to get my model of rational irrationality. The quantity of irrationality demanded, like the quantity of pears demanded, decreases as its material price goes up. As is often the case in economics, however, this mundane assumption raises uncomfortable questions. In daily life, reality gives us material incentives to restrain our irrationality. But what incentive do we have to think rationally about politics?

Almost none. To threaten, "You will get bad policies unless you are rational" is a fallacy of composition. Democracy lets the individual enjoy the psychological benefits of irrational beliefs at no cost to himself. This of course does not deny the value of psychological benefits. But the trade-off is not socially optimal; democracy overemphasizes citizens' psychological payoffs at the expense of their material standard of living.

Migration patterns provide a nice illustration. Citizens of poor countries are often eager to emigrate to rich countries. But they rarely vote for parties that pledge to copy the policies of the rich countries. If an Indian desperately wants to move to the United States but is unable to get a visa, voting to make India more like the United States seems like the next best thing. But there is a crucial difference between the two actions. A migrant who leaves his homeland gives up psychological benefits, such as the belief that his nation is the best in the world, in exchange for a big jump in his material well-being. A voter who turns his back on his nation's political tradition gives up psychological benefits but—since policy is beyond his control—is not a penny richer.

Changing Course

> The Western economics profession has been spoiled
> rotten by rational expectations thinking, by diverting
> our attention away from the profound misunderstandings
> that are part of every deep crisis.
> —*Jeffrey Sachs, "Life in the Economic Emergency Room"*[6]

I am certainly not the first social scientist to disconnect policies' popularity from their effects. A diverse list of thinkers has done the same: Economists like Adam Smith, Frédéric Bastiat, Simon Newcomb, Ludwig von Mises, Frank Knight, Joseph Schumpeter, Charles Schultze, Thomas Sowell, Alan Blinder, and Paul Krugman; political theorists like Niccolò Machiavelli, Gustave Le Bon, Robert Michels, Gaetano Mosca, and Eric Hoffer; even novelists—like George Orwell and Ayn Rand. But my position cuts against the grain of modern social science. If I am right, then a great deal of published research is wrong.

This is primarily true for formal political theory, as practiced in both economics and political science. Models that assume that the average voter understands how the political-economic system works have some value as foils. But there is little point building ever more complicated variations on the theme of rational voting.[7] All models simplify, but that is a poor reason to habitually assume the *opposite* of what we know.

Theorists' unwillingness to relax the rational expectations assumption has forced them to fashion awfully convoluted models.[8] Fernandez and Rodrik's well-known article "Resistance to Reform" is a fine example.[9] Economic reform in developing countries is often unpopular. The simplest and best explanation, in my view, is that most people underestimate the benefits of economic reform.[10] But Rodrik deplores this explanation on methodological grounds: You can't say that.[11] Instead, Fernandez and Rodrik show that a special kind of uncertainty could lead a majority to oppose policies that would benefit a majority. Example: Suppose 40% of voters know that reform will make them $1,000 richer; remaining voters have a 25% chance to gain $1,000, and a 75% chance to lose $1,000. (40% + .25 * 60%) = 55% of the electorate will therefore gain $1,000. But 60% of the electorate *expects* to lose $500, and therefore votes against reform before it happens.

Like most formal political models, Fernandez-Rodrik is internally consistent.[12] The conclusion—a majority of rational voters *may* oppose the adoption of reforms that will *definitely* make a *majority* better off—follows rigorously from the premises. But it is hard to see this as the reason why real people oppose reform. In the absence of professional scruples against voter irrationality, Fernandez and Rodrik would not have bothered with their model. Why wrack your brain to explain why rational voters would do something that *appears* irrational, when you already know that voter irrationality is common?

Considering how many rational voting models are with us, their marginal scientific value has fallen close to zero. Theorists can now teach us far more by exploring the effects of different forms of irrationality. One outstanding example is Timur Kuran and Cass Sunstein's model of "availability cascades."[13] Kuran and Sunstein begin with micro-level evidence that human beings overestimate the probability of memorable events. So what happens, they ask, if the media come across an isolated, vivid, scary anecdote? They lunge for the ratings. Their coverage helps the public remember the anecdote, which amplifies its estimate of the risk, which increases demand for similar stories. Once the scare is widespread, politicians vow to solve the problem, which raises its profile once again. Kuran and Sunstein argue that their mechanism underlies a string of unjustified panics like Love Canal, Alar, and TWA Flight 800. It also helps explain why hysterias vary so much from country to country. A few scary stories about nuclear power snowballed into mass hysteria in the United States, without much impact in Europe; the opposite holds for genetically modified food. Even if Kuran and Sunstein turn out to be wrong, theirs is serious effort to model politics using realistic assumptions about how people think.

If formal political theory is as flawed as I claim, what about empirical work? A great deal of it is immune to my critique. Public opinion research, for example, has rarely succumbed to the strictures of rational choice theory. Not only have experts in this area continued to publish results that formal theorists have trouble accepting; scholars like David Sears have also exposed important holes in rational choice theory—most notably, the assumption of voter selfishness. Furthermore, if voters are half as irrational as I say, we should be open to evidence that politicians have some slack and take advantage of it.[14]

But not all empirical work escapes unscathed. Some investigations limit themselves to "racing" rational choice explanations against each other. If a coefficient is positive, it supports Rational Choice Theory A; if it is negative, it supports Rational Choice Theory B. If higher income predicts support for free trade, that "shows" that it helps the rich at the expense of the poor; if lower income predicts support for free trade, that "shows" the opposite.

This whole brand of theory-driven empirical research is questionable. Despite the pretense of openness to evidence, the answer always supports the rational choice approach. Of course, if this approach had withstood extensive testing against alternatives, there would be no problem. But not only has the rational choice approach *not* endured this kind of scrutiny; when critically examined, it has fared poorly.

Still, even theory-driven empirics can be partly salvaged. Rational choice theory affects the questions that people ask, and skews their interpretation. But as long as the research honestly reports its findings, we can still learn from it. In the rational choice framework one almost automatically treats the fact that higher-income people are less protectionist as proof that protectionism benefits the poor more than the rich. But we can buy the fact without prejudging the explanation. Maybe the rich are less protectionist because they are more rational; or perhaps income is a proxy for education or intelligence, and these make people more rational. Many empirical findings are likely to point in new directions after being liberated from their sterile theoretical milieu.

It is tempting to say that social scientists have wasted so much effort because economics has spread beyond its appropriate domain. But the real problem is that economics, a vital box of analytical tools, has been misused. Markets are the first thing that economists study, but they have plenty of other ways of looking at human behavior. Once a few pioneers analogized politics to markets, however, there was an unfortunate bandwagon effect. It is time to jump off the bandwagon.

Authors often close with a call for further research, and so shall I. There is much to learn about politics, and much to unlearn. Social science has pursued many blind alleys—and ignored many promising ones—out of misguided insistence that every model be a "story without fools," even in areas like politics where folly is central. A proverb tells us that "a wise man learns more from a fool than a fool learns from a wise man." By closing their eyes to fools and folly, the wise men of social science have artificially hobbled the advance of their own learning.

NOTES

INTRODUCTION: THE PARADOX OF DEMOCRACY

1. Simon (2000).
2. On the economics and politics of dictatorship, see Wintrobe (1998).
3. For some discussions of harmful but democratically adopted policies, see Friedman (2002), Krugman (1998), Olson (1996), and Blinder (1987). Irwin (1996) provides a comprehensive history of economists' views on protectionism.
4. Grossman and Helpman (2001, 1996, 1994), Rowley, Tollison, and Tullock (1988), Becker (1983), and Brennan and Buchanan (1980) all question the ability of the majority to control its representatives. Somin (2004), Magee, Brock, and Young (1989), Weingast, Shepsle, and Johnson (1981), and Downs (1957) explore the connection between voters' ignorance and politicians' ability to act against the public interest.
5. See especially Wittman (1995, 1989), and Stigler (1986).
6. For economists and cognitive psychologists on information processing, see Sheffrin (1996), Kahneman, Slovic, and Tversky (1982), and Nisbett and Ross (1980). The main difference between the two disciplines is that cognitive psychologists are much more likely than economists to conclude that people's best information processing is not very good.
7. For interesting experimental evidence of this, see Tetlock (2003).
8. See e.g. Applebaum (2003), Courtois et al. (1999), Becker (1996), Payne (1995), Drèze and Sen (1990), and Conquest (1986).
9. For a wide-ranging survey of critiques of democracy, see Dahl (1989).
10. Eigen and Siegel (1993: 109).
11. See e.g. MacEwan (1999), Soros (1998), Kuttner (1997, 1991, 1984), and Greider (1997, 1992).
12. See e.g. Caplan (2002a), Alston, Kearl, and Vaughn (1992), Blinder (1987), and Schultze (1977).

CHAPTER 1: BEYOND THE MIRACLE OF AGGREGATION

1. Mencken (1995: 375).
2. Olson (1971) and Downs (1957) elegantly explain why ignorant voters are acting in the selfishly optimal way. On voters' low probability of decisiveness, see Edlin, Gelman, and Kaplan (forthcoming), Gelman, Katz, and Bafumi (2004), Fedderson (2004), Mulligan and Hunter (2003), Gelman, King, and Boscardin (1998), and Meehl (1977).
3. Kuttner (1996: xi).
4. See e.g. Kelman (1988), and Rhoads (1985).

5. These terms are near-synonyms, though they carry slightly different connotations. Economists in the tradition of James Buchanan and Gordon Tullock prefer the label *public choice*. Economists less attached to this tradition substitute *political economy* or *positive political economy. Rational choice theory* is more popular among political scientists (Green and Shapiro 1994).

6. See Quirk (1990, 1988).

7. Surowiecki (2004: 11).

8. On random versus systematic error, see e.g. Surowiecki (2004), Austen-Smith and Banks (1996), Wittman (1995, 1989), Page and Shapiro (1993, 1992), Levy (1989), and Muth (1961).

9. For an insightful discussion, see Hoffman (1998).

10. Page and Shapiro (1993: 41).

11. Converse (1990: 383).

12. Brainy Quote (2005b).

13. Surowiecki (2004).

14. Surowiecki (2004: xi–xiii, 3–4, 7–11, 11–15, 17–22).

15. Page and Shapiro (1993: 41).

16. For good overviews, see Somin (2004, 2000, 1999, 1998), Delli Carpini and Keeter (1996), Dye and Zeigler (1996), Bennett (1996), Smith (1989), Neuman (1986), and Converse (1964).

17. Delli Carpini and Keeter (1996: 117).

18. Dye and Zeigler (1992: 206).

19. Delli Carpini and Keeter (1996: 116–22; 89–92).

20. Lecky (1981: 22).

21. For important exceptions, see Althaus (2003, 1998, 1996), Bartels (2004, 1996), Gilens (2001), Wolfers (2001), and Delli Carpini and Keeter (1996).

22. For good overviews, see Rabin (1998) Thaler (1992), Quattrone and Tversky (1988, 1984), Simon (1985), Kahneman, Slovic, and Tversky (1982), and Nisbett and Ross (1980).

23. See e.g. Smith (2003, 1991), Cosmides and Tooby (1996), Barkow, Cosmides, and Tooby (1992), and Cosmides (1989).

24. For my earlier research on this point, see Caplan (2002a, 2002b, 2001d).

25. For simplicity, assume symmetric voter preferences so that the median preference is also the most efficient outcome (Cooter 2000: 32–35).

26. For more examples, see Sowell (2004a, 2004b).

27. See e.g. Krugman (1998) and Siebert (1997).

28. McCloskey (1985: 5).

29. See e.g. Sheffrin (1996).

30. Newcomb (1893: 375).

31. Smith (1981: 488–89).

32. Smith (1981: 493).

33. Smith (1981: 796).

34. Bastiat (1964a: 123).

35. Knight (1960: 19).

36. See e.g. Drazen (2000), Persson and Tabellini (2000), and Rodrik (1996). For an important recent exception, see Romer (2003).

37. Stigler (1986: 309). Earlier in his career, however, Stigler seemed to hold this "singularly obfuscatory" view (Stigler 1959).

38. Skousen (1997: 150).

39. Krugman (1996: 5).

40. For further discussion, see Caplan (2003b).

41. Shermer (2002: 82).

42. Economists who have made this point include Caplan (2001a), Akerlof (1989), and Akerlof and Dickens (1982).

43. Rand (1957: 944).

44. Locke (1977: 570; emphasis added).

45. Locke (1977: 571).

46. Locke (1977: 571).

47. Nietzsche (1954: 635).

48. Le Bon (1960: 73).

49. Hoffer (1951: 26).

50. One fact that makes both religious and political believers less touchy is that many only loosely understand their own doctrines (Converse 1964).

51. For classic treatments of totalitarianism, see Arendt (1973), and Friedrich and Brzezinski (1965).

52. Hoffer (1951: 27).

53. Crossman (1949: 203).

54. Orwell (1983).

55. Hoffer usefully distinguishes between the revolutionary or "active" and institution-building or "consolidation" stages in the life cycle of mass movements. The extreme irrationality of the early phase decays into a more dilute irrationality in the later phase. "The conservatism of a religion—its orthodoxy—is the inert coagulum of a once highly reactive sap" (Hoffer 1951: 14).

56. Shermer (2002) discusses the leading examples.

57. Bastiat (1964a: 84).

58. See Spence (1977) for a formal analysis.

59. Akerlof (1989) is, to the best of my knowledge, the first economist to clearly make this point.

60. Andrews (1993: 229).

61. For overviews of the empirical evidence on the self-interested voter hypothesis, see Mansbridge (1990), Sears and Funk (1990), Citrin and Green (1990), and Sears et al. (1980). On income and party identification, see Gelman et al. (2005), Luttbeg and Martinez (1990), and Kamieniecki (1985). On age and policy preferences, see Ponza et al. (1988). On gender and public opinion about abortion, see Shapiro and Mahajan (1986).

62. Blinder (1987: 89).

63. Le Bon (1960: 110).

64. See e.g. Jacobs and Shapiro (2000) and Bender and Lott (1996).

65. *Merriam-Webster's Collegiate Dictionary* (2003: 330).

66. See Fremling and Lott (1996, 1989).

67. For analysis of, and evidence on, elections as imperfect disciplinary devices, see Matsusaka (2005), Persson and Tabellini (2004, 2000), Gerber and

Lewis (2004), Besley and Case (2003), Persson (2002), Besley and Coate (2000), and Levitt (1996).

68. Admittedly, it is possible that voters are indifferent over a vast range of policies, giving politicians an enormous degree of slack. For this point I am indebted to Ilya Somin.

69. Sutter (2006) is an excellent economic critique of popular misconceptions about the media. For a standard rational choice analysis of the informational role of the media, see Wittman (2005b); for a more skeptical view, see Mullainathan and Shleifer (2005).

70. Abramson, Aldrich, and Rohde (2002: 131).

CHAPTER 2: SYSTEMATICALLY BIASED BELIEFS ABOUT ECONOMICS

1. Le Bon (1960: 114).
2. Becker (1976b: 246).
3. For example, Austen-Smith (1991) "outs" Magee et al. (1989).
4. Coate and Morris (1995: 1212).
5. Rodrik (1996: 38).
6. See e.g. Kruger and Dunning (1999), Camerer (1995), Taylor (1989), Hogarth and Reder (1987), Gigerenzer and Murray (1987), Kahneman, Slovic, and Tversky (1982), Tversky and Kahneman (1982a), Lichtenstein, Fischhoff, and Phillips (1982), and Nisbett and Ross (1980).
7. On overestimation of vivid, memorable events, see Tversky and Kahneman (1982b) and Slovic, Fischhoff, and Lichtenstein (1980). On people's tendency to overestimate themselves, see Kruger and Dunning (1999), and Gilovich (1991).
8. See e.g. Sunstein (2000), Rabin (1998), Babcock and Loewenstein (1997), and Thaler (1992).
9. See Harrison and List (2004) and List (2003).
10. Thus, I am more impressed by the fact that reverse mortgages are unpopular in the real world than I am by experiments showing that "mental budgeting" affects behavior in the lab (Thaler 1992: 107–21).
11. See e.g. Smith (2003), Goldstein and Gigerenzer (2002), Gigerenzer (2001, 2000), and Cosmides and Tooby (1996).
12. See Bartels (2004, 1996), Althaus (2003, 1998, 1996), Gilens (2001), Duch, Palmer, and Anderson (2000), Kuklinski et al. (2000), Krause and Granato (1998), Krause (1997), and Delli Carpini and Keeter (1996). For a somewhat contrary result, see Lau and Redlawsk (1997).
13. Kaiser Family Foundation and Harvard University School of Public Health (1995).
14. Economics and Statistics Administration (2004).
15. Leading examples of the enlightened preference approach include Bartels (2004, 1996), Althaus (2003, 1998, 1996), Gilens (2001), and Delli Carpini and Keeter (1996).
16. Althaus (2003: 60).
17. Althaus (2003: 128–30).
18. Althaus (2003: 130).
19. Althaus (2003: 131, 111).

20. Althaus (2003: 115, 109).

21. Krugman (1996: 118). Krugman is specifically referring to misconceptions about international trade.

22. On modern economists' indifference to history of thought, see Blaug (2001).

23. Of course, this typology is not exhaustive, and some beliefs could sit in more than one category.

24. Herman (1997: 48).

25. See e.g. Sowell (2004a, 2004b), Caplan and Cowen (2004), Mueller (1999), Klein (1999), Shleifer (1998), Cowen (1998), Mises (1998, 1996, 1966), Shiller (1997), Sachs and Warner (1995), Blinder (1987), Henderson (1986), Rhoads (1985), Smith (1981), and Schultze (1977).

26. Schumpeter (1950: 144).

27. Schumpeter (1954: 234).

28. Rubin (2003) elaborates on this theme.

29. Schultze (1977: 18, 47).

30. Mises (1981a: 325).

31. Mises (1966: 854).

32. This is roughly equivalent to what Thomas Sowell (2004a: 4–13) calls "one-stage thinking"—considering only the immediate and obvious effects of a policy, and ignoring the indirect and less obvious effects.

33. Smith (1981: 454).

34. Smith (1981: 456).

35. On usury, see Houkes (2004), and Böhm-Bawerk (1959).

36. Böhm-Bawerk (1959: 10).

37. Kuran (2004: 39).

38. Kuran (2004: 57).

39. Blinder (1987: 136–59).

40. Blinder (1987: 137); for the original study, see Kelman (1981: 98–99).

41. See e.g. Knight (1960: 98–99).

42. See e.g. Scherer and Ross (1990: 208–20).

43. Bastiat (1964b: 19–20).

44. See e.g. Stiglitz (2002b).

45. "We rarely hear, it has been said, of the combinations of masters, though frequently of those of workmen. But whoever imagines, upon this account, that masters rarely combine, is as ignorant of the world as of the subject. Masters are always and everywhere in a sort of tacit, but constant and uniform combination, not to raise the wages of labour above their actual rate. To violate this combination is everywhere a most unpopular action, and a sort of reproach to a master among his neighbours and equals" (Smith 1981: 84).

46. See e.g. Krugman (1998). This is not to deny, of course, that their low productivity may be largely due to poor domestic policies, not to mention the First World's limits on immigration.

47. Mueller (1999: 5).

48. Boublil, Kretzmer, and Natel (1990: 36).

49. Mueller (1999).

50. Krugman (2003); Stiglitz (2003).

51. Greider (1992: 395).

52. See e.g. Hainmueller and Hiscox (forthcoming, 2005a), Poole (2004), Bhagwati (2002), Roberts (2001), Krugman (1996), Irwin (1996), Phelps (1993), Blinder (1987), Henderson (1986), and Taussig (1905).

53. Newcomb (1893: 379).

54. Blinder (1987: 111).

55. Smith (1981: 457).

56. Newcomb (1893: 377).

57. See Irwin (1996).

58. Krugman (1996: 124–25).

59. Landsburg (1993: 197). Landsburg (1993: 197) attributes this argument to David Friedman. Krugman (1996: 119–20) attributes a similar argument to James Ingram's (1983) textbook.

60. See e.g. Bhagwati (2002) and Irwin (1996).

61. Smith (1981: 429).

62. Antidumping laws are another interesting expression of our suspicion of foreigners. It is much easier to prosecute foreign firms for "selling below cost" ("dumping") than it is to prosecute domestic firms for the same offense. As Joseph Stiglitz (2002a: 173–174) explains: "The U.S. estimates costs of production under a peculiar methodology, which, if applied to American firms, would probably conclude that most American firms were dumping as well."

63. See William J. Clinton Foundation (2005).

64. GSS variable identifiers JAPAN, ENGLAND, and CANADA.

65. U.S. Census Bureau (2005a, 2005b). I would like to thank Ilya Somin for alerting me to this fact.

66. Bureau of Economic Analysis (2005).

67. Krugman (1996: 84).

68. Bastiat (1964a: 26–27).

69. See e.g. Cox and Alm (1999), Krugman (1998), Davis, Haltiwanger, and Schuh (1996), Henderson (1986), and Bastiat (1964a, 1964b).

70. Blinder (1987: 17).

71. Bastiat (1964a: 20).

72. Bastiat (1964a: 20).

73. Newcomb (1893: 380).

74. Schlesinger (1957: 462).

75. Cox and Alm (1999: 116). Note the similarity to Schumpeter's (1950: 81–86) notion of "creative destruction."

76. Cox and Alm (1999: 128).

77. Blinder (1987: 124). Blinder is referring to workers displaced by international competition, but his arguments easily extend to workers displaced by technological progress.

78. Cox and Alm (1999: 133).

79. Cox and Alm (1999: 111).

80. Bastiat (1964a: 10).

81. Bastiat (1964a: 10).

82. Herman (1997: 173).

83. See e.g. Kling (2004), Easterbrook (2003), Lomborg (2001), Cox and Alm (1999), Mueller (1999), Whitman (1998), Simon (1996, 1995b), Samuelson (1995), and McCloskey (1993).

84. Rae (1965: 343).

85. See e.g. Krugman (1998, 1996) and Blinder (1987).

86. See e.g. Johnson (2000), Fogel (1999), and Lucas (1993).

87. Herman (1997: 13).

88. Lovejoy and Boas (1965: 7). In Lovejoy and Boas's historical survey, it is striking that the *reasons* for pessimism have varied much more than pessimism itself. While modern pessimists insist that material prosperity is slipping through our fingers, most of the pessimists of antiquity focused not on the impermanence of riches, but its negative effect on virtue and community.

89. Smith (1981: 343; emphasis added).

90. Smith (1981: 343–44; emphasis added).

91. Hume (1987: 464).

92. Hume (1987: 73–74).

93. See e.g. Mises (1981b).

94. Herman (1997: 65).

95. Spencer (1981: 3).

96. Spencer (1981: 6).

97. Herman (1997: 297, 1).

98. For some attempts to answer this question, see Easterbrook (2003), Cox and Alm (1999), Mueller (1999), and Whitman (1998).

99. See e.g. Pew Research Center (1997).

100. Easterbrook (2003: 119).

101. Cox and Alm (1999: 200, 44).

102. Cox and Alm (1999: 197).

103. Krugman (1996: 48).

104. See Krueger and Solow (2001).

105. Krugman (1996: 214).

106. See e.g. Starke (2004). It is also widely believed that life is getting worse because of declining cultural/social quality. For a critique of cultural/social pessimism, see Whitman (1998).

107. Erlich (1968).

108. Simon (1996, 1995a).

109. Simon (1995a: 642–43).

110. See e.g. Dasgupta et al. (2002), Freeman (2002), Lomborg (2001), and Johnson (2000). Even Cole (2003), a critical review of Lomborg, emphasizes exceptions to environmental optimism, but accepts the reality of many positive trends.

111. Kremer (1993). Jared Diamond's (1997) prize-winning *Guns, Germs, and Steel* links population and innovation in essentially the same way, albeit with little fanfare.

112. There is a distinction between (*a*) pessimists who believe that scary scenarios are likely, and (*b*) pessimists who believe that scary scenarios are unlikely, but still worth worrying about. Few economists, myself included, have any strong objection to the second sort of pessimism. It would be foolish to dismiss concerns about nuclear proliferation on the grounds that nuclear weapons will probably never be used. I would like to thank Andrew Gelman for pointing out this distinction.

113. Kirchgässner (2005).

CHAPTER 3: EVIDENCE FROM THE SURVEY OF AMERICANS
AND ECONOMISTS ON THE ECONOMY

1. Krugman (1996: 78).

2. Some of the more important: Blinder and Krueger (2004), Chicago Council on Foreign Relations (2004), Fuller and Geide-Stevenson (2003), Chicago Council on Foreign Relations and the German Marshall Fund of the United States (2002a, 2002b, 2002c), Walstad and Rebeck (2002), Scheve and Slaughter (2001a, 2001b), Fuchs, Krueger, and Poterba (1998), Walstad (1997, 1992), Frey and Eichenberger (1993, 1992), Walstad and Larsen (1992), Alston, Kearl, and Vaughn (1992), Ricketts and Shoesmith (1990), Conover, Feldman, and Knight (1987), Conover and Feldman (1986), Rhoads (1985), Pommerehne et al. (1984), McClosky and Zaller (1984), Chong, McClosky, and Zaller (1983), and Kearl et al. (1979).

3. See Fuller and Geide-Stevenson (2003), Alston, Kearl, and Vaughn (1992), and Kearl et al. (1979).

4. Chicago Council on Foreign Relations and the German Marshall Fund of the United States (2002a).

5. Question 765.

6. Question 575/8. Chicago Council on Foreign Relations and the German Marshall Fund of the United States (2002b) heavily emphasizes the Worldviews 2002 finding that large majorities embrace free trade if combined with assistance for displaced workers. On question 770, respondents' three choices are free trade with worker assistance, free trade without worker assistance, and "I do not favor free trade." Almost 75 percent select the first answer. In my judgment, this is in large part a question-wording effect. The binary choice between "free trade" and "no free trade" probably masks the public's preference for an intermediate policy. Furthermore, the alternative to free trade should have been more positively labeled as e.g. "fair trade." Finally, the last option should have been split into "no free trade + worker assistance" and "no free trade + no worker assistance." It is also noteworthy that Americans overwhelmingly (93%) want trade agreements to regulate minimum working conditions—a deal-breaker for most low-income nations (question 775). For evidence of strong question-wording effects in surveys of trade attitudes, see Hiscox (2006).

7. Kearl et al. (1979: 30).

8. GSS variable identifier PRICECON (General Social Survey 1998).

9. Washington Post, Kaiser Family Foundation, and Harvard University Survey Project (1996).

10. For more information on the SAEE, see Blendon et al. (1997).

11. The total number of questions actually exceeds 37. Some questions were not presented to both groups of respondents, precluding comparison. I omit handful of other questions due to redundancy.

12. Kahneman and Tversky (1982: 493).

13. Greider (1992: 36).

14. Andrews (1993: 262).

15. Kelman (1981: 7).

16. Kelman (1981: 7).

17. See e.g. Dahl and Ransom (1999) and Babcock and Loewenstein (1997).

18. Marx (1965: 609).

19. Mises (1962: 86).

20. Brossard and Pearlstein (1996: A6).

21. See e.g. Soros (1998), Kuttner (1997, 1991, 1984), Greider (1997, 1992), and Lazonick (1991).

22. Kuttner (1997: 3–4).

23. For further discussion, see this chapter's technical appendix.

24. Expert bias is not the *only* reason why adding statistical controls might make belief gaps disappear. If a correct understanding of the economy allows people to prosper, rich noneconomists would agree with professional economists in the absence of self-serving bias. Or suppose that understanding economics *causes* people to become more conservative. Conservatives would tend to agree with economists in the absence of ideological bias.

25. This is a question where my knee-jerk reaction is to side with the public. But my implicit assumption is that lower taxes would be balanced by privatization and cuts in popular programs like Social Security and Medicare. If cuts are limited to "waste" and unpopular programs, my fellow economists are probably right.

26. See e.g. Easterly (2001).

27. Kaiser Family Foundation and Harvard University School of Public Health (1995).

28. On immigration and population growth, see Borjas (1994: 1668); on immigration and wages, see Borjas (1994: 1695–1700); on immigration's net effect on the budget, see Lee and Miller (2000) and Simon (1999: 112–52, 313–21).

29. See e.g. Gruber (2005: 509–10).

30. Given how rarely economists and the public agree, I suspect that their meeting of the minds is a sign that economists have failed to free themselves from popular prejudice. Even if education had significant externalities, why are existing subsidies too small to fully correct for them? More fundamentally, the benefits of education for worker productivity seem almost entirely internalized—you acquire more skills, you earn more money. So there is not much of an efficiency case for *any* subsidies, much less *higher* subsidies. In fact, decades of experience in the education industry have convinced me that education is often mere jumping through hoops—or in technical terms, "signaling" (Weiss 1995). Subsidizing hoop-jumping is wasteful, for it just increases the number of hoops you are expected to jump.

31. Kaiser Family Foundation and Harvard University School of Public Health (1995).

32. Equal Employment Opportunity Commission (2005).

33. Another possibility is that economists read this as a question about "shirking," or, in broader terms, "social capital." The more workers cheat their boss when he looks the other way, the more resources have to be wasted on monitoring. A strong work ethic—an internalized norm against shirking—would therefore have a positive externality.

34. This is another question where I find myself at odds with the professional consensus. There is a plausible economic case for regulation of third-party effects like air pollution. But a great deal of regulation is designed merely to force consumers to buy more safety, health, and other politically correct products than they want. Safety is not free. A worker could always offer to work for a reduced salary in exchange for more on-the-job safety. Safety regulations therefore make workers safer than they want to be. Given standard estimates of the cost of regulation in the hundreds of billions of dollars annually (Office of Management and Budget 1997), and the theoretical conclusion that much of this regulation is not worth its cost, I deem excessive regulation a major problem indeed.

35. For public opinion about the minimum wage, see Gallup Organization (2005); for farm subsidies, see PIPA–Knowledge Networks Poll (2004); for drug testing, see Kaiser Family Foundation (2005).

36. GSS variable identifier SETPRICE.

37. See e.g. Rowley, Tollison, and Tullock (1988), and Weiss and Klass (1986).

38. Washington Post, Kaiser Family Foundation, and Harvard University Survey Project (1996: 4); Walstad and Larsen (1992: 48).

39. Economists would be much more open to the possibility that executive compensation is insufficiently tied to performance. High pay is not a problem, but indiscriminately high pay is.

40. See e.g. Krugman (1998, 1996) and Blinder (1987).

41. See e.g. Cox and Alm (1999).

42. See e.g. Krugman (1998: 62–65), and Kaiser Family Foundation and Harvard University School of Public Health (1995).

43. See Kull (2000) on the public's lukewarm support for trade agreements, and Bhagwati (2002) on economists' support for unilateral free trade.

44. Schumpeter (1950: 145).

45. In my view, economists who predict job *gains* go too far. Trade liberalization increases foreign demand but curtails domestic demand. So there is little reason to expect a short-term employment benefit. A long-term effect is even less likely; macroeconomists doubt that demand shocks have long-run effects on employment (Blinder 1987: 106–7). The theoretically sound response is to focus on living standards, not employment.

46. Note: The response "both" was coded as a 1; "neither" was coded as a 0.

47. See e.g. Blinder (1987).

48. See e.g. Cox and Alm (1999: 139–56).

49. See Gottschalk (1997).

50. See e.g. Cox and Alm (1999: 17–22).

51. See e.g. Fogel (1999), Lucas (1993), and Lebergott (1993).

52. This result further undermines semantic views of lay-expert disagreement. If economists and noneconomists defined "good economic performance" differently, you would expect them to disagree about the *current* state of the economy, not just the past and the future.

53. Kaiser Family Foundation and Harvard University School of Public Health (1995). Similar results appear in the Survey of Americans' Knowledge

and Attitudes about Entitlements (Washington Post, Kaiser Family Foundation, and Harvard University Survey Project, 1997).

54. Anticipating the ambiguity of the "welfare" category, Kaiser asked respondents which programs they define as "welfare." A majority of Americans so categorize Medicaid, food stamps, AFDC, child nutrition programs, and public housing assistance. In the 1993 federal budget, these items add up to 10.2% (Kaiser Family Foundation and Harvard University School of Public Health 1995).

55. A natural defense of the public's good sense is to appeal to definitional ambiguity. In fact, the numbers in table 3.1's last column are deliberately slanted in the public's *favor*. Table 3.1 defines foreign aid broadly to include all spending on international affairs; a narrower definition would pull the budget share down from 1.2% to a mere .4%. Similarly, the measure of health spending omits Medicaid (which is already counted under the "welfare" heading). If you counted Medicaid, health spending would rise to 16.3% of the budget (Office of Management and Budget 2005: 56, 308).

56. Tullock (1987: 28).

57. Blendon et al. (1997: 112–13).

58. Admittedly, the procedure for selecting questions was informal, relying on the judgment calls of the authors. If they wanted to boost their credibility, they could have done a two-stage survey, one to select questions, another to collect answers. But this doubt is hardly strong enough to require us to suspend judgment until someone performs the exercise.

59. Cerf and Navasky (1998).

60. See Klein and Stern (forthcoming).

61. Perhaps the myth of ideological bias originated because people who embrace one extremely right-wing viewpoint usually embrace a lot of them. So when economists summarily dismiss popular complaints about markets, people infer that they subscribe to the whole conservative package.

62. Caplan (2001d: 417).

63. Delli Carpini, and Keeter (1996).

64. Kraus, Malmfors, and Slovic (1992).

65. Caplan (2002a, 2001d).

66. Strictly speaking, our hypothetical student would also be older after completing his Ph.D., so this change in age would have to be factored into the results.

CHAPTER 4: CLASSICAL PUBLIC CHOICE AND THE
FAILURE OF RATIONAL IGNORANCE

1. Edgerton (1992: 197).

2. Tullock (1967: 102). I would like to thank Charles Rowley for guiding me to this reference.

3. Downs (1957: 259).

4. For the classic discussion, see Stigler (1961).

5. See e.g. Edlin, Gelman, and Kaplan (forthcoming), Gelman, Katz, and Bafumi (2004), Fedderson (2004), Mulligan and Hunter (2003), Gelman, King, and Boscardin (1998), Brennan and Lomasky (1993, 1989), and Meehl (1977).

6. See e.g. Stiglitz (2002b).

7. See e.g. Somin (2004), and Bennett (1996).

8. For overviews, see Somin (2004, 2000, 1999, 1998), Delli Carpini and Keeter (1996), Dye and Zeigler (1996), Bennett (1996), Smith (1989), and Neuman (1986).

9. Delli Carpini and Keeter (1996: 117).

10. Dye and Zeigler (1992: 206). Actually, matters are worse: People who can state their senators' name presumably know the answer, but *random guessing* about political parties yields two correct answers a quarter of the time.

11. Delli Carpini and Keeter (1996: 70–71).

12. Delli Carpini and Keeter (1996: 101).

13. See Olson (1982).

14. For analyses of political failure that rely on rational ignorance, see e.g. Coursey and Roberts (1991), Magee, Brock, and Young (1989), Rowley, Tollison, and Tullock (1988), Blinder (1987), Rhoads (1985), Buchanan and Tollison (1984), Weingast, Shepsle, and Johnson (1981), and Olson (1971).

15. Olson (1971: 29).

16. See e.g. Persson and Tabellini (2000), Drazen (2000), Rodrik (1996), Wittman (1995, 1989), Coate and Morris (1999, 1995), Austen-Smith (1991), and Coursey and Roberts (1991).

17. Downs (1957: 10).

18. See e.g. Wittman (2005c).

19. See e.g. Sheffrin (1996), Pesaran (1987), Maddock and Carter (1982), Lucas (1973), and Muth (1961).

20. Downs (1957: 5).

21. Downs (1957: 4).

22. On economists' diverse interpretations of rationality, see Cowen (2001). On Bayesianism, see e.g. Hanson (2002), Howson and Urbach (1989), and Aumann (1976). For experimental evidence against Bayesianism, see Rabin (1998) and Kahneman and Tversky (1982).

23. See Cowen and Hanson (forthcoming), Cowen (2003), and Mele (2001, 1987).

24. The second-most-popular response is to appeal to the distinction between individual and social irrationality. Defection in the Prisoners' Dilemma is said to be "socially" irrational because all players could be better off if they cooperated, but still individually rational because each player is doing as well as possible given the others' behavior.

25. Errors driven by emotional commitments are also known as "motivational biases." An enormous literature on "cognitive biases" further shows that ignorance is not the sole cause of error even on questions where people *lack* emotional precommitments (Gilovich 1991; Nisbett and Ross 1980). I focus on motivational biases because they are both more intuitive and more clearly politically relevant.

26. McCloskey (1985: 177).

27. Crossman (1949: 23).

28. Chambers (1952: 196).

29. For a survey of experimental evidence on evolution, see Bell (1997).

30. Lott (2000).

31. Aristotle (1941: 689).

32. See e.g. Murphy and Shleifer (2004), Mele (2004, 2001, 1987), Tetlock (2003), Redlawsk (2002), Shermer (2002), Taylor (1989), Locke (1977), Hoffer (1951), and Mosca (1939).

33. See e.g. MacEwan (1999), Kuttner (1997, 1996), Hauptmann (1996), and Greider (1992).

34. See e.g. Surowiecki (2004), Wittman (1995), and Page and Shapiro (1992).

35. See e.g. Sutter (2006), Frank (2004), Herman and Chomsky (2002), Murray, Schwartz, and Lichter (2001), Lichter and Rothman (1999), Simon (1996), Kuran (1995), Page and Shapiro (1992), and Geddes and Zaller (1989).

36. Wittman (1995: 15).

37. Johnson (1991: 550).

38. See e.g. Eichenberger and Serna (1996), Wittman (1995, 1989), and Gilovich (1991).

39. See e.g. Posner (2002) and Becker (1968).

40. Becker (1976a: 54).

41. On asymmetric information, see Stiglitz (2003, 2002b) and Akerlof (1970).

42. See e.g. Banks and Weingast (1992), Crew and Twight (1990), Magee, Brock, and Young (1989), and Rowley, Tollison, and Tullock (1988).

43. Akerlof (1970).

44. Some object to the analogy between used cars and government programs because "you do not *have* to buy a car, but you always get a leader." The point, however, if that voters can respond to asymmetric information by saying no to candidates who advocate programs of dubious value.

45. See Caplan (2001c), Wittman (1995: 107), and Breton and Wintrobe (1982).

46. For further discussion, see Lee (1989).

47. On cognitive shortcuts, see e.g. Somin (2004), Cutler (2002), Kuklinski et al. (2001), Lau and Redlawsk (2001), Lupia and McCubbins (1998), Hoffman (1998), Lupia (1994), and Popkin (1991).

48. Lupia and McCubbins (1998: 7).

49. Lupia and McCubbins (1998: 37).

50. See e.g. Nadeau and Lewis-Beck (2001), Lanoue (1994), Lockerbie (1991), and Fiorina (1981).

51. See Achen and Bartels (2004), Somin (2004), and Rudolph (2003).

52. However, some empirical studies also find that shortcuts can lead unsophisticated voters to make *worse* decisions (Lau and Redlawsk 2001).

53. Althaus (2003: 143).

54. Wittman (1989: 1421).

55. For critiques of Wittman, see Lott (1997), Rowley (1997), and Boudreaux (1996), as well as the exchange in *Econ Journal Watch* (Caplan 2005a, 2005b; Wittman 2005c, 2005d).

56. In seminars, I have seen professional game theorists struggle to match what Wittman called the *lowest* level of cognitive ability voters could possibly have!

57. On monopoly power in politics, see e.g. Fiorina (1989), Anderson and Tollison (1988), Brennan and Buchanan (1980), Crain (1977), and Tullock (1965). Posner (2002: 295–347) discusses many reasons to be skeptical about the dangers of "monopoly."

58. Wittman (1995: 25).

59. See e.g. Holcombe (1985) and Shepsle and Weingast (1981).

60. Wittman (1995, 1989).

61. See e.g. Matsusaka (2005), Persson and Tabellini (2004, 2000), Gerber and Lewis (2004), Besley and Case (2003), Persson (2002), Besley and Coate (2000), and Levitt (1996).

62. On direct versus indirect democracy, see Matsusaka (2005). On senators' disagreement, see Levitt (1996). On the effects of open primaries, redistricting, campaign finance rules, and party competition, see Besley and Case (2003).

63. Besley and Case (2003: 68).

64. Besley and Case (2003: 40).

65. See e.g. Alesina and Rosenthal (1994).

66. Wittman (1995: 10–15).

67. For further discussion, see Caplan (2003b, 2001a, 2001c).

68. For an excellent discussion of people's failure to fully adjust for sources' reliability, see Gilovich (1991).

69. Thaler (1992: 198).

CHAPTER 5: RATIONAL IRRATIONALITY

1. Descartes (1999: 6).

2. Wittman (1995: 16–17) argues that irrational minorities fare better under democracy than in markets. Markets let an irrational fringe pursue its self-destructive preferences, but democracy protects the minority from itself. "False political advertising may fool a minority, yet it will have no harmful effect since votes for the minority will not be translated into political power. In contrast, a business does not have to persuade a majority of consumers, only a few, to have any sales." In other words, democracy works better than markets if the median voter is more rational than the mean voter. The opposite holds if—as chapter 3 suggests—the median voter is *less* rational than the mean voter.

3. See Austen-Smith (1991) and Coursey and Roberts (1991).

4. Carroll (1999: 184).

5. Dasgupta and Stiglitz (1988: 570).

6. See e.g. Kuran (1995) and Gilovich (1991).

7. See e.g. Caplan (2001a) and Ainslie (1992).

8. Le Bon (1960: 109).

9. Admittedly, social pressure is also usually at work; coreligionists—who usually include family—rarely approve of those who abandon their religion (Iannaccone 1998). Still, many people cling to their religious views despite social pressure to change them, suggesting that they value the beliefs directly.

10. Mosca (1939: 176–77).

11. Mosca (1939: 175).

12. Helliwell (2003); Donovan and Halpern (2002).

13. Jost et al. (2003: 340).

14. See Stigler and Becker (1977) and Friedman (1953). For a critique, see Caplan (2003a).

15. For a more detailed discussion, see Caplan (2001e, 1999).

16. See e.g. Bertrand and Mullainathan (2001), Kahneman, Ritov, and Schkade (1999), Boulier and Goldfarb (1998), Harrison and Kriström (1995), and LaPiere (1934).

17. See e.g. Vrij (2000) and Frank (1988).

18. Shermer (2002: 82).

19. Samuelson (1946: 187).

20. Chambers (1952: 444).

21. Chambers (1952: 15).

22. Crossman (1949: 23, 56, 162).

23. Caplan (forthcoming a).

24. Nasar (1998: 335).

25. Nasar (1998: 295).

26. Böhm-Bawerk (1959: 320; emphasis added).

27. Mosca (1939: 166).

28. Knox (1967).

29. Thus, social pressure can make the cost of irrationality *negative*. A negative cost is also possible if false beliefs (e.g. overconfidence or overoptimism) increase your abilities by, for example, reducing stress (Compte and Postlewait 2004; Caplan 2000; Taylor 1989). For a rational model of overconfidence, see Van Den Steen (2004).

30. See e.g. Landsburg (1993) and Olson (1971).

31. Of course, the disutility of pollution need not be linear.

32. Notice that the divergence of the private and social costs of false beliefs is conceptually distinct from a more familiar pitfall of group decision-making: conflicting preferences. The mechanism I describe works even if people want the same outcome.

33. Schumpeter (1950: 262).

34. For important exceptions, see Rabin (1998), Thaler (1992), Akerlof (1989), and Akerlof and Dickens (1984, 1982).

35. See e.g. Glaeser (2003) and Caplan (2001a, 2000).

36. Caplan (2000) coined this term, but Mele (2004) and Tirole (2002) have recently used the same label somewhat differently. Mele (2004) in part argues, consistently with my thesis, that it would not be rational to make large material sacrifices in order to become fully rational. Tirole (2002) shows that given

imperfect self-knowledge, imperfect willpower, and/or imperfect recall, apparent irrationality can make people more successful. Another approach that is superficially similar to mine is Schelling (1980), which emphasizes that it may be rational to have a *reputation* for irrationality in order to improve your bargaining power.

37. Rational irrationality is interestingly compatible with Lupia and McCubbins's (1998: 23) equation of rationality with "all human behavior that is directed toward the pursuit of pleasure and the avoidance of pain." On my account, though, voters focus on the pleasure and pain of accepting different beliefs, not the pleasure and pain of living under different policies. If you want more pleasure and less pain, it is far more effective to direct your behavior to something you can control—your beliefs—instead of something you cannot control—policy.

38. Note that to draw a horizontal price line, we must assume that the material cost of irrationality is proportional to the quantity consumed.

39. Indeed, under rarely if ever observed circumstances, demand curves can slope upwards.

40. Still, one would still expect that—like other elasticities—the responsiveness of rationality to incentives would be greater in the long run than the short run.

41. Edgerton (1992: 196).

42. See e.g. Mele (2001, 1987).

43. Orwell (1983: 177).

44. Noss (1974: 114–16).

45. Mosca (1939: 181–82).

46. Caplan (forthcoming c) elaborates on this point.

47. Edgerton (1992: 137).

48. Edgerton (1992: 137).

49. Holloway (1994: 208, 209, 22).

50. Holloway (1994: 208).

51. Becker (1996).

52. Holloway (1994: 211).

53. Holloway (1994: 140).

54. See e.g. Conquest (1991), Bullock (1991), and Tucker (1990, 1973).

55. Holloway (1994: 211–12).

56. Holloway (1994: 148).

57. Holloway (1994: 148).

58. Holloway (1994: 149, 218).

59. Hanson (1995).

60. Hoelzl and Rustichini (2005).

61. Tocqueville (1969: 442).

62. See e.g. Mulligan and Hunter (2003), Brennan and Lomasky (1993: 54–61), and Meehl (1977). If voters choose people instead of policy, the probability of decisiveness shrinks further. *Even if* an election were freakishly decided by one vote, the winning politician could still break the promises that swung the election in his favor.

63. On the recounts, see Ceaser and Busch (2001).

64. See e.g. Weissberg (2002).

65. Highton (2004); Lott and Kenny (1999); Filer, Kenny, and Morton (1993).

66. Furthermore, in contrast to financial and betting markets, democracy lets people with severe biases continue to participate at no extra charge.

67. Le Bon (1960: 175).

68. Tyler and Weber (1982); Lord, Ross, and Lepper (1979).

69. Orwell (1968: 252).

70. For a more detailed discussion, see Caplan (2000).

71. See Prisching (1995).

72. Schumpeter (1950: 258).

73. Schumpeter (1950: 258–59).

74. Bastiat (1964a: 21).

75. See e.g. Kirchgässner and Pommerehne (1993), Kirchgässner (1992), and Akerlof and Yellen (1985).

76. See e.g. Smith and Walker (1993).

77. We were both on the Andrei Shleifer–organized panel on competition. To illustrate his thesis, Thaler summarized his research (Cronqvist and Thaler 2004) on Swedish social-security privatization. Given a choice, most Swedes switched from the default fund (designed by government employees) to plainly inferior funds (higher management fees, higher risk, and lower returns) offered by the private sector. Government made a better decision than the typical market participant did, despite his strong financial incentive to be rational.

An important problem with this study is that it compares private choice to one of the best-designed government pension programs in the world, instead of comparing private choice to *average* government pension programs.

78. Camerer and Hogarth (1999: 7).

79. Harrison and Rutström (forthcoming).

80. Camerer and Hogarth (1999: 34).

81. Hoelzl and Rustichini (2005).

82. Camerer and Hogarth (1999: 35).

83. Camerer and Hogarth (1999: 10).

84. Harrison and List (2004); List (2003).

85. Camerer and Hogarth (1999: 23).

86. Glucksberg (1962). Another common caveat is that high incentives can reduce performance by "stressing people out." Here again, common sense insists on a short-run/long-run distinction. At a given instant, high incentives may reduce performance by increasing stress. But over a longer horizon, people who foresee a high-incentive/high-stress situation work harder to prepare for the challenge.

87. Einhorn and Hogarth (1987: 63). The experimental findings Einhorn and Hogarth are discussing concern utility theory rather than rational expectations; elsewhere in the same volume Hogarth and Reder (1987: 12) apply this point more generally.

88. Brennan and Lomasky (1993, 1989). For another take on expressive voting, see Schuessler (2000a, 2000b). For an experimental test that contradicts Brennan and Lomasky, see Tyran (2004).

89. See e.g. Sowell (2004b), Landsburg (1997), and Becker (1971).
90. Brennan and Lomasky (1993: 48).
91. Brennan and Lomasky (1993: 25; emphasis added).
92. Brennan and Lomasky (1993: 16).
93. This is not to deny that wishful thinking and indifference *never* co-exist: The same people often simultaneously held that "Clinton did not have sexual relations with Lewinsky" and "I don't care if Clinton had sexual relations with Lewinsky." (Posner 1999)
94. Brennan and Lomasky (1993: 50).
95. Brennan and Lomasky (1993: 51; emphasis added). Brennan and Lomasky go on to admit that in their war example, "the assumption of voter 'rationality' seems particularly strained." But this is a reservation about whether their model of expressive voting model fits the example; it does not question the conceptual distinction between expressive preferences and irrational beliefs.
96. Fleming (1939).
97. Brennan and Lomasky (1993: 35–36).
98. See e.g. Barber (1993) and Mansbridge (1990).

CHAPTER 6: FROM IRRATIONALITY TO POLICY

1. Greider (1992: 16).
2. See e.g. Glaeser (2005).
3. See e.g. Greider (1992).
4. Hitler (1943). The depression clearly increased support for Hitler, but Germany was still one of the richest countries in the world.
5. On the Oedipus/Jocasta paradox, see Searle (1983).
6. Böhm-Bawerk (1959: 10).
7. Wittman (1989: 1402).
8. See e.g. Camerer (1987).
9. Krugman (1998: 18).
10. Krugman (1998: 19).
11. For further discussion, see Caplan (2003b).
12. See Becker (1958) for an early answer to this question.
13. Endowments include not only current and expected possessions, but current and expected marketable skills.
14. If the costs of tax collection on imports were the same or lower than on domestic products, they might want a positive tariff. Still, no one would see reducing imports as a benefit.
15. See Brennan and Lomasky (1993).
16. See e.g. Easterbrook (2003), Lichter and Rothman (1999), Whitman (1998), Keeter (1996), and Simon (1996).
17. One reason to be pessimistic even in this scenario is that there could be different tariff rates for different countries.
18. See e.g. Cooter (2000).
19. See e.g. Meltzer and Richard (1981).

20. To be more precise, they are not selfish in the conventional sense of trying to maximize their wealth or income. My analysis *does* assume that people choose their political beliefs based on psychological benefits to themselves, ignoring the costs to society. Thus, my thesis is that voters are selfish in an unusual but non-tautologous sense of the word. I would like to thank philosopher Michael Huemer for highlighting this ambiguity.

21. See Caplan (2001b).

22. For important exceptions, see Peltzman (1990, 1985, 1984).

23. See e.g. Funk (2000), Miller (1999), Funk and García-Monet (1997), Mutz and Mondak (1997), Holbrook and Garand (1996), Mutz (1993, 1992), Mansbridge (1990), Sears and Funk (1990), Citrin and Green (1990), Sears and Lau (1983), Feldman (1982), Sears et al. (1980), Sears, Hensler, and Speer (1979), and Sears et al. (1978).

24. See e.g. Gelman et al. (2005), Manza and Brooks (1999), Luttbeg and Martinez (1990), and Kamieniecki (1985).

25. Caplan (2001b).

26. There is also a large literature finding that voters care a lot more about the nation's economic success than their own (Funk and García-Monet 1997; Markus 1988; Conover, Feldman, and Knight, 1987; Kinder and Kiewiet 1981, 1979). But some (e.g. Kramer 1983) counter that this is perfectly consistent with self-interested voting because personal economic success, unlike national economic success, has a large random component. (Kinder and Kiewiet [1981: 132] recognized this possibility as well.) This leads voters to *selfishly* prefer candidates who *were* good for the country as a whole. Due to this ambiguity, I focus on voters' preferences for specific policies, where the divergence between personal and national benefits is clearer.

27. See e.g. Huddy, Jones, and Chard (2001), Rhodebeck (1993), Sears and Funk (1990), and Ponza et al. (1988).

28. See e.g. Sears and Huddy (1990), and Shapiro and Mahajan (1986).

29. Sears et al. (1980).

30. See e.g. Blinder and Krueger (2004).

31. Sears and Funk (1990); Lau, Brown, and Sears (1978).

32. See e.g. Wolpert and Gimpel (1998), and Sears and Citrin (1985).

33. Green and Gerken (1989).

34. Does this contradict the self-interest assumption? Only if we interpret "People are selfish" to literally mean that "all people are one hundred percent selfish." The contradiction disappears if we interpret "People are selfish" to mean "Most people are highly selfish" (Caplan 2001b).

35. Another reason to expect more altruism in democracy is that charitable giving suffers from a Prisoners' Dilemma (Wittman 2005a).

36. Brennan and Lomasky (1993); Tullock (1981a, 1971).

37. See e.g. Kliemt (1986).

38. My colleague Tyler Cowen poses an interesting challenge to my view that people vote contrary to their self-interest due to low decisiveness: What about the Academy Awards? Would anything change if a voter were decisive? Yes. If a member of the Academy were decisive, he would be far more likely

to vote for projects where he or his friends have a large financial stake. Questions of artistic merit would fade into the background.

39. For more discussion, see Caplan (2002b). Some proponents of the sociotropic voting model distinguish it from altruistic voting (Kinder and Kiewiet 1981), but most of the political science literature now equates the two. I follow the current usage.

40. Held (1990: 303).

41. For more discussion, see Caplan (2002b).

42. On the breakdown of the Median Voter Theorem, see e.g. McLean (2002) and Riker (1988). On the puzzle of stability, see Tullock (1981b).

43. See e.g. Lakoff (2002), Hinich and Munger (1994), Jennings (1992), and Feldman (1988).

44. See e.g. Levitt (1996), Kalt and Zupan (1990, 1984), and Kau and Rubin (1979).

45. See e.g. the seminal work by Poole and Rosenthal (1997, 1991).

46. On partisan voting, see e.g. Bartels (2000) and Miller (1991).

47. See e.g. Blinder and Krueger (2004) and Caplan (2002a). However, it could definitely be argued that the SAEE shows that economic beliefs are *two*-dimensional. The variables that "make people think like economists" are predictively powerful yet orthogonal to left-right ideology (Caplan 2001d).

48. See Poole and Rosenthal (1997: 86–114).

49. For evidence on multidimensionality, see Besley and Coate (2000) and Koford (1994).

50. For more discussion, see Caplan (2001d).

51. For details on the derivation of figure 6.4, see this chapter's technical appendix.

52. See e.g. Hainmueller and Hiscox (forthcoming, 2005b), Walstad and Rebeck (2002), and Walstad (1997).

53. See e.g. Benjamin and Shapiro (2005) and Frey, Pommerehne, and Gygi (1993). For preliminary work on the effect of intelligence on economic beliefs, see Caplan and Miller (2006).

54. On politics, see Delli Carpini and Keeter (1996: 203–9); on toxicology, see Kraus, Malmfors, and Slovic (1992).

55. For a particularly interesting theory of the gender gap on free trade versus protection, see Burgoon and Hiscox (2006).

56. Verba et al. (1993); Leighley and Nagler (1992a, 1992b).

57. See e.g. Meltzer and Richard (1981).

58. Sears and Funk (1990).

59. Mueller and Stratmann (2003) argue that there is empirical evidence in favor of both hypotheses.

60. Is it legitimate to extrapolate from the economic beliefs of the SAEE's random sample to the economic beliefs of self-selected voters? Yes; controlling for voter registration leaves the results virtually unchanged (Caplan 2002b: 429).

61. Surowiecki (2004).

62. Dee (2004).

63. This plausibly assumes that get-out-the-vote campaigns disproportionately influence less-educated voters. Independents are less knowledgeable than partisans (Delli Carpini and Keeter 1996: 172–73), and a field experiment by Gerber and Green (2000) finds that a modest get-out-the-vote campaign has no effect on the turnout of registered Democrats and Republicans, but increases the turnout of independents by 7%.

64. Delli Carpini and Keeter (1996: 199).

65. Caplan (2003c).

66. See e.g. Olson (1996).

67. For further discussion, see Zaller (2003).

68. See e.g. Achen and Bartels (2004), Francis et al. (1994), MacKuen, Erikson, and Stimson (1992), and Fiorina (1981).

69. There is also no trade-off if voters understand which policies work. In fact, if voters know which policies work, they can distinguish bad results caused by bad luck from bad results caused by bad leaders. This allows voters to severely punish incompetence and venality without scaring off qualified candidates (Wolfers 2001).

70. For further discussion, see Caplan (2003b).

71. GSS variable identifiers POLLEFF16 and POLLEFF17.

72. See e.g. Duch, Palmer, and Anderson (2000).

73. See e.g. Buchanan (1998).

74. Conversely, voters may *fail* to punish leaders for problems within their control. Most obviously, they may reward politicians for short-run benefits, but fail to blame them for long-run costs (Achen and Bartels 2004).

75. Achen and Bartels (2004: 6).

76. For a different view, see Groseclose and McCarty (2001).

77. Caplan (forthcoming b; 2002a).

78. See e.g. Gold et al. (2002), Lichter and Rothman (1999), and Kraus, Malmfors, and Slovic (1992).

79. Kraus, Malmfors, and Slovic (1992).

80. Kraus, Malmfors, and Slovic (1992: 228).

81. Kraus, Malmfors, and Slovic (1992: 220–21).

82. Lichter and Rothman (1999) similarly document that cancer researchers' ideology has little effect on their scientific judgment. Liberal cancer researchers who do not work in the private sector still embrace their profession's contrarian views. "As a group, the experts—whether conservative or liberal, Democratic or Republican—viewed cancer risks along roughly the same lines. Thus, their perspectives on this topic do not appear to be 'contaminated' by either narrow self-interest or broader ideological commitments" (1999: 116).

83. See e.g. Viscusi (1996).

84. Kraus, Malmfors, and Slovic (1992).

85. Kraus, Malmfors, and Slovic (1992: 221).

86. Caplan (2001d).

87. Caplan (2001d). I remain indebted to Robin Hanson for suggesting this approach.

CHAPTER 7: IRRATIONALITY AND THE SUPPLY SIDE OF POLITICS

1. Schumpeter (1950: 262–63).
2. See Frey and Eichenberger (1991, 1989).
3. Blinder (1987: 196).
4. Machiavelli (1952: 92–93).
5. For further discussion, see Caplan (2003b).
6. Posner (1999).
7. See e.g. Lee, Moretti, and Butler (2004).
8. Sowell (2004a: 1–2).
9. Madison, Hamilton, and Jay (1966: 432).
10. Machiavelli (1952: 93–94).
11. For an overview, see Vrij (2000).
12. IMDB (2005).
13. See e.g. Klein (1994).
14. Dye and Zeigler (1996: 295).
15. See Amer (1998).
16. The main difference between legal pleading and political pleading is that a lawyer can get rich by defending unpopular clients, but few politicians can succeed by standing up for unpopular causes.
17. Michels (1962: 93).
18. Gregor (1969: 120).
19. Modern History Project (2005).
20. See Zaller (1992).
21. Krugman (2003: 196).
22. Langer (2002).
23. For a rational model of this and related phenomenon, see Alesina and Cukierman (1990).
24. It is logically possible—though implausible—that voters are simply risk-preferrers. They would rather have a gamble whose expected value is the moderate position than receive the moderate position with certainty. Howitt and Wintrobe (1995) use the opposite assumption to explain why politicians avoid raising issues in the first place: they prefer the status quo with certainty to the gamble of a fresh political contest.
25. See e.g. Burstein (2003), Bender and Lott (1996), and Bernstein (1989).
26. Machiavelli (1952: 93).
27. See e.g. Klein and Tabarrok (2001) and Tabarrok (2000).
28. Food and Drug Administration (1997).
29. Machiavelli (1952: 98).
30. For an overview, see Sappington (1991).
31. For a rational model in which voters actually prefer unresponsive politicians, see Maskin and Tirole (2004).
32. The fact that Supreme Court justices usually stay on the bench long after the president who appointed them leaves office only marginally changes matters. Think about it this way. After the president retires, it is hard to punish

him for unpopular rulings by his appointees. But if the public realizes this, it should be hypersensitive about any unpopular rulings that happen while the appointing president is still in office. Unpopular decisions now—when the president responsible for the appointments can still be punished—tell people to expect a series of unpopular decisions in the future—when it will be too late for the public to express its displeasure. It is only common sense to conclude: "No time like the present!" Now is the time to punish the president not only for the current unpopular choices of his subordinates, but for the whole series of unpopular choices you expect his subordinates to make during their tenure.

33. Richmond (1997: 133).

34. Tullock (1987: 74).

35. Siprut (2004).

36. Greider (1992: 89).

37. For further discussion, see Caplan (2001c).

38. See e.g. Matsusaka (2005), Besley and Case (2003), Besley and Coate (2000), Levitt (1996), Rowley, Tollison, and Tullock (1988), Buchanan and Tollison (1984), Brennan and Buchanan (1980), Olson (1971), Tullock (1967), and Downs (1957). For more optimistic views, see Burstein (2003), Cannes-Wrone, Brady, and Cogan (2002), and Jacobs and Shapiro (2000).

39. Becker (1983: 392).

40. Wittman (1995, 1989).

41. On the economics of media bias, see Sutter (2006). On persuasion by repetition, see DeMarzo, Vayanos, and Zweibel (2003).

42. Hitler (1943: 180–81).

43. Simon (1996: 220).

44. On the history of publishing, see Encyclopedia Britannica (2005).

45. Murphy and Shleifer (2004: 7–8).

46. Schumpeter (1950: 263).

47. Rubin (2003: 164).

48. On the evolutionary basis of xenophobia, see Reynolds, Falger, and Vine (1987). For a wide-ranging attempt to link modern economic biases with our evolutionary heritage, see Rubin (2003).

49. Simon (1995a: 655).

50. For a particularly insightful model of this process, see Kuran and Sunstein (1999).

51. See e.g. Mullainathan and Shleifer (2005) and Glaeser (2003).

52. On the Alar scare, see Kuran and Sunstein (1999).

53. See e.g. Murray, Schwartz, and Lichter (2001).

54. Kuttner (1997: 345).

55. Wittman (2005b).

56. See e.g. Stratmann (2005), and Ansolabehere, de Figueiredo, and Snyder (2002).

57. See e.g. Glaeser (2003).

58. Krugman (2003: 145).

CHAPTER 8: "MARKET FUNDAMENTALISM" VERSUS
THE RELIGION OF DEMOCRACY

1. Brainy Quote (2005a).
2. Colander (2005) shows that the degree of consensus perceived by the latest generation of economists has substantially increased.
3. Reder (1999: 236).
4. Tucker (1978: 461; 460; 475).
5. Waters (1970: 249).
6. Kuttner (1997: 37).
7. Soros (1998: 20).
8. Kuttner (1997: 6).
9. Kuttner (1997: 6, 9; emphasis added).
10. Kuttner (1997: 7; emphasis added).
11. Stiglitz (2002a: 221).
12. Friedman (2002: 32).
13. Friedman (2002: 28).
14. Rothbard (1962: 887). Even at the libertarian extreme of the economic profession, however, the charge of "market fundamentalism" does not exactly fit. On closer reading, Rothbard only makes the agnostic claim that the effect of government intervention on social welfare is ambiguous because every act of government hurts at least one person (Caplan 1999: 833–35).
15. Bork (1990: 139).
16. Shermer (2002: 142).
17. Shermer (2002: 143).
18. Eigen and Siegel (1993: 115).
19. Kamber (1995).
20. Bardhan (1999: 109).
21. Greider (1992: 407).
22. Bardhan (1999).
23. Bardhan (1999: 93; 109).
24. Shapiro (1996: 9).
25. Shapiro (1996: 9; emphasis added).
26. Shapiro (1996: 128).
27. Shapiro (1996: 128).
28. See e.g. Somin (2004), Delli Carpini and Keeter (1996), Dye and Zeigler (1996), Bennett (1996), Smith (1989), and Neuman (1986).
29. Shapiro (1996: 129).
30. Robert Bork (1990: 36–58) actually takes a more fundamentalist position than Shapiro. Bork largely accepts the economists' view of the world. But if economics and the public disagree, he maintains that judges should *still* side with the public.
31. Tetlock (2003: 320; emphasis added).
32. Kuttner (1997: 37).
33. Kuttner (1997: xi–xii).
34. Council of Economic Advisers (2005: 304).
35. Eigen and Siegel (1993: 109).

REFERENCES

Abramson, Paul, John Aldrich, and David Rohde. 2002. *Change and Continuity in the 2000 Elections*. Washington, DC: CQ Press.

Achen, Christopher, and Larry Bartels. 2004. "Musical Chairs: Pocketbook Voting and the Limits of Democratic Accountability." URL http://www.princeton.edu/~bartels/chairs.pdf.

Ainslie, George. 1992. *Piconomics*. Cambridge: Cambridge University Press.

Akerlof, George. 1970. "The Market for 'Lemons': Quality Uncertainty and the Market Mechanism." *Quarterly Journal of Economics* 84(3): 488–500.

———. 1989. "The Economics of Illusion." *Economics and Politics* 1(1): 1–15.

Akerlof, George, and William Dickens. 1982. "The Economic Consequences of Cognitive Dissorance." *American Economic Review* 72(3): 307–19.

———. 1984. "The Economic Consequences of Cognitive Dissonance." In George Akerlof. *An Economic Theorist's Book of Tales*. Cambridge: Cambridge University Press: 123–44.

Akerlof, George, and Janet Yellen. 1985. "Can Small Deviations from Rationality Make Significant Differences to Economic Equilibria?" *American Economic Review* 75(4): 708–20.

Alesina, Alberto, and Alex Cukierman. 1990. "The Politics of Ambiguity." *Quarterly Journal of Economics* 105(4): 829–50.

Alesina, Alberto, and Howard Rosenthal. 1994. *Partisan Politics, Divided Government, and the Economy*. Cambridge: Cambridge University Press.

Alston, Richard, J. R. Kearl, and Michael Vaughan. 1992. "Is There a Consensus Among Economists in the 1990's?" *American Economic Review* 82(2): 203–9.

Althaus, Scott. 1996. "Opinion Polls, Information Effects, and Political Equality: Exploring Ideological Biases in Collective Opinion." *Political Communication* 13(1): 3–21.

———. 1998. "Information Effects in Collective Preferences." *American Political Science Review* 92(2): 545–58.

———. 2003. *Collective Preferences in Democratic Politics: Opinion Surveys and the Will of the People*. Cambridge: Cambridge University Press.

Amer, Mildred. 1998. "Membership of the 105th Congress: A Profile." Government Division. Order No. 97–37 GOV, July 17.

Anderson, Gary, and Robert Tollison. 1988. "Legislative Monopoly and the Size of Government." *Southern Economic Journal* 54(3): 529–45.

Andrews, Robert, ed. 1993. *The Columbia Dictionary of Quotations*. New York: Columbia University Press.

Ansolabehere, Stephen, John de Figueiredo, and James Snyder. 2002. "Why Is There So Little Money in U.S. Politics?" NBER Working Paper No. 9409.

Applebaum, Anne. 2003. *Gulag: A History*. New York: Doubleday.

Arendt, Hannah. 1973. *The Origins of Totalitarianism*. New York: Harcourt, Brace & World.

Aristotle. 1941. *The Basics Works of Aristotle*. Ed. Richard McKeon. New York: Random House.

Aumann, Robert. 1976. "Agreeing to Disagree." *Annals of Statistics* 4(6): 1236–39.

Austen-Smith, David. 1991. "Rational Consumers and Irrational Voters: A Review Essay on *Black Hole Tariffs and Endogenous Policy Theory*." *Economics and Politics* 3(1): 73–92.

Austen-Smith, David, and Jeffrey Banks. 1996. "Information Aggregation, Rationality, and the Condorcet Jury Theorem." *American Political Science Review* 90(1): 34–45.

Babcock, Linda, and George Loewenstein. 1997. "Explaining Bargaining Impasse: The Role of Self-Serving Biases." *Journal of Economic Perspectives* 11(1): 109–26.

Banks, Jeffrey, and Barry Weingast. 1992. "The Political Control of Bureaucracies under Asymmetric Information." *American Journal of Political Science* 36(2): 509–24.

Barber, Benjamin. 1993. "Reductionist Political Science and Democracy." In George Marcus and Russell Hanson, eds., *Reconsidering the Democratic Public*. University Park: Pennsylvania State University Press: 65–72.

Bardhan, Pranab. 1999. "Democracy and Development: A Complex Relationship." In Ian Shapiro and Casiano Hacker-Cordón, eds., *Democracy's Value*. Cambridge: Cambridge University Press: 93–111.

Barkow, Jerome, Leda Cosmides, and John Tooby, eds. 1992. *The Adapted Mind*. New York: Oxford University Press.

Bartels, Larry. 1996. "Uninformed Voters: Information Effects in Presidential Elections." *American Journal of Political Science* 40(1): 194–230.

———. 2000. "Partisanship and Voting Behavior, 1952–1996." *American Journal of Political Science* 44(1): 35–50.

———. 2004. "Homer Gets a Tax Cut: Inequality and Public Policy in the American Mind." URL http://www.princeton.edu/~bartels/homer.pdf.

Bastiat, Frédéric. 1964a. *Economic Sophisms*. Irvington-on-Hudson, NY: Foundation for Economic Education.

———. 1964b. *Selected Essays on Political Economy*. Irvington-on-Hudson, NY: Foundation for Economic Education.

Becker, Gary. 1958. "Competition and Democracy." *Journal of Law and Economics* 1: 105–9.

———. 1968. "Crime and Punishment: An Economic Approach." *Journal of Political Economy* 76(2): 169–217.

———. 1971. *The Economics of Discrimination*. Chicago: University of Chicago Press.

———. 1976a. *The Economic Approach to Human Behavior*. Chicago: University of Chicago Press.

———. 1976b. "Toward a More General Theory of Regulation: Comment." *Journal of Law and Economics* 19(2): 245–48.

———. 1983. "A Theory of Competition Among Pressure Groups for Political Influence." *Quarterly Journal of Economics* 98(3): 371–400.

———. 1985. "Public Policies, Pressure Groups, and Dead Weight Costs." *Journal of Public Economics* 28(3): 329–47.

Becker, Jasper. 1996. *Hungry Ghosts: Mao's Secret Famine.* New York: Free Press.

Bell, Graham. 1997. *Selection: The Mechanism of Evolution.* New York: Chapman and Hall.

Bender, Bruce, and John Lott. 1996. "Legislator Voting and Shirking: A Critical Review of the Literature." *Public Choice* 87(1–2): 67–100.

Benjamin, Daniel, and Jesse Shapiro. 2005. "Does Cognitive Ability Reduce Psychological Bias?" URL http://home.uchicago.edu/~jmshapir/iq022605.pdf.

Bennett, Stephen. 1996. " 'Know-Nothings' Revisited Again." *Political Behavior* 18(3): 219–33.

Bernstein, Robert. 1989. *Elections, Representation, and Congressional Voting Behavior: The Myth of Constituency Control.* Englewood Cliffs, NJ: Prentice Hall.

Bertrand, Marianne, and Sendhil Mullainathan. 2001. "Do People Mean What They Say? Implications for Subjective Survey Data." *American Economic Review* 91(2): 67–72.

Besley, Timothy, and Anne Case. 2003. "Political Institutions and Policy Choices: Evidence from the United States." *Journal of Economic Literature* 41(1): 7–73.

Besley, Timothy, and Stephen Coate. 2000. "Issue Unbundling Via Citizens' Initiatives." NBER Working Paper No. 8036.

Bhagwati, Jagdish. 2002. *Free Trade Today.* Princeton, NJ: Princeton University Press.

Blaug, Mark. 2001. "No History of Ideas, Please, We're Economists." *Journal of Economic Perspectives* 15(1): 145–64.

Blendon, Robert, John Benson, Mollyann Brodie, Richard Morin, Drew Altman, Daniel Gitterman, Mario Brossard, and Matt James. 1997. "Bridging the Gap Between the Public's and Economists' Views of the Economy." *Journal of Economic Perspectives* 11(3): 105–88.

Blinder, Alan. 1987. *Hard Heads, Soft Hearts: Tough-Minded Economics for a Just Society.* Reading, MA: Addison-Wesley.

Blinder, Alan, and Alan Krueger. 2004. "What Does the Public Know about Economic Policy, and How Does It Know It?" *Brookings Papers on Economic Activity* 1: 327–87.

Böhm-Bawerk, Eugen von. 1959. *Capital and Interest.* South Holland, IL: Libertarian Press.

Borjas, George. 1994. "The Economics of Immigration." *Journal of Economic Literature* 32(4): 1667–1717.

Bork, Robert. 1990. *The Tempting of America.* New York: Free Press.

Boublil, Alain, Herbert Kretzmer, and Jean-Marc Natel. 1990. *Les Misérables: The Complete Symphonic Recording.* N.P.: Alain Boublil Music.

Boudreaux, Donald. 1996. "Was Your High-School Civics Teacher Right After All? Donald Wittman's *The Myth of Democratic Failure.*" *Independent Review* 1(1): 111–28.

Boulier, Bryan, and Robert Goldfarb. 1998. "On the Use and Nonuse of Surveys in Economics." *Journal of Economic Methodology* 5(1): 1–21.

Brainy Quote. 2005a. "Bertrand Russell Quotes." URL http://www.brainyquote .com/quotes/authors/b/bertrand_russell.html.

———. 2005b. "H. L. Mencken Quotes." URL http://www.brainyquote.com/ quotes/authors/h/h_l_mencken.html.

Brennan, Geoffrey, and James Buchanan. 1980. *The Power to Tax: Analytical Foundations of a Fiscal Constitution.* Cambridge: Cambridge University Press.

Brennan, Geoffrey, and Loren Lomasky. 1989. "Large Numbers, Small Costs: The Uneasy Foundations of Democratic Rule." In Geoffrey Brennan and Loren Lomasky, eds., *Politics and Process: New Essays in Democratic Thought.* Cambridge: Cambridge University Press: 42–59.

———. 1993. *Democracy and Decision: The Pure Theory of Electoral Preference.* Cambridge: Cambridge University Press.

Breton, Albert, and Ronald Wintrobe. 1982. *The Logic of Bureaucratic Conduct: An Economic Analysis of Competition, Exchange, and Efficiency in Private and Public Organizations.* New York: Cambridge University Press.

Brossard, Mario, and Steven Pearlstein. 1996. "Great Divide: Economists vs. Public: Data and Daily Life Tell Different Stories." *Washington Post,* October 15, A1.

Buchanan, James, and Robert Tollison, eds. 1984. *The Theory of Public Choice II.* Ann Arbor: University of Michigan Press.

Buchanan, Patrick. 1998. *The Great Betrayal: How American Sovereignty and Social Justice are Being Sacrificed to the Gods of the Global Economy.* Boston: Little, Brown.

Bullock, Alan. 1991. *Hitler and Stalin: Parallel Lives.* New York: Vintage Books.

Bureau of Economic Analysis. 2005. "Foreign Direct Investment in the U.S." URL http://www.bea.doc.gov/bea/di/di1fdibal.htm.

Burgoon, Brian, and Michael Hiscox. 2006. "The Mysterious Case of Female Protectionism: Gender Bias in Attitudes Toward International Trade." URL http://www.people.fas.harvard.edu/~hiscox/FemaleProtectionism.pdf.

Burstein, Paul. 2003. "The Impact of Public Opinion on Public Policy: A Review and an Agenda." *Political Research Quarterly* 56(1): 29–40.

Camerer, Colin. 1987. "Do Biases in Probability Judgment Matter in Markets? Experimental Evidence." *American Economic Review* 77(5): 981–97.

———. 1995. "Individual Decision Making." In John Kagel and Alvin Roth, eds., *The Handbook of Experimental Economics.* Princeton, NJ: Princeton University Press: 587–703.

Camerer, Colin, and Robin Hogarth. 1999. "The Effects of Financial Incentives in Experiments: A Review and Capital-Labor-Production Framework." *Journal of Risk and Uncertainty* 19(1–3): 7–42.

Cannes-Wrone, Brandice, David Brady, and John Cogan. 2002. "Out of Step, Out of Office: Electoral Accountability and House Member Voting." *American Political Science Review* 96(1): 127–40.

Caplan, Bryan. 1999. "The Austrian Search for Realistic Foundations." *Southern Economic Journal* 65(4): 823–38.

———. 2000. "Rational Irrationality: A Framework for the Neoclassical-Behavioral Debate." *Eastern Economic Journal* 26(2): 191–211.

———. 2001a. "Rational Ignorance versus Rational Irrationality." *Kyklos* 54(1): 3–26.

———. 2001b. "Libertarianism Against Economism: How Economists Misunderstand Voters and Why Libertarians Should Care." *Independent Review* 5(4): 539–63.

———. 2001c. "Rational Irrationality and the Microfoundations of Political Failure." *Public Choice* 107 (3–4): 311–31.

———. 2001d. "What Makes People Think Like Economists? Evidence on Economic Cognition from the Survey of Americans and Economists on the Economy." *Journal of Law and Economics* 44(2): 395–426.

———. 2001e. "Probability, Common Sense, and Realism: A Reply to Hülsmann and Block." *Quarterly Journal of Austrian Economics* 4(2): 69–86.

———. 2002a. "Systematically Biased Beliefs About Economics: Robust Evidence of Judgemental Anomalies from the Survey of Americans and Economists on the Economy." *Economic Journal* 112(479): 433–58.

———. 2002b. "Sociotropes, Systematic Bias, and Political Failure: Reflections on the Survey of Americans and Economists on the Economy." *Social Science Quarterly,* 83(2): 416–35.

———. 2002c. "Economic Illiteracy: A Modest Plea Against Humility." *Royal Economic Society Newsletter* 119:9–10.

———. 2003a. "Stigler-Becker versus Myers-Briggs: Why Preference-Based Explanations Are Scientifically Meaningful and Empirically Important." *Journal of Economic Behavior and Organization* 50(4): 391–405.

———. 2003b. "The Logic of Collective Belief." *Rationality and Society* 15(2): 218–42.

———. 2003c. "The Idea Trap: The Political Economy of Growth Divergence." *European Journal of Political Economy* 19(2): 183–203.

———. 2005a. "From Friedman to Wittman: The Transformation of Chicago Political Economy." *Econ Journal Watch* 2(1): 1–21.

———. 2005b. "Rejoinder to Wittman: True Myths." *Econ Journal Watch* 2(2): 165–85.

———. Forthcoming a. "The Economics of Szasz: Preferences, Constraints, and Mental Illness." *Rationality and Society.* URL http://www.gmu.edu/departments/economics/bcaplan/szaszjhe.doc.

———. Forthcoming b. "How Do Voters Form Positive Economic Beliefs? Evidence from the Survey of Americans and Economists on the Economy." *Public Choice.* URL http://www.gmu.edu/departments/economics/bcaplan/econbelfin.doc.

———. Forthcoming c. "Terrorism: The Relevance of the Rational Model." *Public Choice.* URL http://www.gmu.edu/departments/economics/bcaplan/relevance6.doc.

Caplan, Bryan, and Tyler Cowen. 2004. "Do We Underestimate the Benefits of Cultural Competition?" *American Economic Review* 94(2): 402–7.

Caplan, Bryan, and Stephen Miller. 2006. "Economic Beliefs, Intelligence, and Ability Bias: Evidence from the General Social Survey." URL http://www.gmu.edu/departments/economics/bcaplan/iqbeliefej.doc.

Caplan, Bryan, and Edward Stringham. 2005. "Mises, Bastiat, Public Opinion, and Public Choice: What's Wrong With Democracy." *Review of Political Economy* 17(1): 79–105.

Carroll, Lewis. 1999. *Alice's Adventures in Wonderland and Through the Looking-Glass.* New York: Barnes and Noble.

Cawley, John, and Tomas Philipson, 1999. "An Empirical Examination of Information Barriers to Trade in Insurance." *American Economic Review* 89(4): 827–46.

Ceaser, James, and Andrew Busch. 2001. *The Perfect Tie: The True Story of the 2000 Presidential Election.* Lanham, MD: Rowman & Littlefield.

Cerf, Christopher, and Victor Navasky. 1998. *The Experts Speak: The Definitive Compendium of Authoritative Misinformation.* New York: Villard.

Chambers, Whittaker. 1952. *Witness.* New York: Random House.

Chiappori, Pierre-Andre, and Bernard Salanie, 2000. "Testing for Asymmetric Information in Insurance Markets." *Journal of Political Economy* 108(1): 56–78.

Chicago Council on Foreign Relations. 2004. "Global Views 2004." URL http://www.ccfr.org/globalviews2004/sub/pdf/Global_Views_2004_US.pdf.

Chicago Council on Foreign Relations and the German Marshall Fund of the United States. 2002a. "Worldviews: Topline Data from U.S. Public Survey." URL http://www.worldviews.org/detailreports/usreport/public_topline_report.pdf.

———. 2002b. "Worldviews: American Public Opinion & Foreign Policy." URL http://www.worldviews.org/detailreports/usreport.pdf.

———. 2002c. "Worldviews: American and European Public Opinion & Foreign Policy." URL http://www.worldviews.org/detailreports/compreport.pdf.

Chong, Dennis, Herbert McClosky, and John Zaller. 1983. "Patterns of Support for Democratic and Capitalist Values in the United States." *British Journal of Political Science* 13(4): 401–40.

Citrin, Jack, and Donald Green. 1990. "The Self-Interest Motive in American Public Opinion." *Research in Micropolitics* 3:1–28.

Citrin, Jack, Eric Schickler, and John Sides. 2003. "What If Everyone Voted? Simulating the Impact of Increased Turnout in Senate Elections." *American Journal of Political Science* 47(1): 75–90.

Coase, Ronald. 1998. "Comment on Thomas W. Hazlett: Assigning Property Rights to Radio Spectrum Users: Why Did FCC License Auctions Take 67 Years?" *Journal of Law and Economics* 41(2): 577–80.

———. 1999. "Economists and Public Policy." In Daniel Klein, ed., *What Do Economists Contribute?* New York: New York University Press: 33–52.

Coate, Stephen, and Stephen Morris. 1995. "On the Form of Transfers to Special Interests." *Journal of Political Economy* 103(6): 1210–35.

———. 1999. "Policy Persistence." *American Economic Review* 89(5): 1327–36.

Colander, David. 2005. "The Making of an Economist Redux." *Journal of Economic Perspectives* 19(1): 175–98.

Fiorina, Morris. 1989. *Congress: Keystone of the Washington Establishment.* New Haven: Yale University Press.

Fischhoff, Baruch. 1982. "Debiasing." In Daniel Kahneman, Paul Slovic, and Amos Tversky, eds., *Judgment under Uncertainty: Heuristics and Biases.* Cambridge: Cambridge University Press: 422–44.

Fleming, Victor, dir. 1939. *Gone with the Wind.* DVD. MGM.

Fogel, Robert. 1999. "Catching Up with the Economy." *American Economic Review* 89(1): 1–21.

Food and Drug Administration. 1997. "FDA Talk Paper." URL http://www.fda .gov/bbs/topics/ANSWERS/ANS00819.html.

Francis, Wayne, Lawrence Kenny, Rebecca Morton, and Amy Schmidt. 1994. "Retrospective Voting and Political Mobility." *American Journal of Political Science* 38(4): 999–1024.

Frank, Robert. 1988. *Passions Within Reason: The Strategic Role of the Emotions.* New York: Norton.

Frank, Thomas. 2004. *What's the Matter with Kansas? How Conservatives Won the Heart of America.* New York: Metropolitan Books.

Freeman, A. Myrick, III. 2002. "Environmental Policy since Earth Day I: What Have We Gained?" *Journal of Economic Perspectives* 16(1): 125–46.

Fremling, Gertrud, and John Lott. 1989. "Time Dependent Information Costs, Price Controls, and Successive Government Intervention." *Journal of Law, Economics and Organization* 5(2): 293–306.

———. 1996. "The Bias Towards Zero in Aggregate Perceptions: An Explanation Based on Rationally Calculating Individuals." *Economic Inquiry* 34(2): 276–95.

Frey, Bruno. 2000. "Does Economics Have an Effect? Toward an Economics of Economics." Institute for Empirical Research in Economics Working Paper No. 36.

———. 2002. "Do Economists Affect Policy Outcomes?" Working Paper Series, Institute for Empirical Research, University of Zürich.

Frey, Bruno, and Reiner Eichenberger. 1989. "Anomalies and Institutions." *Journal of Economic Behavior and Organization* 145(3): 423–37.

———. 1991. "Anomalies in Political Economy." *Public Choice* 68(1–3): 71–89.

———. 1992. "Economics and Economists: A European Perspective." *American Economic Review* 82(2): 216–20.

———. 1993. "American and European Economics and Economists." *Journal of Economic Perspectives* 7(4): 185–93.

Frey, Bruno, Werner Pommerehne, and Beat Gygi. 1993. "Economics Indoctrination or Selection? Some Empirical Results." *Journal of Economic Education* 24(3): 271–81.

Friedman, Jeffrey, ed. 1996. *The Rational Choice Controversy: Economic Models of Politics Reconsidered.* New Haven: Yale University Press.

Friedman, Milton. 1953. "The Methodology of Positive Economics." In *Essays in Positive Economics.* Chicago: University of Chicago Press: 3–43.

———. 2002. *Capitalism and Freedom.* Chicago: University of Chicago Press.

Cole, Matthew. 2003. "Environmental Optimists, Environmental Pessimists and the Real State of the World—An Article Examining *The Skeptical Environmentalist: Measuring the Real State of the World* by Bjorn Lomborg." *Economic Journal* 113(488): F362–F380.

Compte, Olivier, and Andrew Postlewait. 2004. "Confidence-Enhanced Performance." *American Economic Review* 94(5): 1536–57.

Conover, Pamela, and Stanley Feldman. 1986. "Emotional Reactions to the Economy: I'm Mad as Hell and I'm Not Going to Take It Anymore." *American Journal of Political Science* 30(1): 50–78.

Conover, Pamela, Stanley Feldman, and Kathleen Knight. 1987. "The Personal and Political Underpinnings of Economic Forecasts." *American Journal of Political Science* 31(3): 559–83.

Conquest, Robert. 1986. *Harvest of Sorrow: Soviet Collectivization and the Terror-Famine.* New York: Oxford University Press.

———. 1991. *Stalin: Breaker of Nations.* New York: Penguin.

Converse, Philip. 1964. "The Nature of Belief Systems in Mass Publics." In David Apter, ed., *Ideology and Discontent.* New York: Free Press: 206–61.

———. 1990. "Popular Representation and the Distribution of Information." In John Ferejohn and James Kuklinski, eds., *Information and Democratic Processes.* Urbana: University of Illinois Press: 369–88.

Cooter, Robert. 2000. *The Strategic Constitution.* Princeton, NJ: Princeton University Press.

Cosmides, Leda. 1989. "The Logic of Social Exchange: Has Natural Selection Shaped How Humans Reason? Studies with the Wason Selection Task." *Cognition* 31(3): 187–276.

Cosmides, Leda, and John Tooby. 1996. "Are Humans Good Intuitive Statisticians After All? Rethinking Some Conclusions from the Literature on Judgment under Uncertainty." *Cognition* 58(1): 1–73.

Council of Economic Advisers. 2005. *Economic Report of the President.* Washington, DC: U.S. Government Printing Office.

Coursey, Don, and Russell Roberts. 1991. "Competition in Political and Economic Markets." *Public Choice* 70(1): 83–88.

Courtois, Stéphane, Nicolas Werth, Jean-Louis Panné, Andrzej Paczkowski, Karel Bartošek, and Jean-Louis Margolin. 1999. *The Black Book of Communism: Crimes, Terror, Repression.* Cambridge: Harvard University Press.

Cowen, Tyler. 1998. *In Praise of Commercial Culture.* Cambridge: Harvard University Press.

———. 2001. "How Do Economists Think About Rationality?" URL http://www.gmu.edu/jbc/Tyler/rationality.pdf.

———. 2003. "Self-Deception as the Root of Political Failure." URL http://www.gmu.edu/jbc/Tyler/PrideandSelf.pdf.

Cowen, Tyler, and Robin Hanson. Forthcoming. "Are Disagreements Honest?" *Journal of Economic Methodology.* URL http://hanson.gmu.edu/deceive.pdf.

Cox, W. Michael, and Richard Alm. 1999. *Myths of Rich and Poor.* New York: Basic Books.

Crain, W. Mark. 1977. "On the Structure and Stability of Political Markets." *Journal of Political Economy* 85(4): 829–42.

Crew, Michael, and Charlotte Twight. 1990. "On the Efficiency of Law: A Public Choice Perspective." *Public Choice* 66(1): 15–36.

Cronqvist, Henrik, and Richard Thaler. 2004. "Design Choices in Privatized Social-Security Systems: Learning from the Swedish Experience." *American Economic Review* 94(2): 424–28.

Crossman, Richard, ed. 1949. *The God That Failed.* New York: Harper and Brothers.

Cutler, Fred. 2002. "The Simplest Shortcut of All: Sociodemographic Characteristics and Electoral Choice." *Journal of Politics* 64(2): 466–90.

Dahl, Gordon, and Michael Ransom. 1999. "Does Where You Stand Depend on Where You Sit?" *American Economic Review* 89(4): 703–27.

Dahl, Robert. 1989. *Democracy and Its Critics.* New Haven: Yale University Press.

Dasgupta, Partha, and Joseph Stiglitz. 1988. "Potential Competition, Actual Competition, and Economic Welfare." *European Economic Review* 32(2–3): 569–77.

Dasgupta, Susmita, Benoit Laplante, Hua Wang, and David Wheeler. 2002. "Confronting the Environmental Kuznets Curve." *Journal of Economic Perspectives* 16(1): 147–68.

Davis, Steven, John Haltiwanger, and Scott Schuh. *Job Creation and Destruction.* Cambridge: MIT Press.

Dee, Thomas. 2004. "Are There Civic Returns to Education?" *Journal of Public Economics* 88(9): 1697–1720.

Delli Carpini, Michael, and Scott Keeter. 1996. *What Americans Know About Politics and Why It Matters.* New Haven: Yale University Press.

DeMarzo, Peter, Dimitri Vayanos, and Jeffrey Zwiebel. 2003. "Persuasion Bias, Social Influence, and Unidimensional Opinions." *Quarterly Journal of Economics* 68(3): 909–68.

Descartes, René. 1999. *Discourse on Method.* Indianapolis: Hackett

Diamond, Jared. 1997. *Guns, Germs, and Steel: The Fates of Human Societies.* New York: Norton.

Donovan, Nick, and David Halpern. 2002. *Life Satisfaction: The State of Knowledge and Implications for Government.* London: Cabinet Office/ Prime Minister's Strategy Unit.

Downs, Anthony. 1957. *An Economic Theory of Democracy.* New York: Harper and Row.

Drazen, Allan. 2000. *Political Economy in Macroeconomics.* Princeton, NJ: Princeton University Press.

Drèze, Jean, and Amartya Sen, eds. 1990. *The Political Economy of Hunger.* New York: Oxford University Press.

Duch, Raymond, Harvey Palmer, and Christopher Anderson. 2000. "Heterogeneity in Perceptions of National Economic Conditions." *American Journal of Political Science* 44(4): 635–52.

Dye, Thomas, and Harmon Zeigler. 1992. *The Irony of D... common Introduction to American Politics.* 7th editio Brooks/Cole.

———. 1996. *The Irony of Democracy: An Uncommon Intr... can Politics.* 10th ed. New York: Wadsworth.

Easterbrook, Gregg. 2003. *The Progress Paradox: How Lif... People Feel Worse.* New York: Random House.

Easterly, William. 2001. *The Elusive Quest for Growth: Eco... and Misadventures in the Tropics.* Cambridge: MIT Pres...

Economics and Statistics Administration. 2004. *Statisti... United States, 2003.* Washington, DC: U.S. Department...

Edgerton, Robert. 1992. *Sick Societies: Challenging the My... mony.* New York: Free Press.

Edlin, Aaron, Andrew Gelman, and Noah Kaplan. Forthc... Rational Choice: Why and How People Vote to Impro... Others." *Rationality and Society.* URL http://www... ~gelman/research/published/rational_final5.pdf.

Ehrlich, Paul. 1968. *The Population Bomb.* New York: Bal...

Eichenberger, Reiner, and Angel Serna. 1996. "Random E... tion, and Politics." *Public Choice* 86(1–2): 137–56.

Eigen, Lewis, and Jonathan Siegel, eds. 1993. *The Mac... Political Quotations.* New York: Macmillan.

Einhorn, Hillel, and Robin Hogarth. 1987. "Decision Ma... ity." In Robin Hogarth and Melvin Reder, eds., *Ratio... trast Between Economics and Psychology.* Chicago: U... Press: 41–66.

Emerson, Ralph. N.d. *Essays.* New York: Grosset and Du...

Encyclopedia Britannica. 2005. "Publishing." 26: 415–4...

Equal Employment Opportunity Commission. 2005. "S... www.eeoc.gov/stats.

Erikson, Robert, Gerald Wright, and John McIver. 1989. ... lic Opinion, and State Policy in the United States." ... ence Review* 83(3): 729–50.

Fedderson, Timothy. 2004. "Rational Choice Theory a... Voting." *Journal of Economic Perspectives* 18(1): 99–...

Feldman, Stanley. 1982. "Economic Self-Interest an... *American Journal of Political Science* 26(3): 446–66.

———. 1988. "Structure and Consistency in Public Op... Beliefs and Values." *American Journal of Political S...

Fernandez, Raquel, and Rodrik, Dani. 1991. "Resist... Quo Bias in the Presence of Individual-Specific U... Economic Review* 81(5): 1146–55.

Filer, John, Lawrence Kenny, and Rebecca Morton. 19... come, and Voting." *American Journal of Political S...

Fiorina, Morris. 1981. *Retrospective Voting in Ameri... New Haven: Yale University Press.

Friedrich, Carl, and Zbigniew Brzezinski. 1965. *Totalitarian Dictatorship and Autocracy.* New York: Praeger.

Fuchs, Victor, Alan Krueger, and James Poterba. 1998. "Economists' Views about Parameters, Values, and Policies: Survey Results in Labor and Public Economics." *Journal of Economic Literature* 36(3): 1387–1425.

Fuller, Dan, and Doris Geide-Stevenson. 2003. "Consensus Among Economists: Revisited." *Journal of Economic Education* 34(4): 369–87.

Funk, Carolyn. 2000. "The Dual Influence of Self-Interest and Societal Interest in Public Opinion." *Political Research Quarterly* 53(1): 37–62.

Funk, Carolyn, and Patricia García-Monet. 1997. "The Relationship between Personal and National Concerns in Public Perceptions about the Economy." *Political Research Quarterly* 50(2): 317–42.

Gallup Organization. 2005. "Create a Trend: Minimum Wage." URL http://institution.gallup.com/documents/trendQuestion.aspx?QUESTION=119914&Advanced=0&SearchConType=1&SearchTypeAll=minimum%20wage.

Geddes, Barbara, and John Zaller. 1989. "Sources of Popular Support for Authoritarian Regimes." *American Journal of Political Science* 33(2): 319–47.

Gelman, Andrew, Jonathan Katz, and Joseph Bafumi. 2004. "Standard Voting Power Indexes Do Not Work: An Empirical Analysis." *British Journal of Political Science* 34(4): 657–74.

Gelman, Andrew, Gary King, and W. John Boscardin. 1998. "Estimating the Probability of Events That Have Never Occurred: When Is Your Vote Decisive?" *Journal of the American Statistical Association* 93(441): 1–9.

Gelman, Andrew, Boris Shor, Joseph Bafumi, and David Park. 2005. "Rich State, Poor State, Red State, Blue State: What's the Matter with Connecticut?" URL http://www.stat.columbia.edu/~gelman/research/unpublished/redblue11.pdf.

General Social Survey. 1998. URL http://www.icpsr.umich.edu/GSS/home.htm.

Gerber, Alan, and Donald Green. 2000. "The Effect of a Nonpartisan Get-Out-the-Vote Drive: An Experimental Study of Leafleting." *Journal of Politics* 62(3): 846–57.

Gerber, Elisabeth, and Jeffrey Lewis. 2004. "Beyond the Median: Voter Preferences, Distinct Heterogeneity, and Political Representation." *Journal of Political Economy* 112(6): 1364–83.

Gigerenzer, Gerd. 2000. *Adaptive Thinking: Rationality in the Real World.* New York: Oxford University Press.

———. 2001. "The Adaptive Toolbox: Toward a Darwinian Rationality." In Jeffrey French, Alan Kamil, Daniel Leger, Richard Dienstbier, and Martin Daly, eds., *Evolutionary Psychology and Motivation.* Lincoln: University of Nebraska Press: 113–43.

Gigerenzer, Gerd, and David Murray. 1987. *Cognition as Intuitive Statistics.* Hillsdale, NJ: Lawrence Erlbaum Associates.

Gilens, Martin. 2001. "Political Ignorance and Collective Policy Preferences." *American Political Science Review* 95(2): 379–96.

Gillman, Howard. 1993. *The Constitution Besieged: The Rise and Demise of Lochner Era Police Powers Jurisprudence*. Durham, NC: Duke University Press.

Gilovich, Thomas. 1991. *How We Know What Isn't So*. New York: Macmillan.

Glaeser, Edward. 2003. "Psychology and the Market." NBER Working Paper No. 10203.

———. 2005. "The Political Economy of Hatred." *Quarterly Journal of Economics* 70(1): 45–86.

Glucksberg, Sam. 1962. "The Influence of Strength and Drive on Functional Fixedness and Perceptual Recognition." *Journal of Experimental Psychology* 63: 36–41.

Gold, Lois, Thomas Slone, Neela Manley, and Bruce Ames. 2002. *Misconceptions About the Causes of Cancer*. Vancouver, BC: Fraser Institute.

Goldstein, Daniel, and Gerd Gigerenzer. 2002. "Models of Ecological Rationality: The Recognition Heuristic." *Psychological Review* 109(1): 75–90.

Gottschalk, Peter. 1997. "Inequality, Income Growth, and Mobility: The Basic Facts." *Journal of Economic Perspectives* 11(2): 21–40.

Green, Donald, and Ann Gerken. 1989. "Self-Interest and Public Opinion Toward Smoking Restrictions and Cigarette Taxes." *Public Opinion Quarterly* 53(1): 1–16.

Green, Donald, and Ian Shapiro. 1994. *Pathologies of Rational Choice Theory: A Critique of Applications in Political Science*. New Haven: Yale University Press.

Gregor, A. James. 1969. *The Ideology of Fascism*. New York: Free Press.

Greider, William. 1992. *Who Will Tell the People?* New York: Simon and Schuster.

———. 1997. *One World, Ready or Not: The Manic Logic of Global Capitalism*. New York: Simon and Schuster.

Groseclose, Tim, and Nolan McCarty. 2001. "The Politics of Blame: Bargaining Before an Audience." *American Journal of Political Science* 45(1): 100–19.

Grossman, Gene, and Elhanan Helpman. 1994. "Protection for Sale." *American Economic Review* 84(4): 833–50.

———. 1996. "Electoral Competition and Special Interest Politics." *Review of Economic Studies* 63(2): 265–88.

———. 2001. *Special Interest Politics*. Cambridge: MIT Press.

Gruber, Jonathan. 2005. *Public Finance and Public Policy*. New York: Worth.

Hainmueller, Jens, and Michael Hiscox. 2005a. "Educated Preferences: Explaining Attitudes Toward Immigration in Europe." URL http://www.people.fas.harvard.edu/~hiscox/EducatedPreferences.pdf.

———. 2005b. "Learning to Love Globalization? Education and Individual Attitudes Toward International Trade. Supplement II: What Drives the Education Effect? Economic Literacy or Tolerance?" Unpub.

———. Forthcoming. "Learning to Love Globalization: Education and Individual Attitudes Toward International Trade." *International Organization*. URL http://www.people.fas.harvard.edu/~hiscox/HainmuellerHiscox Education.pdf.

Hanson, Robin. 1995. "Could Gambling Save Science? Encouraging an Honest Consensus." *Social Epistemology* 9(1): 3–33.

———. 2002. "Disagreement is Unpredictable." *Economics Letters* 77(3): 365–69.

———. 2005. "The Policy Analysis Market (and FutureMAP) Archive." URL http://hanson.gmu.edu/policyanalysismarket.html.

———. 2006. "Decision Markets for Policy Advice." In Eric Patashnik and Alan Gerber, eds., *Promoting the General Welfare: American Democracy and the Political Economy of Government Performance.* Washington, DC: Brookings Institution Press, forthcoming.

Harberger, Arnold. 1993. "Secrets of Success: A Handful of Heroes." *American Economic Review* 83(2): 343–50.

Harrison, Glenn, and Bengt Kriström. 1995. "On the Interpretation of Responses in Contingent Valuation Surveys." In Per-Olav Johansson, Bengt Kriström, and Karl-Göran Mäler, eds., *Current Issues in Environmental Economics.* Manchester: Manchester University Press: 35–57.

Harrison, Glenn, and John List. 2004. "Field Experiments." *Journal of Economic Literature* 42(4): 1009–55.

Harrison, Glenn, and E. Elisabet Rutström. Forthcoming. "Experimental Evidence of Hypothetical Bias in Value Elicitation Methods." In Charles Plott and Vernon Smith, eds., *Handbook of Experimental Economics Results.*

Hauptmann, Emily. 1996. *Putting Choice Before Democracy: A Critique of Rational Choice Theory.* Albany: State University of New York Press.

Held, Virginia. 1990. "Mothering versus Contract." In Jane Mansbridge, ed., *Beyond Self-Interest.* Chicago: University of Chicago Press: 287–304.

Helliwell, John. 2003. "How's Life: Combining Individual and National Variables to Explain Subjective Well-Being." *Economic Modelling* 20(2): 331–60.

Hemenway, David. 1990. "Propitious Selection." *Quarterly Journal of Economics* 16(4): 1063–69.

Henderson, David. 1986. *Innocence and Design: The Influence of Economic Ideas on Policy.* New York: Basil Blackwell.

Herman, Arthur. 1997. *The Idea of Decline in Western History.* New York: Free Press.

Herman, Edward, and Noam Chomsky. 2002. *Manufacturing Consent: The Political Economy of the Mass Media.* New York: Pantheon.

Highton, Benjamin. 2004. "Voter Registration and Turnout in the United States." *Perspectives on Politics* 2(3): 507–15.

Hinich, Melvin, and Michael Munger. 1994. *Ideology and the Theory of Political Choice.* Ann Arbor: University of Michigan Press.

Hiscox, Michael. 2006. "Through a Glass and Darkly: Attitudes Toward International Trade and the Curious Effects of Issue Framing." *International Organization*, forthcoming.

Hitler, Adolf. 1943. *Mein Kampf.* Boston: Houghton Mifflin.

Hoelzl, Erik, and Aldo Rustichini. 2005. "Overconfident: Do You Put Your Money On It?" *Economic Journal* 115(503): 305–18.

Hoffer, Eric. 1951. *The True Believer: Thoughts on the Nature of Mass Movements.* New York: New American Library.

Hoffman, Tom. 1998. "Rationality Reconceived: The Mass Electorate and Democratic Theory." *Critical Review* 12(4): 459–80.

Hogarth, Robin, and Melvin Reder. 1987. "Introduction: Perspectives from Economics and Psychology." In Robin Hogarth and Melvin Reder, eds., *Rational Choice: The Contrast Between Economics and Psychology.* Chicago: University of Chicago Press: 1–23.

Holbrook, Thomas, and James Garand. 1996. "Homo Economus? Economic Information and Economic Voting." *Political Research Quarterly* 49(2): 351–75.

Holcombe, Randall. 1985. *An Economic Analysis of Democracy.* Carbondale: Southern Illinois University Press.

Holloway, David. 1994. *Stalin and the Bomb: The Soviet Union and Atomic Energy, 1939–1956.* New Haven: Yale University Press.

Holmes, Stephen, and Cass Sunstein. 1999. *The Cost of Rights: Why Liberty Depends on Taxes.* New York: Norton.

Houkes, John. 2004. *An Annotated Bibliography on the History of Usury and Interest from the Earliest Times Through the Eighteenth Century.* Lewiston, NY: E. Mellen Press.

Howitt, Peter, and Ronald Wintrobe. 1995. "The Political Economy of Inaction." *Journal of Public Economics* 56(2): 329–53.

Howson, Colin, and Peter Urbach. 1989. *Scientific Reasoning: The Bayesian Approach.* LaSalle, IL: Open Court.

Huddy, Leonie, Jeffrey Jones, and Richard Chard. 2001. "Compassion v. Self-Interest: Support for Old-Age Programs among the Non-Elderly." *Political Psychology* 22(3): 443–72.

Hume, David. 1987. *Essays: Moral, Political and Literary.* Indianapolis: LibertyClassics.

Iannaccone, Laurence. 1998. "Introduction to the Economics of Religion." *Journal of Economic Literature* 36(3): 1465–95.

IMDB. 2005. "Memorable Quotes from 'Seinfeld.' " URL http://www.imdb .com/title/tt0098904/quotes.

Ingram, James. 1983. *International Economics.* New York: Wiley.

Irwin, Douglas. 1996. *Against the Tide: An Intellectual History of Free Trade.* Princeton, NJ: Princeton University Press.

Jacobs, Lawrence, and Robert Shapiro. 2000. *Politicians Don't Pander: Political Manipulation and the Loss of Democratic Responsiveness.* Chicago: University of Chicago Press.

Jennings, M. Kent. 1992. "Ideological Thinking Among Mass Publics and Political Elites." *Public Opinion Quarterly* 56(4): 419–41.

Johnson, D. Gale. 2000. "Population, Food, and Knowledge." *American Economic Review* 90(1): 1–14.

Johnson, Paul. 1991. *Modern Times: The World from the Twenties to the Nineties.* New York: HarperCollins.

Jost, John, Jack Glaser, Arie Kruglanski, and Frank Sulloway. 2003. "Political Conservatism as Motivated Social Cognition." *Psychological Bulletin* 129(3): 339–75.

Kahneman, Daniel, Ilana Ritov, and David Schkade. 1999. "Economic Preferences or Attitude Expressions? An Analysis of Dollar Responses to Public
Issues." *Journal of Risk and Uncertainty* 19(1–3): 203–35.

Kahneman, Daniel, Paul Slovic, and Amos Tversky, eds. 1982. *Judgment under
Uncertainty: Heuristics and Biases.* Cambridge: Cambridge University Press.

Kahneman, Daniel, and Amos Tversky. 1982. "On the Study of Statistical Intu-
itions." In Daniel Kahneman, Paul Slovic, and Amos Tversky, eds., *Judgment under Uncertainty: Heuristics and Biases.* Cambridge: Cambridge
University Press: 493–508.

Kaiser Family Foundation. 2005. "Views On Prescription Drugs And The Pharmaceutical Industry." URL http://www.kff.org/healthpollreport/feb_2005/
index.cfm.

Kaiser Family Foundation and Harvard University School of Public Health.
1995. "National Survey of Public Knowledge of Welfare Reform and the
Federal Budget." January 12, #1001. URL http://www.kff.org/kaiserpolls/
1001-welftbl.cfm.

Kalt, Joseph, and Mark Zupan. 1984. "Capture and Ideology in the Economic
Theory of Politics." *American Economic Review* 74(3): 279–300.

———. 1990. "The Apparent Ideological Behavior of Legislators: Testing for
Principal-Agent Slack in Political Institutions." *Journal of Law and Economics* 33(1): 103–31.

Kamber, Victor. 1995. *Giving Up on Democracy: Why Term Limits Are Bad for
America.* Washington, DC: Regency.

Kamieniecki, Sheldon. 1985. *Party Identification, Political Behavior, and the
American Electorate.* Westport, CT: Greenwood Press.

Kau, James, and Paul Rubin. 1979. "Self-Interest, Ideology, and Logrolling in
Congressional Voting." *Journal of Law and Economics* 22(2): 365–84.

Kearl, J. R., Clayne Pope, Gordon Whiting, and Larry Wimmer. 1979. "A Confusion of Economists?" *American Economic Review* 69(2): 28–37.

Keeter, Scott. 1996. "The Origins of the Disjuncture of Perception and Reality:
The Cases of Racial Equality and Environmental Protection." Unpub.

Kelman, Mark. 1988. "On Democracy-Bashing: A Skeptical Look At the Theoretical and 'Empirical' Practice of the Public Choice Movement." *University
of Virginia Law Review* 74(2): 199–273.

Kelman, Steven. 1981. *What Price Incentives? Economists and the Environment.* Boston: Auburn House.

Keynes, John Maynard. 1963. *Essays in Persuasion.* New York: Norton.

Kinder, Donald, and Roderick Kiewiet. 1979. "Economic Discontent and Political Behavior: The Role of Personal Grievances and Collective Economic
Judgments in Congressional Voting." *American Journal of Political Science*
23(3): 495–527.

———. 1981. "Sociotropic Politics: The American Case." *British Journal of
Political Science* 11(2): 129–61.

Kirchgässner, Gebhard. 1992. "Towards a Theory of Low-Cost Decisions." *European Journal of Political Economy* 8(2): 305–20.

———. 2005. "(Why) Are Economists Different?" *European Journal of Political
Economy* 21(3): 543–62.

Kirchgässner, Gebhard, and Werner Pommerehne. 1993. "Low-Cost Decisions as a Challenge to Public Choice." *Public Choice* 77(1): 107–15.

Klein, Daniel. 1994. "If Government is So Villainous, How Come Government Officials Don't Seem Like Villains?" *Economics and Philosophy* 10(1) 91–106.

Klein, Daniel. 1999. *What Do Economists Contribute?* New York: New York University Press.

Klein, Daniel, and Charlotta Stern. Forthcoming. "How Politically Diverse Are the Social Sciences and Humanities? Survey Evidence from Six Fields." *Academic Questions.* URL http://www.ratio.se/pdf/wp/dk_ls_diverse.pdf.

Klein, Daniel, and Alexander Tabarrok. 2001. "Theory, Evidence and Examples of FDA Harm." *FDA Review.* URL http://www.fdareview.org/harm.shtml.

Kliemt, Hartmut. 1986. "The Veil of Insignificance." *European Journal of Political Economy* 2(3): 333–44.

Kling, Arnold. 2004. *Learning Economics.* Philadelphia: Xlibris Corporation.

Knight, Frank. 1951. "The Role of Principles in Economics and Politics." *American Economic Review* 41(1): 1–29.

———. 1960. *Intelligence and Democratic Action.* Cambridge: Harvard University Press.

Knox, R. Buck. 1967. *James Ussher: Archbishop of Armagh.* Cardiff: University of Wales Press.

Koford, Kenneth. 1994. "What Can We Learn About Congressional Politics From Dimensional Studies of Roll-Call Voting?" *Economics and Politics* 6(2): 173–86.

Kramer, Gerald. 1983. "The Ecological Fallacy Revisited: Aggregate- versus Individual-level Findings on Economics and Elections, and Sociotropic Voting." *American Political Science Review* 77(1): 92–111.

Kraus, Nancy, Torbjörn Malmfors, and Paul Slovic. 1992. "Intuitive Toxicology: Expert and Lay Judgments of Chemical Risks." *Risk Analysis* 12(2): 215–32.

Krause, George. 1997. "Voters, Information Heterogeneity, and the Dynamics of Aggregate Economic Expectations." *American Journal of Political Science* 41(4): 1170–1200.

Krause, George, and Jim Granato. 1998. "Fooling Some of the Public Some of the Time? A Test for Weak Rationality With Heterogeneous Information Levels." *Public Opinion Quarterly* 62(2): 135–51.

Kremer, Michael. 1993. "Population Growth and Technological Change: One Million B.C. to 1990." *Quarterly Journal of Economics* 108(3): 681–716.

Krueger, Alan, and Robert Solow, eds. 2001. *The Roaring Nineties: Can Full Employment Be Sustained?* New York: Russell Sage Foundation.

Kruger, Justin, and David Dunning. 1999. "Unskilled and Unaware of It: How Difficulties in Recognizing One's Own Incompetence Lead to Inflated Self-Assessments." *Journal of Personality and Social Psychology* 77(6): 1121–34.

Krugman, Paul. 1996. *Pop Internationalism.* Cambridge: MIT Press.

———. 1998. *The Accidental Theorist.* New York: Norton.

———. 2003. *The Great Unraveling.* New York: Norton.

Kuklinksi, James, Paul Quirk, Jennifer Jerit, and Robert Rich. 2001. "The Political Environment and Citizen Competence." *American Journal of Political
Science* 45(2): 410–24.

Kuklinksi, James, Paul Quirk, Jennifer Jerit, David Schwieder, and Robert Rich.
2000. "Misinformation and the Currency of Democratic Citizenship." *Journal of Politics* 62(3): 790–816.

Kull, Steven. 2000. "Americans on Globalization: A Study of U.S. Public Attitudes." *Program on International Policy Attitudes.* URL http://www.
pipa.org/OnlineReports/Globalization/contents.html.

Kuran, Timur. 1995. *Private Truths, Public Lies: The Social Consequences of
Preference Falsification.* Cambridge: Harvard University Press.

———. 2004. *Islam and Mammon: The Economic Predicaments of Islamism.*
Princeton, NJ: Princeton University Press.

Kuran, Timur, and Cass Sunstein. 1999. "Availability Cascades and Risk Regulation." *Stanford Law Review* 51(4): 683–768.

Kuttner, Robert. 1984. *The Economic Illusion: False Choices Between Prosperity and Social Justice.* Philadelphia: University of Pennsylvania Press.

———. 1991. *The End of Laissez-Faire: National Purpose and the Global Economy After the Cold War.* New York: Knopf.

———. 1997. *Everything for Sale: The Virtues and Limits of Markets.* New York:
Knopf.

———. ed. 1996. *Ticking Time Bombs: The New Conservative Assault on Democracy.* New York: New Press.

Lakoff, George. 2002. *Moral Politics: How Liberals and Conservatives Think.*
Chicago: University of Chicago Press.

Landsburg, Steven. 1993. *The Armchair Economist: Economics and Everyday
Life.* New York: Free Press.

———. 1997. *Fair Play.* New York: Free Press.

Langer, Gary. 2002. "Trust in Government . . . To Do What?" *Public Perspective,*
July–August, 7–10.

Lanoue, David. 1994. "Retrospective and Prospective Voting in Presidential-
Year Elections." *Political Research Quarterly* 47(1): 193–205.

LaPiere, Richard. 1934. "Attitudes vs. Actions." *Social Forces* 13(2): 230–37.

Lau, Richard, Thad Brown, and David Sears. 1978. "Self-Interest and Civilians'
Attitudes Toward the Vietnam War." *Public Opinion Quarterly* 42(4):
464–83.

Lau, Richard, and David Redlawsk. 1997. "Voting Correctly." *American Political Science Review* 91(3): 585–98.

———. 2001. "Advantages and Disadvantages of Cognitive Heuristics in Political Decision Making. *American Journal of Political Science* 45(4): 951–71.

Lazonick, William. 1991. *Business Organization and the Myth of the Market
Economy.* Cambridge: Cambridge University Press.

Lebergott, Stanley. 1993. *Pursuing Happiness: American Consumers in the
Twentieth Century.* Princeton, NJ: Princeton University Press.

Le Bon, Gustave. 1960. *The Crowd: A Study of the Popular Mind.* New York:
Viking Press.

Lecky, William. 1981. *Liberty and Democracy.* Vol. 1. Indianapolis: Liberty Classics.

Lee, David, Enrico Moretti, and Matthew Butler. 2004. "Do Voters Affect or Elect Policies? Evidence from the U.S. House." *Quarterly Journal of Economics* 69(3): 807–59.

Lee, Dwight. 1989. "The Impossibility of a Desirable Minimal State." *Public Choice* 61(3): 277–84.

Lee, Ronald, and Timothy Miller. 2000. "Immigration, Social Security, and Broader Fiscal Impacts." *American Economic Review* 90(2): 350–54.

Leighley, Jan, and Jonathan Nagler. 1992a. "Socioeconomic Class Bias in Turnout, 1964–1988: The Voters Remain the Same." *American Political Science Review* 86(3): 725–36.

————. 1992b. "Individual and Systemic Influences on Turnout: Who Votes? 1984. *Journal of Politics* 54(3): 718–40.

Levitt, Steven. 1996. "How Do Senators Vote? Disentangling the Role of Voter Preferences, Party Affiliation, and Senator Ideology." *American Economic Review* 86(3): 425–41.

Levy, David. 1989. "The Statistical Basis of Athenian-American Constitutional Theory." *Journal of Legal Studies* 18(1): 79–103.

Lichtenstein, Sarah, Baruch Fischhoff, and Lawrence Phillips. 1982. "Calibration of Probabilities: The State of the Art to 1980." In Daniel Kahneman, Paul Slovic, and Amos Tversky, eds., *Judgment under Uncertainty: Heuristics and Biases.* Cambridge: Cambridge University Press: 306–34.

Lichter, S. Robert, and Stanley Rothman. 1999. *Environmental Cancer—A Political Disease?* New Haven: Yale University Press.

List, John. 2003. "Does Market Experience Eliminate Market Anomalies?" *Quarterly Journal of Economics* 68(1): 41–71.

Locke, John. 1977. "An Essay Concerning Human Understanding." In Steven Cahn, ed., *Classics of Western Philosophy.* Indianapolis: Hackett Publishing Company: 479–574.

Lockerbie, Brad. 1991. "The Influence of Levels of Information on the Use of Prospective Evaluations." *Political Behavior* 13(3): 223–35.

Lomborg, Bjorn. 2001. *The Skeptical Environmentalist: Measuring the Real State of the World.* Cambridge: Cambridge University Press.

Lord, Charles, Lee Ross, and Mark Lepper. 1979. "Biased Assimilation and Attitude Polarization: The Effect of Prior Theories on Subsequently Considered Evidence." *Journal of Personality and Social Psychology* 37(11): 2098–109.

Lott, John. 1997. "Donald Wittman's *The Myth of Democratic Failure.*" *Public Choice* 92(1–2): 1–13.

————. 2000. *More Guns, Less Crime: Understanding Crime and Gun-Control Laws.* Chicago: University of Chicago Press.

Lott, John, and Lawrence Kenny. 1999. "Did Women's Suffrage Change the Size and Scope of Government?" *Journal of Political Economy* 107(6): 1163–98.

Lovejoy, Arthur, and George Boas. 1965. *Primitivism and Related Ideas in Antiquity.* New York: Octagon Books.

Lucas, Robert. 1973. "Some International Evidence on Output-Inflation Tradeoffs." *American Economic Review* 63(3): 326–34.

———. 1993. "Making a Miracle." *Econometrica* 61(2): 251–72.

Lupia, Arthur. 1994. "Shortcuts Versus Encyclopedias: Information and Voting Behavior in California Insurance Reform Elections." *American Political Science Review* 88(1): 63–76.

Lupia, Arthur, and Matthew McCubbins. 1998. *The Democratic Dilemma: Can Citizens Learn What They Need to Know?* Cambridge: Cambridge University Press.

Luttbeg, Norman, and Michael Martinez. 1990. "Demographic Differences in Opinion." *Research in Micropolitics* 3:83–118.

MacEwan, Arthur. 1999. *Neoliberalism or Democracy? Economic Strategy, Markets, and Alternatives for the 21st Century.* New York: St. Martin's Press.

Machiavelli, Niccolò. 1952. *The Prince.* New York: NAL Penguin.

MacKuen, Michael, Robert Erikson, and James Stimson. 1992. "Peasants or Bankers? The American Electorate and the U.S. Economy." *American Political Science Review* 86(3): 597–611.

Maddock, Rodney, and Michael Carter. 1982. "A Child's Guide to Rational Expectations." *Journal of Economic Literature* 20(1): 39–51.

Madison, James, Alexander Hamilton, and John Jay. 1966. *The Federalist Papers.* New Rochelle, NY: Arlington House.

Magee, Stephen, William Brock, and Leslie Young. 1989. *Black Hole Tariffs and Endogenous Policy Theory: Political Economy in General Equilibrium.* Cambridge: Cambridge University Press.

Mansbridge, Jane, ed. 1990. *Beyond Self-Interest.* Chicago: University of Chicago Press.

Manza, Jeff, and Clem Brooks. 1999. *Social Cleavages and Political Change: Voter Alignments and U.S. Party Coalitions.* New York: Oxford University Press.

Markus, Gregory. 1988. "The Impact of Personal and National Economic Conditions on the Presidential Vote: A Pooled Cross-Sectional Analysis." *American Journal of Political Science* 32(1): 137–54.

Marx, Karl. 1965. *Capital.* Vol. 1. Moscow: Progress Publishers.

Maskin, Eric, and Jean Tirole. 2004. "The Politician and the Judge: Accountability in Government." *American Economic Review* 94(4): 1034–54.

Matsusaka, John. 2005. "Direct Democracy Works." *Journal of Economic Perspectives* 19(2): 185–206.

McChesney, Robert. 1999. *Rich Media, Poor Democracy: Communication Politics in Dubious Times.* Urbana: University of Illinois Press.

McCloskey, Donald. 1985. *The Rhetoric of Economics.* Madison: University of Wisconsin Press.

———. 1993. "Competitiveness and the Antieconomics of Decline." In Donald McCloskey, ed., *Second Thoughts: Myths and Morals of U.S. Economic History.* New York: Oxford University Press: 167–73.

McClosky, Herbert, and John Zaller. 1984. *The American Ethos: Public Attitudes Towards Capitalism and Democracy.* Cambridge: Harvard University Press.

McLean, Iain. 2002. "William H. Riker and the Invention of Heresthetic(s)." *British Journal of Political Science* 32(3): 535–58.

Meehl, Paul. 1977. "The Selfish Voting Paradox and the Thrown-Away Vote Argument." *American Political Science Review* 71(1): 11–30.

Mele, Alfred. 1987. *Irrationality: An Essay on Akrasia, Self-Deception, and Self-Control.* New York: Oxford University Press.

———. 2001. *Self-Deception Unmasked.* Princeton, NJ: Princeton University Press.

———. 2004. "Rational Irrationality." *Philosophers' Magazine* 26(2): 31–32.

Meltzer, Allan, and Scott Richard. 1981. "A Rational Theory of the Size of Government." *Journal of Political Economy* 89(5): 914–27.

Mencken, H. L. 1995. *A Second Mencken Chrestomathy.* New York: Knopf.

Merriam-Webster's Collegiate Dictionary. 2003. Springfield, MA: Merriam-Webster.

Michels, Robert. 1962. *Political Parties: A Sociological Study of the Oligarchical Tendencies of Modern Democracy.* New York: Free Press.

Miller, Dale. 1999. "The Norm of Self-Interest." *American Psychologist* 54(12): 1053–60.

Miller, Warren. 1991. "Party Identification, Realignment, and Party Voting: Back to the Basics." *American Political Science Review* 85(2): 557–68.

Mises, Ludwig von. 1962. *Bureaucracy.* New Haven: Yale University Press.

———. 1966. *Human Action: A Treatise on Economics.* Chicago: Contemporary Books.

———. 1981a. "A New Treatise on Economics." In *New Individualist Review.* Indianapolis: Liberty Fund: 323–26.

———. 1981b. *Socialism.* Indianapolis: Liberty Classics.

———. 1996. *Liberalism: The Classical Tradition.* Irvington-on-Hudson, NY: Foundation for Economic Education.

———. 1998. *Interventionism: An Economic Analysis.* Irvington-on-Hudson, NY: Foundation for Economic Education.

Modern History Project. 2005. "Rudolph Hess." URL http://modernhistory project.org/mhp/EntityDisplay.php?Entity=HessR.

Monroe, Alan. 1983. "American Party Platforms and Public Opinion." *American Journal of Political Science* 27(1): 27–42.

———. 1998. "Public Opinion and Public Policy, 1980–1993." *Public Opinion Quarterly* 62(1): 6–28.

Mosca, Gaetano. 1939. *The Ruling Class.* New York: McGraw-Hill.

Mueller, Dennis, and Thomas Stratmann. 2003. "The Economic Effects of Democratic Participation." *Journal of Public Economics* 87(9): 2129–55.

Mueller, John. 1999. *Capitalism, Democracy, and Ralph's Pretty Good Grocery.* Princeton, NJ: Princeton University Press.

Mullainathan, Sendhil, and Andrei Shleifer. 2005. "The Market for News." *American Economic Review* 95(4): 1031–53.

Mulligan, Casey, and Charles Hunter. 2003. "The Empirical Frequency of a Pivotal Vote." *Public Choice* 116(1–2): 31–54.

Murphy, Kevin, and Andrei Shleifer. 2004. "Persuasion in Politics." NBER Working Paper No. 10248.

Murray, David, Joel Schwartz, and S. Robert Lichter. 2001. *It Ain't Necessarily So: How Media Make and Unmake the Scientific Picture of Reality.* Lanham, MD: Rowman and Littlefield.

Muth, John. 1961. "Rational Expectations and the Theory of Price Movements." *Econometrica* 29(3): 315–35.

Mutz, Diana. 1992. "Mass Media and the Depoliticization of Personal Experience." *American Journal of Political Science* 36(2): 483–508.

———. 1993. "Direct and Indirect Routes to Politicizing Personal Experience: Does Knowledge Make a Difference?" *Public Opinion Quarterly* 57(4): 483–502.

Mutz, Diana, and Jeffrey Mondak. 1997. "Dimensions of Sociotropic Behavior: Group-Based Judgements of Fairness and Well-Being." *American Journal of Political Science* 41(1): 284–308.

Nadeau, Richard, and Michael Lewis-Beck. 2001. "National Economic Voting in U.S. Presidential Elections." *Journal of Politics* 63(1): 159–81.

Nasar, Sylvia. 1998. *A Beautiful Mind.* New York: Simon and Schuster.

National Commission on Terrorist Attacks Upon the United States. 2004. *The 9/11 Commission Report.* URL http://www.9–11commission.gov/report/911Report.pdf.

Neuman, W. Russell. 1986. *The Paradox of Mass Politics: Knowledge and Opinion in the American Electorate.* Cambridge: Harvard University Press.

Newcomb, Simon. 1893. "The Problem of Economic Education." *Quarterly Journal of Economics* 7(4): 375–99.

Nietzsche, Friedrich. 1954. *The Portable Nietzsche.* Ed. Walter Kaufmann. New York: Viking Press.

Nisbett, Richard, and Lee Ross. 1980. *Human Inference: Strategies and Shortcomings of Social Judgment.* Englewood Cliffs, NJ: Prentice-Hall.

Noss, John. 1974. *Man's Religions.* New York: Macmillan.

Office of Management and Budget. 1997. "Report to Congress on the Costs and Benefits of Federal Regulation." URL http://www.whitehouse.gov/omb/inforeg/rcongress.html.

———. 2005. *Historical Tables: Budget of the United States, F.Y. 2006.* Washington, DC: U.S. Government Printing Office.

Olson, Mancur. 1971. *The Logic of Collective Action: Public Goods and the Theory of Groups.* Cambridge: Harvard University Press.

———. 1982. *The Rise and Decline of Nations: Economic Growth, Stagflation and Social Rigidities.* New Haven: Yale University Press.

———. 1996. "Big Bills Left on the Sidewalk: Why Some Nations are Rich and Others are Poor." *Journal of Economic Perspectives* 10(2): 3–24.

Orwell, George. 1968. "Looking Back on the Spanish War." In Sonia Orwell and Ian Angus, eds., *The Collected Essays, Journalism and Letters of George Orwell.* Vol. 2. New York: Harcourt, Brace, and World: 249–67.

———. 1983. *1984.* New York: Signet Classic.

Page, Benjamin, and Robert Shapiro. 1983. "Effects of Public Opinion on Policy." *American Political Science Review* 77(1): 175–90.

———. 1992. *The Rational Public: Fifty Years of Trends in Americans' Policy Preferences.* Chicago: University of Chicago Press.

———. 1993. "The Rational Public and Democracy." In George Marcus and Russell Hanson, eds., *Reconsidering the Democratic Public.* University Park: Pennsylvania State University Press: 33–64.

Pashigian, B. Peter. 2000. "Teaching Microeconomics in Wonderland." George J. Stigler Center for the Study of Economy and the State Working Paper No. 161.

Payne, Stanley. 1995. *A History of Fascism: 1914–1945.* Madison: University of Wisconsin Press.

Peltzman, Sam. 1984. "Constituent Interest and Congressional Voting." *Journal of Law and Economics* 27(1): 181–210.

———. 1985. "An Economic Interpretation of the History of Congressional Voting in the Twentieth Century." *American Economic Review* 75(4): 656–75.

———. 1990. "How Efficient Is the Voting Market?" *Journal of Law and Economics* 33(1): 27–63.

Persson, Torsten. 2002. "Do Political Institutions Shape Economic Policy?" *Econometrica* 70(3): 883–905.

Persson, Torsten, and Guido Tabellini. 2000. *Political Economics: Explaining Economic Policy.* Cambridge: MIT Press.

———. 2004. "Constitutions and Economic Policy." *Journal of Economic Perspectives* 18(1): 75–98.

Pesaran, M. Hashem. 1987. *The Limits to Rational Expectations.* Oxford: Blackwell.

Pew Research Center. 1997. "The Optimism Gap Grows." January 17. URL http://people-press.org/reports/display.php3?ReportID=115.

Phelps, Richard. 1993. "American Public Opinion on Trade, 1950–1990." *Business Economics* 28(3): 35–40.

Pinker, Steven. 2002. *The Blank Slate: The Modern Denial of Human Nature.* New York: Viking.

PIPA–Knowledge Networks Poll. 2004. "Americans on Farm Subsidies." URL http://www.pipa.org/OnlineReports/Economics/FarmQnnaire_01_04.pdf.

Pommerehne, Werner, Friedrich Schneider, Guy Gilbert, and Bruno Frey. 1984. "Concordia Discors: Or: What Do Economists Think?" *Theory and Decision* 16(3): 251–308.

Ponza, Michael, Greg Duncan, Mary Corcoran, and Fred Groskind. 1988. "The Guns of Autumn? Age Differences in Support for Income Transfers to the Young and Old." *Public Opinion Quarterly* 52(4): 441–66.

Poole, Keith, and Howard Rosenthal. 1991. "Patterns of Congressional Voting." *American Journal of Political Science* 35(1): 228–78.

———. 1997. *Congress: A Political-Economic History of Roll Call Voting.* New York: Oxford University Press.

Poole, William. 2004. "Free Trade: Why Are Economists and Noneconomists So Far Apart?" *Federal Reserve Bank of St. Louis Review* 6(5): 1–6.

Popkin, Samuel. 1991. *The Reasoning Voter: Communication and Persuasion in Presidential Campaigns.* Chicago: University of Chicago Press.

Posner, Richard. 1999. *An Affair of State: The Investigation, Impeachment, and Trial of President Clinton.* Cambridge: Harvard University Press.

———. 2002. *Economic Analysis of Law.* New York: Aspen Publishers.

Prisching, Manfred. 1995. "The Limited Rationality of Democracy: Schumpeter as the Founder of Irrational Choice Theory." *Critical Review* 9(3): 301–23.

Quattrone, George, and Amos Tversky. 1984. "Causal Versus Diagnostic Contingency: On Self-Deception and on the Voter's Illusion." *Journal of Personality and Social Psychology* 46(2): 237–48.

———. 1988. "Contrasting Rational and Psychological Analysis of Political Choice." *American Political Science Review* 82(3): 716–36.

Quirk, Paul. 1988. "In Defense of the Politics of Ideas." *Journal of Politics* 50(1): 31–41.

———. 1990. "Deregulation and the Politics of Ideas." In Jane Mansbridge, ed., *Beyond Self-Interest.* Chicago: University of Chicago Press: 183–99.

Rabin, Matthew. 1998. "Psychology and Economics." *Journal of Economic Literature* 36(1): 11–46.

Rae, John. 1965. *Life of Adam Smith.* New York: Augustus M. Kelley.

Rand, Ayn. 1957. *Atlas Shrugged.* New York: Signet.

Reder, Melvin. 1999. *Economics: The Culture of a Controversial Science.* Chicago: University of Chicago Press.

Redlawsk, David. 2002. "Hot Cognition or Cool Consideration? Testing the Effects of Motivated Reasoning on Political Decision Making." *Journal of Politics* 64(2): 1021–44.

Reynolds, Vernon, Vincent Falger, and Ian Vine. 1987. *The Sociobiology of Ethnocentrism: Evolutionary Dimensions of Xenophobia, Discrimination, Racism and Nationalism.* Athens: University of Georgia Press.

Rhoads, Steven. 1985. *The Economist's View of the World: Government, Markets, and Public Policy.* Cambridge: Cambridge University Press.

Rhodebeck, Laurie. 1993. "The Politics of Greed? Political Preferences among the Elderly." *Journal of Politics* 55(2): 342–64.

Richmond, Ray. 1997. *The Simpsons: A Complete Guide to Our Favorite Family.* New York: HarperCollins.

Ricketts, Martin and Edward Shoesmith. 1990. *British Economic Opinion: A Survey of a Thousand Economists.* London: Institute of Economic Affairs.

Riker, William. 1988. *Liberalism Against Populism: A Confrontation between the Theory of Democracy and the Theory of Social Choice.* Prospect Heights, IL: Waveland Press.

Roberts, Russell. 2001. *The Choice: A Fable of Free Trade and Protectionism.* Upper Saddle River, NJ: Prentice Hall.

Rodrik, Dani. 1996. "Understanding Economic Policy Reform." *Journal of Economic Literature* 34(1): 9–41.

Romer, David. 2003. "Misconceptions and Political Outcomes." *Economic Journal* 113(484): 1–20.

Rothbard, Murray. 1962. *Man, Economy, and State: A Treatise on Economic Principles.* Los Angeles: Nash.

Rowley, Charles. 1997. "Donald Wittman's *The Myth of Democratic Failure*." *Public Choice* 92(1–2): 15–26.

Rowley, Charles, Robert Tollison, and Gordon Tullock, eds. 1988. *The Political Economy of Rent-Seeking*. Boston: Kluwer Academic Publishers.

Rubin, Paul. 2003. "Folk Economics." *Southern Economic Journal* 70(1): 157–71.

Rudolph, Thomas. 2003. "Who's Responsible for the Economy? The Formation and Consequences of Responsibility Attributions." *American Journal of Political Science* 47(4): 697–712.

Sachs, Jeffrey. 1994. "Life in the Economic Emergency Room." In John Williamson, ed., *The Political Economy of Policy Reform*. Washington, DC: Institute for International Economics: 503–23.

Sachs, Jeffrey, and Andrew Warner. 1995. "Economic Reform and the Process of Global Integration." *Brookings Papers on Economic Activity* 1:1–118.

Saint-Paul, Gilles. 2000. "The 'New Political Economy': Recent Books by Allen Drazen and by Torsten Persson and Guido Tabellini." *Journal of Economic Literature* 38(4): 915–25.

Samuelson, Paul. 1946. "Lord Keynes and the General Theory." *Econometrica* 14(3): 187–200.

———. 1966. "What Economists Know." In *The Collected Scientific Papers of Paul A. Samuelson*. Vol. 1. Cambridge: MIT Press: 1619–49.

Samuelson, Robert. 1995. *The Good Life and Its Discontents: The American Dream in the Age of Entitlement*. New York: Random House.

Sappington, David. 1991. "Incentives in Principal-Agent Relationships." *Journal of Economic Perspectives* 5(2): 45–66.

Schelling, Thomas. 1980. *The Strategy of Conflict*. Cambridge: Harvard University Press.

Scherer, F. M., and David Ross. 1990. *Industrial Market Structure and Economic Performance*. Boston: Houghton Mifflin.

Scheve, Kenneth, and Matthew Slaughter. 2001a. *Globalization and the Perceptions of American Workers*. Washington, DC: Institute for International Economics.

———. 2001b. "What Determines Individual Trade Policy Preferences?" *Journal of International Economics* 54(2): 267–92.

Schlesinger, Arthur. 1957. *The Crisis of the Old Order, 1919–1933*. Boston: Houghton Mifflin.

Schuessler, Alexander. 2000a. "Expressive Voting." *Rationality and Society* 12(1): 87–119.

———. 2000b. *A Logic of Expressive Choice*. Princeton, NJ: Princeton University Press.

Schultze, Charles. 1977. *The Public Use of Private Interest*. Washington, DC: Brookings Institution.

Schumpeter, Joseph. 1950. *Capitalism, Socialism, and Democracy*. New York: Harper and Brothers.

Schumpeter, Joseph. 1954. *History of Economic Analysis*. New York: Oxford University Press.

Searle, John. 1983. *Intentionality: An Essay in the Philosophy of Mind.* Cambridge: Cambridge University Press.

Sears, David, and Jack Citrin. 1985. *Tax Revolt: Something for Nothing in California.* Cambridge: Cambridge University Press.

Sears, David, and Carolyn Funk. 1990. "Self-Interest in Americans' Political Opinions." In Jane Mansbridge, ed., *Beyond Self-Interest.* Chicago: University of Chicago Press: 147–70.

Sears, David, Carl Hensler, and Leslie Speer. 1979. "Whites' Opposition to 'Busing': Self-Interest or Symbolic Politics?" *American Political Science Review* 73(2): 369–84.

Sears, David, and Leonie Huddy. 1990. "On the Origins of the Political Disunity of Women." In Patricia Gurin and Louise Tilly, eds., *Women, Politics, and Change.* New York: Russell Sage Foundation: 249–77.

Sears, David, and Richard Lau. 1983. "Inducing Apparently Self-Interested Political Preferences." *American Journal of Political Science* 27(2): 223–52.

Sears, David, Richard Lau, Tom Tyler, and Harris Allen. 1980. "Self-Interest vs. Symbolic Politics in Policy Attitudes and Presidential Voting." *American Political Science Review* 74(3): 670–84.

Sears, David, Tom Tyler, Jack Citrin, and Donald Kinder. 1978. "Political System Support and Public Response to the Energy Crisis." *American Journal of Political Science* 22(1): 56–82.

Shapiro, Ian. 1996. *Democracy's Place.* Ithaca, NY: Cornell University Press.

———. 1999. *Democratic Justice.* New Haven: Yale University Press.

Shapiro, Ian, and Casiano Hacker-Cordón. 1999. "Reconsidering Democracy's Value." In Ian Shapiro and Casiano Hacker-Cordón, eds., *Democracy's Value.* Cambridge: Cambridge University Press: 1–19.

Shapiro, Robert, and Harpreet Mahajan. 1986. "Gender Differences in Policy Preferences: A Summary of Trends From the 1960s to the 1980s." *Public Opinion Quarterly* 50(1): 42–61.

Sheffrin, Steven. 1996. *Rational Expectations.* Cambridge: Cambridge University Press.

Shepsle, Kenneth, and Barry Weingast. 1981. "Political Preferences for the Pork Barrel: A Generalization." *American Journal of Political Science* 25(1): 96–111.

Shermer, Michael. 2002. *Why People Believe Weird Things: Pseudoscience, Superstition, and Other Confusions of Our Time.* New York: Henry Holt.

Shiller, Robert. 1997. "Public Resistance to Indexation: A Puzzle." *Brookings Papers on Economic Activity* 1: 159–228.

Shleifer, Andrei. 1998. "State versus Private Ownership." *Journal of Economic Perspectives* 12(4): 133–50.

Siebert, Horst. 1997. "Labor Market Rigidities: At the Root of Unemployment in Europe." *Journal of Economic Perspectives* 11(3): 37–54.

Simon, Herbert. 1985. "Human Nature in Politics: The Dialogue of Psychology with Political Science." *American Political Science Review* 79(2): 293–304.

Simon, Julian. 1995a. "What Does the Future Hold? The Forecast in a Nutshell." In Julian Simon, ed., *The State of Humanity.* Cambridge: Blackwell: 642–60.

Simon, Julian, ed. 1995b. *The State of Humanity.* Cambridge: Blackwell.
———. 1996. *The Ultimate Resource 2.* Princeton, NJ: Princeton University Press.
———. 1999. *The Economic Consequences of Immigration.* Ann Arbor: University of Michigan Press.
Simon, Scott. 2000. "Music Cues: Adlai Stevenson." National Public Radio. URL http://www.npr.org/programs/wesat/000205.stevenson.html.
Siprut, Joseph. 2004. "Rational Irrationality: Why Playing The World Trade Organization as a Scapegoat Reduces the Social Costs of Armchair Economics." *Brooklyn Journal of International Law* 29(2): 709–45.
Skousen, Mark. 1997. "The Perseverance of Paul Samuelson's Economics." *Journal of Economic Perspectives* 11(2): 137–52.
Slovic, Paul, Baruch Fischhoff, and Sarah Lichtenstein. 1980. "Facts and Fears: Understanding Perceived Risk." In Richard Schwing and Walter Albers, eds., *Societal Risk Assessment: How Safe is Safe Enough?* New York: Plenum Press: 181–216.
Smith, Adam. 1981. *An Inquiry Into the Nature and Causes of the Wealth of Nations.* Indianapolis: Liberty Classics.
Smith, Eric. 1989. *The Unchanging American Voter.* Berkeley and Los Angeles: University of California Press.
Smith, Vernon. 1991. "Rational Choice: The Contrast Between Economics and Psychology." *Journal of Political Economy* 99(4): 877–97.
———. 2003. "Constructivist and Ecological Rationality in Economics." *American Economic Review* 93(3): 465–508.
Smith, Vernon, and James Walker. 1993. "Monetary Rewards and Decision Cost in Experimental Economics." *Economic Inquiry* 31(2): 245–61.
Somin, Ilya. 1998. "Voter Ignorance and the Democratic Ideal." *Critical Review* 12(4): 99–111.
———. 1999. "*Resolving the Democratic Dilemma?*" *Yale Journal on Regulation* 16(2): 401–14.
———. 2000. "Do Politicians Pander?" *Critical Review* 14(2–3): 147–55.
———. 2004. "Political Ignorance and The Countermajoritarian Difficulty: A New Perspective on the 'Central Obsession' of Constitutional Theory." *Iowa Law Review* 89(4): 1287–1372.
Soros, George. 1998. *The Crisis of Global Capitalism: Open Society Endangered.* New York: Public Affairs.
Sowell, Thomas. 2004a. *Applied Economics: Thinking Beyond Stage One.* New York: Basic Books.
———. 2004b. *Basic Economics: A Citizen's Guide to the Economy.* New York: Basic Books.
Speck, W. A. 1993. *A Concise History of Britain, 1707–1975.* Cambridge: Cambridge University Press.
Spence, Michael. 1977. "Consumer Misperceptions, Product Failure, and Producer Liability." *Review of Economic Studies* 44(3): 561–72.
Spencer, Herbert. 1981. "From Freedom to Bondage." In Thomas Mackay, ed., *A Plea for Liberty: An Argument Against Socialism and Socialistic Legislation.* Indianapolis: Liberty Fund: 3–34.

Starke, Linda, ed. 2004. *State of the World, 2004*. New York: Norton.

Stigler, George. 1959. "The Politics of Political Economists." *Quarterly Journal of Economics* 73(4): 522–32.

———. 1961. "The Economics of Information." *Journal of Political Economy* 69(3): 213–25.

———. 1986. "Economics or Ethics?" In Kurt Leube and Thomas Gale Moore, eds., *The Essence of Stigler*. Stanford, CA: Hoover Institution Press: 303–36.

Stigler, George, and Gary Becker. 1977. "De Gustibus Non Est Disputandum." *American Economic Review* 67(2): 76–90.

Stiglitz, Joseph. 2002a. *Globalization and Its Discontents*. New York: Norton.

———. 2002b. "Information." In David Henderson, ed., *The Concise Encyclopedia of Economics*. URL http://www.econlib.org/library/Enc/Information.html.

———. 2003. *The Roaring Nineties. A New History of the World's Most Prosperous Decade*. New York: Norton.

Stratmann, Thomas. 2005. "Some Talk: Money in Politics. A (Partial) Review of the Literature." *Public Choice* 124(1/2): 135–56.

Sunstein, Cass, ed. 2000. *Behavioral Law and Economics*. New York: Cambridge University Press.

Surowiecki, James. 2004. *The Wisdom of Crowds*. New York: Doubleday.

Sutter, Daniel. 2006. Political Bias in the News: A Critical Examination. Unpub.

Tabarrok, Alexander. 2000. "Assessing the FDA Via the Anomaly of Off-Label Drug Prescribing." *Independent Review* 5(1): 25–53.

Taussig, Frank. 1905. "The Present Position of the Doctrine of Free Trade." *Publications of the American Economic Association* 6(1): 29–65.

Taylor, Shelley. 1989. *Positive Illusions: Creative Self-Deception and the Healthy Mind*. New York: Basic Books.

Tetlock, Philip. 2003. "Thinking the Unthinkable: Sacred Values and Taboo Cognitions." *Trends in Cognitive Science* 7(7): 320–24.

Thaler, Richard. 1992. *The Winner's Curse: Paradoxes and Anomalies of Economic Life*. Princeton, NJ: Princeton University Press.

Tirole, Jean. 2002. "Rational Irrationality: Some Economics of Self-Management." *European Economic Review* 46(4–5): 633–55.

Tocqueville, Alexis de. 1969. *Democracy in America*. New York: Harper-Perennial.

Tollison, Robert, and Richard Wagner. 1991. "Romance, Realism, and Policy Reform." *Kyklos* 44(1): 57–70.

Tucker, Robert. 1973. *Stalin as Revolutionary: 1879–1929*. New York: Norton.

———. 1990. *Stalin in Power: The Revolution From Above 1928–1941*. New York: Norton.

———. ed. 1978. *The Marx-Engels Reader*. New York: Norton.

Tullock, Gordon. 1965. "Entry Barriers in Politics." *American Economic Review* 55(1/2): 458–66.

———. 1967. *Toward a Mathematics of Politics*. Ann Arbor: University of Michigan Press.

———. 1971. "Charity of the Uncharitable." *Western Economic Journal* 9(4): 379–92.

————. 1981a. "The Rhetoric and Reality of Redistribution." *Southern Economic Journal* 47(4): 895–907.

————. 1981b. "Why So Much Stability?" *Public Choice* 37(2): 189–202.

————. 1987. *The Politics of Bureaucracy.* Lanham, MD: University Press of America.

————. 1988. "Further Directions for Rent-Seeking Research." In Charles Rowley, Robert Tollison, and Gordon Tullock, eds., *The Political Economy of Rent-Seeking.* Boston: Kluwer Academic Publishers: 465–80.

————. 1999. "How to Do Well While Doing Good!" In Daniel Klein, ed., *What Do Economists Contribute?* New York: New York University Press: 87–103.

Tversky, Amos, and Daniel Kahneman. 1982a. "Judgment under Uncertainty: Heuristics and Biases." In Daniel Kahneman, Paul Slovic, and Amos Tversky, eds., *Judgment under Uncertainty: Heuristics and Biases.* Cambridge: Cambridge University Press: 3–20.

————. 1982b. "Availability: A Heuristic for Judging Frequency and Probability." In Daniel Kahneman, Paul Slovic, and Amos Tversky, eds., *Judgment under Uncertainty: Heuristics and Biases.* Cambridge: Cambridge University Press: 163–78.

Tyler, Tom, and Renee Weber. 1982. "Support for the Death Penalty: Instrumental Response to Crime, or Symbolic Attitude?" *Law and Society Review* 17(1): 21–46.

Tyran, Jean-Robert. 2004. "Voting When Money and Morals Conflict: An Experimental Test of Expressive Voting." *Journal of Public Economics* 88(7–8): 1645–64.

U.S. Census Bureau. 2005a. "U.S. Trade Balance With Canada." URL http://www.census.gov/foreign-trade/balance/c1220.html.

————. 2005b. "U.S. Trade Balance With Mexico." URL http://www.census.gov/foreign-trade/balance/c2010.html.

Van Den Steen, Eric. 2004. "Rational Overoptimism (and Other Biases)." *American Economic Review* 94(4): 1141–51.

Verba, Sidney, Kay Schlozman, Henry Brady, and Norman Nie. 1993. "Citizen Activity: Who Participates? What Do They Say?" *American Political Science Review* 87(2): 303–18.

Viscusi, W. Kip. 1996. *Rational Risk Policy.* New York: New York University Press.

Vrij, Aldert. 2000. *Detecting Lies and Deceit: The Psychology of Lying and the Implications for Professional Practice.* New York: John Wiley and Sons.

Walstad, William. 1992. "Economics Instruction in High Schools." *Journal of Economic Literature* 30(4): 2019–51.

————. 1997. "The Effect of Economic Knowledge on Public Opinion of Economic Issues." *Journal of Economic Education* 28(3): 195–205.

Walstad, William, and Max Larsen. 1992. *A National Survey of American Economic Literacy.* Lincoln, NE: Gallup Organization.

Walstad, William, and Ken Rebeck. 2002. "Assessing the Economic Knowledge and Economic Opinions of Adults." *Quarterly Review of Economics and Finance* 42(5): 921–34.

Washington Post, Kaiser Family Foundation, and Harvard University Survey Project. 1996. "Survey of Americans and Economists on the Economy." October 16, #1199. URL http://www.kff.org/kaiserpolls/1199-econgen.cfm.

———. 1997. "Survey of Americans' Knowledge and Attitudes about Entitlements." URL http://www.kff.org/medicare/loader.cfm?url=/commonspot/security/getfile.cfm&PageID=14513.

Waters, Mary-Alice, ed. 1970. *Rosa Luxemburg Speaks*. New York: Pathfinder Press.

Weingast, Barry, Kenneth Shepsle, and Christopher Johnsen. 1981. "The Political Economy of Benefits and Costs: A Neoclassical Approach to Distributive Politics." *Journal of Political Economy* 89(4): 642–64.

Weiss, Andrew. 1995. "Human Capital vs. Signalling Explanations of Wages." *Journal of Economic Perspectives* 9(4): 133–54.

Weiss, Leonard, and Michael Klass. 1986. *Regulatory Reform: What Actually Happened*. Boston: Little, Brown.

Weissberg, Robert. 2002. *Polling, Policy, and Public Opinion: The Case Against Heeding the "Voice of the People."* NY: Palgrave.

Whitman, David. 1998. *The Optimism Gap*. New York: Walker.

William J. Clinton Foundation. 2005. "Facts Sheet on NAFTA Notes." URL http://www.clintonfoundation.org/legacy/101293-fact-sheet-on-nafta-notes.htm.

Wintrobe, Ronald. 1987. "The Market for Corporate Control and the Market for Political Control." *Journal of Law, Economics, and Organization* 3(2): 435–48.

———. 1998. *The Political Economy of Dictatorship*. Cambridge: Cambridge University Press.

Wittman, Donald. 1989. "Why Democracies Produce Efficient Results." *Journal of Political Economy* 97(6): 1395–1424.

———. 1995. *The Myth of Democratic Failure: Why Political Institutions Are Efficient*. Chicago: University of Chicago Press.

———. 2005a. "Voting on Income Redistribution: How a Little Bit of Altruism Creates Transitivity." URL http://repositories.cdlib.org/ucscecon/586/

———. 2005b. "Pressure Groups and Political Advertising: How Uninformed Voters Can Use Strategic Rules of Thumb." URL http://people.ucsc.edu/~wittman/working.papers/ruleofthumb.2005.pdf.

———. 2005c. "Reply to Caplan: On the Methodology of Testing for Voter Irrationality." *Econ Journal Watch* 2(1): 22–31.

———. 2005d. "Second Reply to Caplan: The Power and Glory of the Median Voter." *Econ Journal Watch* 2(2): 186–95.

Wolfers, Justin. 2001. "Are Voters Rational? Evidence from Gubernatorial Elections." Stanford University Graduate School of Business Working Paper No. 1730.

Wolfers, Justin, and Eric Zitzewitz. 2004. "Prediction Markets." *Journal of Economic Perspectives* 18(2): 107–26.

Wolpert, Robin, and James Gimpel. 1998. "Self-Interest, Symbolic Politics, and Public Attitudes toward Gun Control." *Political Behavior* 20(3): 241–62.

Wright, Gerald, Robert Erikson, and John McIver. 1987. "Public Opinion and Policy Liberalism in the American States." *American Journal of Political Science* 31(4): 980–1001.

Wyden, Ron. 2003. "Wyden, Dorgan Call For Immediate Halt to Tax-Funded 'Terror Market' Scheme." URL http://wyden.senate.gov/media/2003/07282003_terrormarket.html.

Zaller, John. 1992. *The Nature and Origins of Mass Opinion.* Cambridge: Cambridge University Press.

———. 2003. "Coming to Grips with V.O. Key's Concept of Latent Opinion." In MacKuen, Michael, and George Rabinowitz, eds. *Electoral Democracy.* Ann Arbor: University of Michigan Press: 311–36.

INDEX

abortion, 28, 149
Achen, Christopher, 160
Adams, Henry, 43
adverse selection, 196
advertising, 176; political, 179–80
affirmative action, SAEE question
  regarding, 61
agency, principal-agent relations, 172
aggregation. *See* Miracle of Aggregation
agriculture, 30, 42, 129
Akerlof, George, 105
Alm, Richard, 42–43, 47
Althaus, Scott, 27–28, 108
altruism, 35, 195; "unselfish voters"
  thought experiment, 151–53, 161–62
antiforeign bias, 30, 36–39, 49, 146; defined, 36; evidence for existence of, 51,
  58–59, 66, 68, 70–71; immigration policy and, 38–39; as matter of degree, 39;
  rational irrationality and situational
  abandonment of, 137; systematic
  error and, 10
antimarket bias, 30–36, 49, 146, 201;
  competition and, 71–72; debt market
  and prejudice against interest, 32–33,
  142–43; defined, 30; evidence for existence of, 51, 59–60, 62–63, 64–65, 72–
  73; market payments conflated with
  transfers, 32; monopoly theories of
  price and, 34; profit motive and, 30–
  32; rational irrationality and situational abandonment of, 137; systematic error and, 10
antitrust laws, 175
Aristotle, 102
asymmetric information, 105–6, 112

Bardhan, Pranab, 187
Bartels, Larry, 160
Bastiat, Frédéric, 17, 29, 34, 40, 197, 199;
  Candlemakers' Petition, 202; eco-
  nomic education and, 200, 203; on
  make-work bias, 40, 41, 43, 134–35; on
  sophisms (systematic error), 12
Baudelaire, Charles, 30

Bayesianism and Bayes' Rule, 99
Becker, Gary, 23, 104, 117
behavioral economics. *See* psychology
  and economics
belief: bad policies linked to false beliefs,
  142–43, 146–47, 161–62; bias as predisposition to belief, 20; consumption
  value of, 206; dogmatic belief and systematic error, 100–102; false beliefs as
  comforting or consoling, 206–7; "heterogeneity of belief" thought experiment, 147–48, 161; irrationality linked
  to, 2. *See also* lay/expert belief gap;
  preference over beliefs
beliefs, false beliefs about political responsibility, 31, 51, 174
Bentham, Jeremy, 54
Berkeley, George, 117
Besley, Timothy, 111
betting, 130–31; Policy Analysis Market
  (PAM), 190–92
bias: democratic fundamentalism, 186–
  90, 193; ideological, 54–56, 82, 83;
  market fundamentalism among
  economists, 183–85; in the media, 176;
  as predisposition to belief, 20; projection of bias onto opposition, 186;
  self-serving bias, 54, 55, 56, 63–64, 82,
  83; of voters *vs.* nonvoters, 157. *See
  also* antiforeign bias; antimarket bias;
  bias, systematic; make-work bias;
  pessimistic bias
bias, systematic: about toxicology, 160–
  62; bad policy linked to, 146–47; democracy as polluted by, 206; economists and refutation of bias, 203;
  economists as biased, 48–49, 183–85;
  education's role in eliminating, 198; of
  experts, 81–82; as innate, 31, 178; media's role in promulgating foolish beliefs, 177–79; objections to use of SAEE
  as measure of, 70–81; preference over
  beliefs as cause of, 101–2; psychology
  research and evidence of, 24–30; public opinion research and evidence of,

preferences: democracy and aggregation of, 144; "enlightened preferences," 25–28, 55; irrationality and, 122; policy preferences, 158–59. *See also* preference over beliefs
presidential influence over economy, SAEE question regarding, 73
price: full price, 17; of ideological loyalty, 18; monopoly theories of, 34; support policies, 34–35; wage and, 34–35
price supports, 30
Primitivism and Related Ideas In Antiquity (Lovejoy and Boas), 45
The Prince (Machiavelli), 167, 168, 171, 172
principal-agent relations, 172
Prisoner's Dilemma, 127
private choice, 192–94, 197; private action in relationship to collective action, 193–94
private costs, 121
probability of decisiveness, 150
productivity, SAEE question regarding, 65
profits: antimarket bias and profit motive, 30–32; SAEE question regarding, 63–64
progress, 45
propaganda, 176–80, 181; political advertising, 179–80
protectionism: Candlemakers' Petition as critique of, 202; as example of socially harmful policy, 1; as popular, 12, 50–51, 69, 81, 100, 139, 142–43, 178; rational irrationality and, 124, 139
psychology: of conviction or blind faith, 16, 189; economics and, 24, 135–37; evidence of systematic bias from research in, 24–30; expressive voting as psychologically rewarding, 138; irrationality as comfort or consolation, 118–19, 145–46, 206–7; pessimistic bias as rooted in, 46, 47; plausibility of rational irrationality, 125–31; "sacred values," 189
psychology and economics, 24, 135–37
public choice theory. *See* rational choice theory
public interest, Paradox of Democracy and, 2, 3
public opinion: dimensionality of public opinion in multi-issue democracy, 153–54; economists and influence of,

203; PAM betting market and, 191–92; politicians general compliance with, 195; research, 208; research in, 24–30
punishment, 109, 112; death penalty, 132–33; optimal, 104–5; of shirking politicians, 171

Rand, Ayn, 14–15
rational choice theory, 6, 14, 19; empirical research as theory-driven, 208–9; inability to explain political failure, 102–11; preference over beliefs and, 21–22; public opinion research and, 208–9. *See also* Classical Public Choice
rational expectations, 98–99, 207
rational ignorance, 5–6; Classical Public Choice (rational choice theory) and, 94–96; flaws in "ignorance only" as explanation of systematic error, 100–102; as inadequate explanation, 108–9; rational irrationality compared to, 123
rational irrationality, 17–18, 206; case studies in, 127–31; cognitive shortcuts and, 126; experimental evidence indicating, 135–37; as explanation for political behavior, 141; expressive voting and, 137–40, 138–39; fluctuating incentives and, 124; politics and, 131–35; rational ignorance compared to, 123; sincerity of commitment to beliefs and, 140; situational examples of, 124–25; systematic bias and, 137; tacit knowledge and, 126
rationality: Bayesian, 99; ends *vs.* means and, 98–99; incentives for, 206; as truth-seeking, 99, 101
receptivity to ideas, 201; preference over beliefs as obstruction, 103–4; propaganda and, 177–78; rhetoric as persuasive, 170
regulation: deregulation and privatization, 6, 183, 189, 192–93; insurance industry and, 196; of markets, 27–28; SAEE questions regarding, 62–63, 73; supply and demand consequences of, 11; systematic bias and, 19–21, 31, 62–63, 73, 133, 146, 161
religion: "creation science" and objectivity, 186; doctrinal disputes within, 127–28; as political issue, 27; preference over beliefs and, 15–16, 19, 116–17; rational irrationality and religious

wealth, 63–64; gap between rich and poor, 74, 157; prejudice against, 37–38; ratio of result to effort linked to, 41
Wealth of Nations (Smith), 12, 32, 37–38
welfare, 79–80; SAEE question regarding, 60–61
"What Do Undergrads Need to Know About Trade" (Krugman), 199
Who Will Tell the People (Greider), 36, 142
"wisdom of crowds," 191
The Wisdom of Crowds (Surowiecki), 6

Wittman, Donald, 103, 109–11, 143, 175–76, 179–80
Wittman's fork, 108–11
women in workforce, SAEE question regarding, 68
work ethic, SAEE question regarding, 61–62
World Trade Organization (WTO), 174
Worldviews survey, 51
Wyden, Ron, 190, 192

Zeigler, Harmon, 169